Leadership at a Distance

Research in
Technologically-Supported Work

Leadership at a Distance

Research in Technologically-Supported Work

<small>EDITED BY</small>

Suzanne P. Weisband
University of Arizona

 Lawrence Erlbaum Associates
Taylor & Francis Group

New York   London

Cover design by Tomai Maridou.

Lawrence Erlbaum Associates
Taylor & Francis Group
270 Madison Avenue
New York, NY 10016

Lawrence Erlbaum Associates
Taylor & Francis Group
2 Park Square
Milton Park, Abingdon
Oxon OX14 4RN

© 2008 by Taylor & Francis Group, LLC
Lawrence Erlbaum Associates is an imprint of Taylor & Francis Group, an Informa business

Printed in the United States of America on acid-free paper
10 9 8 7 6 5 4 3 2 1

International Standard Book Number-13: 978-0-8058-5097-0 (Softcover) 978-0-8058-5096-3 (Hardcover)

Visit the Taylor & Francis Web site at
http://www.taylorandfrancis.com

and the LEA Web site at
http://www.erlbaum.com

DEDICATION

To Nate, Mara and Sami

Contents

Foreword

Thomas W. Malone
Massachusetts Institute of Technology

Imagine what leadership in a group of our hunting and gathering ancestors must have looked like tens of thousands of years ago. These early humans supported themselves by hunting for wild animals and gathering fruits, berries, and other foods. Anthropologists tell us that they often lived in bands of 15–25 people and that decision-making in these face-to-face groups was relatively egalitarian. Because of age, experience, or other personal characteristics, some members of the band had more influence on group decisions than others. But most decisions were made by group consensus, and no one had absolute power over others.

We can speculate that effective leaders in these groups must have had many of the characteristics we would still recognize in leaders of small groups of peers today: credibility based on achievements important to the group, persuasiveness based on personal charisma, and enough social skill to sense what the group wants and not try to lead in a direction the group won't follow.

Now imagine what leadership looked like in the government and armies of ancient Rome. Small groups of peers still existed, and leadership in these groups was probably very similar to leadership in similar small groups before and since.

But now new forms of leadership had been added. New technologies—especially writing—now enabled a small group of people in Rome to "lead" an empire of tens of millions of others spread over parts of three continents. And the Roman army was—for its time—a masterpiece of organizational design. With carefully defined ways of grouping, linking, and controlling tens of thousands of people, it anticipated many of the organizational principles that still underlie the largest corporations of today.

Effective leadership in these new kinds of organizations required many new leadership skills. Not only did (at least some of) the new leaders need to master new communication technologies (like writing). But very different kinds of skills were needed to do things like issue orders that would be carried out by thousands of people, hundreds of miles away, after being filtered through several levels of intermediate leaders.

Today, we are in the early stages of another profound change in leadership. New communication technologies (like email, the Web, instant messaging, videoconferencing, inexpensive voice communication, and the Internet in general) are now making it possible to communicate with vastly more people, almost instantly, almost anywhere in the world, and often at almost no cost. Just as the Roman Empire did not emerge immediately after writing was invented, it will take a while for all the new organizational forms enabled by these new technologies to be invented.

But I think—and I suspect many of the contributors to this book would agree—that the kinds of leadership that will be needed in these new organizations may be as different from leadership in 20th century organizations, as leadership in the Roman Empire was from leadership in a hunter-gatherer band. Not that the old kinds of leadership will go away. They won't. But they will be joined by some very new kinds of leadership, too.

For instance, leading a small group of software developers spread around the world, communicating only by email and telephone, requires some very different skills from leading the same small group if they all worked in a single room. And, as a number of chapters in this volume suggest, leadership is becoming more distributed in another sense, too: Not only is it more distributed *geographically*; it is also becoming more distributed *organizationally*.

That is, as information is more widely distributed throughout an organization, so, too, is leadership. Many of the leadership skills that used to be concentrated at the top of an organization (such as sensemaking and visioning) are now becoming critical for more and more leaders throughout an organization.

Of course, no one knows all the answers about how leadership will change as we enter this new world of distributed leadership. In fact, many of the answers haven't even been invented yet. But this volume contains provocative work by some of the leading researchers in this area today. If anyone can help us see how things are changing, it should be them!

Thomas W. Malone is the Patrick J. McGovern Professor of Management at the MIT Sloan School of Management. He is also the founder and director of the MIT Center for Collective Intelligence and author of the book *The Future of Work* (Harvard Business School Press, 2004) which elaborates—and provides references for—some of the points made in this Foreword.

Preface

When learning that Colin Powell conducted his work using wireless and computer technologies, Thomas Friedman wrote, "Your boss can do his job and your job. He can be secretary of state and his own secretary. He can give you instructions day or night. So you are never out. You are always in. Therefore, you are always on. Bosses, if they are inclined, can collaborate more directly with more of their staff than ever before—no matter who they are or where they are in the hierarchy" (Friedman, 2005, p. 213).

Like Friedman, the researchers in this book have noticed that the world of leadership in distributed work environments has changed in dramatic ways. There are hundreds of books and studies and much media attention on leadership, yet leaders and organizations are still floundering about what to do in this new, "flatter" world of work. In a recent survey of 440 human resource professionals, more than 70% of the respondents rated their virtual team member-training as "not at all effective" or only "slightly effective." Similarly, more than 75% of the respondents rated their training as a virtual team leader as "not at all effective" or only "slightly effective." In fact, only 7% of respondents rated their current virtual team member and leader training programs as "very effective" or "extremely effective" (Rosen, Furst, & Blackburn, 2006).

This book examines the complex phenomenon of leadership in distributed work settings, or leadership at a distance. The study of leadership at a distance is complex because of the ubiquitous roles that leaders play, the scale of the work in which leaders find themselves, and the range of technologies available to them. Two goals of this book are to address this complexity and to set new directions in studying leadership at a distance. The chapters in this book show that leaders head distant teams; they are engineers, physicians, and webmasters who work in a wide range of work settings, from temporary arrangements with individuals, small sets of individuals, or large online communities to large-scale collaboration efforts to provide aid to Hurricane Katrina victims, and they conduct science as well. This book also examines the range of technologies leaders employ to do their work, including email, videoconferencing, group support systems, websites, blogs, web forums, and software development.

The scholars who contributed to this book are located with disciplinary and interdisciplinary programs in psychology, organizational behavior, information systems, computer science, human–computer interaction, cognitive science, management, and other hybrid fields. Because of their diverse backgrounds and separate venues for publication and research networks, there have been few opportunities for these researchers to meet and work together to understand the field of distant leadership from a broader perspective. A group of the authors met for this purpose at a workshop in Scottsdale, Arizona, to share papers and ideas. This workshop was sponsored by the U.S. Army Research Institute to better help Army officers and researchers understand the new world of leading at a distance.

This book, based on some of the papers presented at the workshop as well as recent work in large-scale collaboration and international leadership, offers a unique perspective of empirical research representing a variety of fields and methods. It is intended for researchers and others who seek to understand leadership in distributed teams, organizations, and large-scale collaboration. Through this book, we hope to stimulate more research on this topic and on studies related to the design of technologies for leaders.

The chapters are organized to offer very different perspectives on leading at a distance. The book begins with an overview of the challenges leaders face in the 21st century. We then present three chapters describing field studies and new ways of thinking about leadership in distributed work settings. The next three chapters describe experiments on the group dynamics and social processes involved in leading teams at a distance. Finally, four chapters present research on leadership in large-scale distributed collaborations. They test previous theories of leadership and question whether leaders need to know in advance their roles and responsibilities, or have the right training, or have the right skills and personal characteristics. We end with a concluding chapter that highlights the lessons learned about leadership at a distance and future research directions.

Because of space limitations, some areas of work have been not been included here. We do not include studies of the effects of leadership training and development in distributed work. We also do not include studies of leadership in knowledge networks or how leadership affects the distribution of knowledge in organizations. We believe this work has been covered well elsewhere. Many of the chapters discuss technologies to support distant leadership, but we do not focus on technology itself. Rather, this book is designed to foster understanding of the role technology plays in leadership, and how leadership is shaped by the use of technology. Although this book was sponsored by the U.S. Army Research Institute, it does not focus on any individual leaders from the Army. Instead, we offer new perspectives on leadership at a distance to inform the Army and other organizations of the challenges and lessons of leadership in the 21st century.

ACKNOWLEDGMENTS

Through the support of the Army Research Institute for the Behavioral and Social Sciences (#DASW01-01-K-0001), we were able to host a workshop for most of the authors represented in this book, and to present their work. I thank Leanne Atwater for her help in organizing the workshop, her comments on earlier drafts, and her willingness to do anything I asked at a moment's notice. Karl Wiers handled workshop logistics, technical support, and website design and maintenance. Michele Pesnell made all financial arrangements. I could not have finished this book without the prodding, care, and constant support of Sara Kiesler. I am grateful to her and to the contributors of this book for their hard work and, mostly, for their patience.

REFERENCES

Friedman, T. L. (2005). *The world is flat: A brief history of the twenty-first century.* New York, NY: Farrar, Straus & Giroux.

Rosen, B., Furst, S., & Blackburn, R. (2006). Training for virtual teams: An investigation of current practices and future needs. *Human Resource Management, 45*(2), 229–247.

Leadership at a Distance

Research in
Technologically-Supported Work

I

New Challenges for Leading at a Distance

1

Research Challenges for Studying Leadership at a Distance

Suzanne Weisband
University of Arizona

OVERVIEW

Globalization and the spread of advanced information and communication technologies are fueling a transition to distributed work practices. Now many more people have the information they need to make decisions for themselves. Leadership is no longer the sole responsibility of the CEO or vice president; it can be found at every level of an organization. It becomes a special challenge, then, to understand how shifts to distributed forms of work are changing the nature of leadership. When leaders have direct access to information and to the people with whom they collaborate, it will change the way they interact with others and what they talk about. When leaders come to rely on and use sophisticated computer technologies, there will be a greater reliance on the infrastructure supporting the work and the technology. When collaboration involves hundreds of researchers, engineers, programmers, and software developers, the world of work shifts to a very different perspective on how to lead and work together. This chapter offers a new perspective on leadership at a distance, from the research that considers the role of single leaders with special traits and attributes to a more nuanced role of leadership emergence, technical expertise, and new authority structures in large-scale collaborations. The new challenge for researchers interested in leadership is to keep up with this flatter, global, highly interconnected, world of work. The contributions from this book should convince and inspire you to realize that research on leadership at a distance is thriving and moving in new directions.

Two weeks after New Orleans flooded, *Time* magazine's website published a cartoon of a man standing in waist-deep water, holding a sign that said, "Leadership Please" (Garcia, 2006). The next day Michael Brown, the embattled head of the Federal Emergency Management Agency (FEMA) resigned. These are indications that our nation's leadership is in crisis. News headlines of financial and ethical scandals, bankruptcies, and forced resignations of leaders in corporate, educational, and political institutions may exaggerate the problem, yet there is growing concern that our nation is not producing enough future leaders able to deal in the "flat world" of international experience and outlook (Treverton & Bikson, 2003; Friedman, 2005).

Globalization and the spread of advanced information and communication technologies have encouraged a transition to distributed, virtual work practices. By reducing the costs of communication, these technologies now make it possible for many more people, even in large, multinational organizations, to have the information they need to make decisions for themselves instead of just following orders from the boss. This has made it possible for more people than ever before to collaborate and compete in real time with more people on different kinds of work from anywhere in the world—using computers, email, networks, teleconferencing, and dynamic new software applications. Thus, according to Thomas Friedman in his book, *The World is Flat*, "The global competitive playing field was being leveled. The world was being flattened" (Friedman, 2005, p. 8).

Friedman contends that the world, over time, has been flattened by ten forces, or "flatteners": the opening of the Berlin Wall, Netscape going public, work flow, outsourcing, offshoring, open-sourcing, insourcing, supply-chaining, in-forming, and the steroids of the "digital, mobile, virtual and personal" amplifying the other flatteners. The result of the convergence of these ten forces "was the creation of a global, Web-enabled playing field that allows for multiple forms of collaboration—the sharing of knowledge and work—in real time, without regard to geography, distance, or, in the near future, even language" (Friedman, 2005, p. 176).

Although many of the ten flatteners have been around for years, what we need, according to Friedman, is the emergence of a large cadre of managers, innovators, IT specialists, CEOs, and business schools to get comfortable with this new flatter playing field. In short, we need "a set of business practices and skills that would get the most out of the flat world" (Friedman, 2005, p. 178).

DEFINING LEADERSHIP

Up until the late 1940s, leadership theory emphasized leader traits; that is, the characteristics of the leader make all the difference. This view of leadership remains yoked to the concept of "leader as commander." Yet with the proliferation of self-managed work groups (Wolff, Pescosolido, & Druskat, 2002) as well as the increase in globalization and decentralized organizational forms, researchers and organizations may have been forced to rethink traditional views of leadership. Today, theories of leadership have shifted from vertical leadership to shared or distributed leadership (e.g., Ensley, Hmieleski, & Pearce, 2006; Gronn, 2002). Vertical leadership may be viewed as an influence on team processes, dependent on the wisdom of an individual leader. In contrast, shared leadership is a team process by which leadership is carried out by the team as a whole, and the leadership draws from the knowledge of a collective.

This is not to say that vertical leadership is the way of the past, but rather that new thinking about leadership must encompass a fuller view of leadership processes and outcomes (e.g., Day, Gronn, & Salas, 2004). That is, leaders may be either appointed or emerge from a group of workers, and they can influence others beyond their formal authority in the organization. Leadership is not the sole responsibility of the CEO or vice president; it can be found at every level of an organization. Leadership is the process of influencing others to understand and agree about what needs to be done and how it can be done effectively, and the process of facilitating individual and collective efforts to accomplish a shared objective (Yukl, 2002). According to Gronn (2002), leadership is a status ascribed to one individual, an aggregate of separate individuals, small groups of individuals acting in concert, or larger plural-member organizational units.

LEADING AT A DISTANCE

Technological advances and changes in the global economy are motivating and enabling an increasing geographic distribution of work. Many leaders today communicate regularly with individuals, with their team members, and with larger organizational units at a distance. Distant leaders lead military missions from remote locations, use videoconferencing to learn about breaking news, resolve conflicts without compensation or authority to do so (see chapter 10 in this volume), manage local and remote teams, and oversee online communities (see chapter 9 in this volume).

Distributed work teams differ from traditional work teams on many dimensions, including the location of the workers, where and how the work is done, and what the relationships are among workers in multiple organizations, as well as among organizations. The label "virtual" has often been employed to work environments such as these, where individuals and team members are physically or temporally distributed or distant. A virtual team can include as members individuals working at home and employees in different geographic locations in nonoverlapping times (e.g., global or multinational teams, or software development teams) (Meadows, 1996; Townsend, DeMarie, & Hendrickson, 1998; Watson-Manheim, Crowston, & Chudoba, 2002). Members of these teams may be located in different countries and have very different cultural backgrounds (Carmel, 1999; Maznevski & DiStefano, 2000).

The Challenges of Leading at a Distance

Numerous challenges face teams engaged in distributed work. Often, they are expected to perform as well as or better than physically collocated teams: to provide deliverables, meet project schedules, and to generate feasible and even innovative problem solutions. And yet all this must be done at a distance. Team members come from different departments, organizations, countries, and sometimes even competitor companies. Sometimes teams meet face-to-face on a regular basis, sometimes rarely, often not at all (Mark, 2001). Challenges are more likely to occur when distributed work occurs in different time zones, when local communication and human infrastructures fail (Lee, Dourish, & Mark, 2006), when team members' hardware and software platforms are different (Star & Ruhleder, 1996), or when local work demands requires the immediate attention of collocated managers and workers, thereby creating pressure to pursue local priorities over the objectives of distant collaborators (Kerner & Buono, 2004; Mark, 2001).

 According to recent research on leadership in distributed work teams, or e-leadership, these coordination problems could be mitigated if virtual team leaders had better skills and received more training (e.g., Avolio, Kahai, & Dodge, 2001; Maznevski & DiStefano, 2000; Rosen, Furst, & Blackburn, 2006), behaved within appropriate roles (e.g., Zaccaro & Bader, 2003; Zigurs, 2003), developed trust (e.g., Gibson & Manual, 2003; Jarvenpaa, Knoll, & Leidner, 1998; Jarvenpaa & Leidner, 1999), monitored group process and performance (Weisband, 2002), or successfully used technologies appropriate for specific tasks (Rosen et al., 2006; Martins, Gilson, & Maynard, 2004, May & Carter, 2001). That many distant leaders do not do these things or have these skills is apparent from recent studies of distributed work (e.g., Cramton, 2001; Cummings & Kiesler, 2005; Hinds & Bailey, 2003; Mark 2005; Olson & Olson, 2000).

A growing literature has focused on the special challenges facing electronically-connected ("e") leaders and the dynamic context leaders now face. Avolio and Kahai (2003) make the strong point that the "e" in e-leadership is critical to understanding how shifts in the new—flattened—world of work are changing the nature of leadership. First, leaders have more access to information and to the people they collaborate with, and this is changing the way people interact and what they talk about. Second, leadership is no longer bounded by hierarchical structures; it is moving to lower levels of the organization, as well as out to external networks like customers, suppliers, competitors (Ancona, Bresman, & Kaeufer, 2002). Third, leadership creates and exists in networks that cross organizational and community boundaries. In crossing both physical and social boundaries, leaders can confuse or anger team members. Antonakis and Atwater (2002) define leader distance as leader–follower physical distance, perceived social distance, and perceived interaction frequency. Especially, leaders can appear to be very distant if they are physically distant, they maximize their status and power differentials by virtue of their elevated social position, and they maintain infrequent contact with team members. Fourth, through hidden networks of many people and little accountability, unethical leaders can have a much broader negative impact on more people. Fifth, and finally, leaders' uses of sophisticated information technologies will depend on the infrastructure supporting the work and the technology.

TECHNICAL AND INFRASTRUCTURE CHALLENGES

The development of new technologies offers new opportunities and resources for distant leaders and the people they work with by offering access to expertise around the world (Boh, Ren, Kiesler, & Bussjaeger, in press), responding to business opportunities quickly wherever they arise (e.g., Carmel, 1999), and overcoming organizational inertia (Armstrong & Peter, 2002). Tools and technical infrastructure make electronic communication between leaders, teams, and online public spaces possible (see chapters 9, 10, and 11 in this volume). Yet, technology is not a routine resource. Technical infrastructure not only involves special technical expertise to install, develop, and maintain the basic system, but it also involves managing software versions and monitoring the content to make sure it is up-to-date and used appropriately.

The development of technologies may solve some immediate problems, but it can also result in higher order effects. For example, good connectivity does not necessarily help in integrating the work of the virtual and local working spheres (Mark, 2001). Work is continuous and complex; people move from one task to another, and remote people and tasks are typically not part of the day-to-day work that most people find themselves doing locally. Local managers tend to favor local employees and work (Boh et al., in press). New technologies may encourage the emergence of a distant leader, which may in turn unleash conflict forces on team members, who may have to choose between local and distant leadership.

Many of us have developed some competence in working together face-to-face. For example, we can establish relations with one another, maintain awareness of work activities, hold group discussions, and produce quality joint products. But when we move to distant, geographically distributed teams, we have to develop new ways of work and new competencies. We also have to become technically competent, not just in figuring out how to operate the technology but also in knowing how to use it to interact effectively with others. Thus, we need new competencies in leadership. These include styles of leadership (see chapter 4 in this volume), good interpersonal skills (Mankin, Cohen, & Fitzgerald, 2004), effective strategies for integrating local work with remote work, and ways to keep track of what distant members are doing (Weisband, 2002).

According to Star and Ruhleder's early vision of distributed leadership (1996), an infrastructure can evolve such that local practices are brought into alignment with a larger-scale technology in order for global work to be accomplished. In these cases, local and global tensions are resolved. In these dynamic, interdisciplinary, and multifunctional arrangements that cross organizational boundaries and geography, human infrastructure is a "synergistic collaboration of hundreds of researchers, programmers, software developers, tool builders, and others who understand the difficulties of developing applications and software for a complex, distributed, and dynamic environment. These people are able to work together to develop the software infrastructure, tools, and applications . . . required to prototype, integrate, harden, and nurture ideas from concept to maturity" (Berman, 2001, p. 1).

Star and Ruhleder's vision remains an ideal. People who work in large-scale collaboration efforts often do not feel that they are part of a distributed team. Team boundaries are not clear (Mortenson & Hinds, 2002), and people do not know if they are members of a team or organizational work group. Scaffidi, Myers, and Shaw (chapter 11 in this volume) found that problems sharing data among team leaders and members had less to do with an individual leader's ineptness or ego and more to do with the difficulty of collaborating on widely distributed, time-critical projects.

In short, in the flat world of globalization, where networks of individuals work across boundaries, we have to advance a perspective on what we mean by leadership at a distance that complicates any overly-simplistic heuristic of virtual teams or distributed collaboration. We need to investigate the detailed processes and conditions of leadership at a distance, such as authority structures (see chapter 12 in this volume) and leadership emergence (see chapter 10 in this volume). Leadership at a distance as it is practiced today reinvented what researchers traditionally meant by leadership.

PLAN OF THE BOOK

Technology may allow for the flattening of the world, but understanding how leaders and workers adapt to these new technologies and networked forms of complex collaboration requires that we see the range of leadership at a distance. Several cross-cutting questions and perspectives about leadership at a distance are presented in the book and suggest where promising research in distant leadership is heading. We begin with an overview of the field and new directions in international leadership and globalization (chapters 1 and 2). These chapters set the stage for the rest of the book and for discussion of ways that leaders in distributed arrangements manage teams and others.

The effectiveness of leading groups at a distance is important to discern. Informal and frequent communication among work group members is more effective when geographic dispersion is high as compared to when work group members are less dispersed (chapter 3). In contrast, leaders who use their status and rank to intimidate group members will limit communication and knowledge flow, which can have serious consequences in times of crisis (chapter 5). Early face-to-face communication prior to working apart can allow for important information about who is part of the group, as well as information about who has expertise that can be accessed later (chapter 4). Creating norms for how to effectively communicate with distant team members is an important implication for remote leadership (chapters 3, 4, and 5).

We learn about leadership styles, including differences between transformational and transactional leadership when communicating over computer networks (chapters 6), as well as interaction style (chapters 7 and 8). In this view of leadership, there is one member who displays certain leadership characteristics as either a confederate acting as transformational or transactional leader (chapter 6), or who is rated by others as having leadership qualities (chapter 7), or who is identified as the expert (chapter 8), or who is assigned the role of leader because of his or her high rank and status (chapter 5).

The field studies describing new ways of leading in distributed work settings and in large-scale distributed collaborations reflect the wide range of distant leadership arrangements. Some leaders are in charge of local and remote members (chapters 3 and 4); others are responsible for large online communities (chapter 9); still others provide direct leadership through the use of videoconferencing (chapter 5). Many authors note that leaders often emerge when current structures and strategies prove ineffective (chapter 10), or because of technical expertise (chapter 11), a need to help others (chapter 12), or the expert can resolve conflicts among different groups and has the leadership characteristics to take on the task, knowing that important work will flounder if someone doesn't step in and do something (chapter 10). These emergent leaders in distributed work typically have no formal leadership training or formal authority, yet they have an urgent need to help others (chapters 10, 11, and 12).

Finally, many authors in this book address the question of whether and how technology can support leadership at a distance. Although not everyone agrees on this question, many authors discuss the requirements of new technology to support leaders and their dispersed teams and collaborators. They include requirements for supporting blogs and web forums in crisis situations (chapter 12); the need to reduce redundancy among multiple websites all trying to help people find each other, as in the wake of Hurricane Katrina (chapter 11); the constraints of having to work with certain kinds of technologies, not all of which are effective (chapter 5); and the infrastructure that technology should provide for social interaction (chapters 11 and 12), as well as the human infrastructure that mediates local and global concerns (chapter 10). Clearly, the increase in globalization requires that we think carefully about the kinds of leaders we are going to need in the 21st century (chapter 2). This book is intended as an important and critical step in that direction.

REFERENCES

Ancona, D. G., Bresman, H., & Kaeufer, K. (2002). The comparative advantage of X-teams. *MIT Sloan Management Review, 43*, 33–40.

Antonakis, J., & Atwater, L. (2002). Leader distance: A review and proposed theory. *The Leadership Quarterly, 13*, 673–704.

Armstrong, D. J., & Peter, E. B. (2002). Virtual proximity, real teams. In P. Hinds and S. Kiesler (Eds), *Distributed work* (pp. 187–189). Cambridge, MA: MIT Press.

Avolio, B. J., & Kahai, S. S. (2003). Adding the "E" to E-Leadership: How it may impact your leadership. *Organizational Dynamics, 31*(4), 325–338

Avolio, B. J., Kahai, S., & Dodge, G. E. (2001). E-leadership: Implications for theory, research, and practice. *The Leadership Quarterly, 11*, 615–668.

Berman, F. (2001). The human side of cyberinfrastructure. *EnVision, 17*(2), 1.

Boh, W. F., Ren, Y., Kiesler, S., & Bussjaeger, R. (in press). Expertise and collaboration in the geographically dispersed organization. *Organization Science.*

Carmel, E. (1999). *Global software teams: Collaborating across borders and time zones.* Upper Saddle River, NJ: Prentice Hall.

Cramton, C. D. (2001). The mutual knowledge problem and its consequences in geographically dispersed teams. *Organization Science, 12*, 346–371.

Cummings, J. N., & Kiesler, S. (2005). Collaborative research across disciplinary and organizational boundaries. *Social Studies of Science, 35*, 703–722.

Day, D. V., Gronn, P., & Salas, E. (2004). Leadership capacity in teams. *The Leadership Quarterly, 15*(6), 857–880.

Ensley, M. D., Hmieleski, K. M., & Pearce, C. L. (2006). The importance of vertical and shared leadership within new venture top management teams: Implications for the performance of startups. *The Leadership Quarterly, 17*, 217–231

Friedman, T. L. (2005). *The world is flat: A brief history of the twenty-first century.* New York, NY: Farrar, Straus & Giroux.

Garcia, H. F. (2006). Effective leadership response to crisis. *Strategy & Leadership, 34*, 4–10.

Gibson, C. B., & Manuel, J. A. (2003). Building trust: Effective multicultural communication processes in virtual teams. In C. Gibson & S. Cohen (Eds.), *Virtual teams that work: Creating conditions for virtual team effectiveness* (pp. 59–86). San Francisco: Jossey-Bass.

Gronn, P. (2002). Distributed leadership as a unit of analysis. *The Leadership Quarterly, 13*, 423–451.

Hinds, P., & Bailey, D. (2003). Out of sight, out of sync: Understanding conflict in distributed teams: An empirical investigation. *Organization Science, 14*(6), 615–632.

Jarvenpaa, S. L., Knoll, K., & Leidner, D. E. (1998). Is anybody out there? Antecedents of trust in global virtual teams. *Journal of Management Information Systems, 14*, 29–64.

Jarvenpaa, S., & Leidner, D. E. (1999). Communication and trust in global virtual teams. *Organization Science, 10*, 791–815.

Kerner, K. W., & Buono, A. F. (2004). Leadership challenges in global virtual teams: Lessons from the field. *S.A.M. Advanced Management Journal, 69*(4), 4–10.

Lee, C., Dourish, P., & Mark, G. (2006). The human infrastructure of cyberinfrastructure. *Proceedings of the ACM Conference on Computer Supported Cooperative Work (CSCW'06)*, Banff, Alberta, Canada, November 4–8, New York: ACM.

Mankin, D., Cohen, S., & Fitzgerald, S. P. (2004). Developing complex collaborations: Basic principles to guide design and implementation. In M. Beyerlein, D. A. Johnson, & S. T. Beyerlein (Eds.), *Complex Collaboration: Building the capabilities for working across boundaries. Advances in Interdisciplinary Studies of Work Teams, 10*, 1–26.

Mark, G. (2001). Meeting current challenges for virtually collocated teams: Participation, culture, and integration. In L. Chidambaram & I. Zigurs (Eds). *Our virtual world : The transformation of work, play, and life via technology* (pp. 74–93). Hershey, PA: Idea Group Publishing.

Mark, G. (2005). Large-scale distributed collaboration: Tension in a new interaction order. *Proceedings of the Social Informatics Workshop*, Irvine, CA. Paper available at http://crito.uci.edu/2/si/resources.asp.

Martins, L. L., Gilson, L. L., & Maynard, M. T. (2004). Virtual teams: What do we know and where do we go from here? *Journal of Management, 30*(6), 805–835.

May, A., & Carter, C. (2001). A case study of a virtual team working in the European automotive industry. *International Journal of Industrial Ergonomics, 27*(3), 171–186.

Maznevski, M. L., & DiStefano, J. J. (2000). Global leaders are team players: Developing global leaders through membership on global teams. *Human Resource Management, 39*(2&3), 195–208.

Meadows, C. J. (1996). Globalizing software development, *Journal of Global Information Management, 4*(1), 5–14.

Mortensen, M., & Hinds, P. (2002). Fuzzy teams: Boundary disagreement in distributed and collocated teams. In P. Hinds & S. Kiesler (Eds), *Distributed work* (pp. 283–308). Cambridge, MA: MIT Press.

Olson, G. M., & Olson, J. S. (2000). Distance matters. *Human Computer Interaction, 15*, 139–179.

Rosen, B., Furst, S., & Blackburn, R. (2006). Training for virtual teams: An investigation of current practices and future needs. *Human Resource Management, 45*(2), 229–247.

Star, L., & Ruhleder, K. (1996). Steps toward an ecology of infrastructure: Design and access for large information spaces. *Information Systems Research, 7*(1), 111–134.

Townsend, A. M., DeMarie, S. M., & Hendrickson, A. R. (1998). Virtual teams: Technology and the workplace of the future, *Academy of Management Executive, 12*(3), 17–29.

Treverton, G. F., & Bikson, T. K. (2003). New challenges for international leadership: Positioning the United States for the 21st Century. RAND, IP–233.

Watson-Manheim, M. B., Crowston, K., & Chudoba, K. M. (2002). A new perspective on "virtual": Analyzing discontinuities in the work environment. *Hawaii International Conference on Systems Science (HICSS)*, Kona, Hawaii, January 7–10, 2002.

Weisband, S. (2002). Maintaining awareness in distributed team collaboration: Implications for leadership and performance. In P. Hinds & S. Kiesler (Eds.), *Distributed work* (pp. 311–333). Cambridge, MA: MIT Press.

Wolff, S. B., Pescosolido, A. T., & Druskat, V. U. (2002). Emotional intelligence as the basis of leadership emergence in self-managing teams. *The Leadership Quarterly, 13*(5), 505–522.

Yukl, G. (2002). *Leadership in organizations*. Upper Saddle River, NJ: Prentice Hall.

Zaccaro, S. J., & Bader, P. (2003). E-leadership and the challenges of leading e-teams: Minimizing the bad and maximizing the good. *Organizational Dynamics, 31*(4), 377–387.

Zigurs, I. (2003). Leadership in Virtual Teams: Oxymoron or Opportunity? *Organizational Dynamics, 31*(4), 339–351.

2

Leadership in International Organizations: 21st Century Challenges

Tora K. Bikson, Greg F. Treverton and Joy S. Moini
RAND Corporation, Santa Monica, CA

Gustav Lindstrom
EU Institute for Strategic Studies, Paris, France

OVERVIEW

Is the United States producing the leaders it will need in the 21st century? No issue is more critical for America's role in the world than its capacity to develop among its people the intellectual and professional expertise that will be required for leadership in international affairs, and that issue has never been more important than it is today.

Our world now bears little resemblance to that of a few decades ago. The bipolar worldview that characterized the cold war period has given way to a global perspective in which national boundaries no longer define the limits of daily interaction in business, government, and nongovernmental organizations. Advances in information and communication technology have facilitated this process, linking countries and organizations in unprecedented ways, but cultural, political, and economic differences remain significant barriers to international understanding. Today's world is both networked and fractured, both full of promise and full of danger. Exercising leadership in this environment presents new and daunting challenges.

The global role of the United States in the century ahead will demand a broader and deeper understanding of the differing societal forces that shape the world. And, while the aftermath of September 11, 2001, has given new urgency to the role of national governments, it has also called attention to the significant parts played in world affairs by the private sectors. International leadership is not for governments alone; it is exerted as well by corporations, nongovernmental institutions, and intergovernmental organizations. Thus, the need for a globally competent workforce spans these sectors, characterizing all organizations with an international reach.

This chapter aims to improve our understanding of the challenges the United States faces in building the cross-cultural expertise required for international leadership in the 21st century (see Bikson, Treverton, Moini, & Lindstrom, 2003, for a more detailed report of this research). We explored the following research questions:

- What kinds of competencies are now required for career professionals in organizations whose missions demand international leadership?
- How well are these leadership needs being met?
- What are the prospects for meeting future internationally oriented human resource needs?

BACKGROUND

In addressing these research objectives, we relied on prior RAND studies that examined the supply of and demand for international expertise in public sector institutions (Berryman, Langer, Pincus, & Solomon, 1979) and private sector firms (Bikson & Law, 1994) with international missions. We also reviewed more recent literature in this field to take into account the growing significance of globalization (see Lindstrom, Bikson, & Treverton, 2003 for a summary of that review and the references for a sample of relevant resources on which that review relied). The themes that emerged from this background are summarized briefly below.

Globalization

Globalization is a comparatively recent driver of human resource needs in U.S. organizations. We define globalization as the expansion of networks of interdependence spanning national boundaries that follows the increasingly rapid movement of information, ideas, money, goods, services, and people across those borders (Nye & Keohane, 1987). Globalization, in this sense, is accelerated by advances in information and communication technologies (Malone & Crowston, 2001). Although its economic implications received greatest initial attention (Bikson & Law, 1994), its political, legal, and sociocultural dimensions have increased in salience in recent years.

So defined, globalization has several important implications. First, in previous decades, international leadership was mainly viewed as the province of a small number of federal entities—the State Department, the Department of Defense, and the National Security Agency. Presently, however, a great many federal agencies have missions that incorporate significant and far-reaching international dimensions—the Department of Agriculture, the Environmental Protection Agency, the Department of Commerce, the Department of Health and Human Services, and the Department of Labor, among others. Besides broadening the demand for international leadership in the federal workforce, these changes eventuate in some blurring of the boundaries between domestic and foreign policy.

Second, globalization also entails substantial de facto sharing of international leadership among a much broader range of stakeholders. Although national governments continue to play key roles, international leadership is also exercised by multinational corporations as well as by major intergovernmental and private nongovernmental organizations. As a result, both formal and collegial partnerships that span sectors as well as national borders are increasingly in evidence. In this chapter, we take all three sectors and their relationships into account.

New Competency Needs

The changes stimulated by globalization should lead to changed human resource requirements in the affected organizations. In their study of multinational corporations, for example, Bikson and Law (1994) reported a demand for two generic new characteristics. One was cognitive—a revolutionary way of understanding the world economy and the position of U.S. firms within it (a "Copernican revolution" in which the U.S.-centric perspective gives way to an astronaut's view of the global business environment). The other was operational, reflecting the skills and attitudes necessary to translate that understanding into new ways of performing business missions that were more responsive to local opportunities and threats. In our literature review, we found a threefold categorization of desired employee qualifications into knowledge, skills, and attitudes. Adapting from Arnold, Robertson, and Cooper (1991), we construed these categories in the following way (see also Levy et al., 2001b).

- *Knowledge:* Understanding and recalling facts, information, and concepts necessary for successful performance.
- *Skills:* Behaviors, including higher-order cognitive or interpersonal processes, involved in the effective execution or management of specific tasks.
- *Attitudes:* Socioemotional or affective feelings and dispositions, including the level of motivation to carry out tasks, as well as orientation toward coworkers and team processes.

The new generic competencies sought by international corporations taking part in the Bikson and Law (1994) study, for example, would entail knowledge (understanding globalism in the cognitive sense) as well as skills and attitudes (for translating that understanding into successful context-specific performance). The research reported below made use of this typology.

RESEARCH CONTEXT

Our research efforts focused chiefly on how globalization changes the leadership requirements of organizations with an international reach; it assumed that these organizations' increasingly global missions could provide an appropriate basis for assessing the adequacy of the supply of desired competencies. Second, the research targeted individuals who are moving toward higher-level managerial and professional positions—those in the leadership pipeline. Finally, we emphasized on managers and professionals who were thought to be successful at directing mission-based activities with international implications. While this orientation excludes attention to human resource needs at the lower levels of organizational hierarchies, it is not restricted to the very top tiers. Rather it addresses the larger cadre of career employees that influences in significant ways the nature of critical business processes that have an international reach.

RESEARCH APPROACH

Primary data were gathered through structured interviews, supplemented by unstructured discussions of emerging issues with knowledgeable experts.

Participants

For this study, our sample comprised 76 organizations divided equally among the public, for-profit, and nonprofit sectors. Organizations had to meet two criteria for inclusion. First, they had to have international missions that engaged them in interactions spanning national boundaries. Second, they had to have been in existence long enough to have experienced the effects of increasing globalization. We set the cutoff at five years, but most of the organizations in our sample had been in operation far longer.

Within these fairly broad criteria we sought, in each sector, variation in mission orientations. For instance, in the for-profit sector, we included both manufacturing and service firms, representing both traditional and high-technology industries. Examples included Accenture, Cisco, Deloitte and Touche, Halliburton, Microsoft, and Procter & Gamble. In the public sector, we enrolled agencies involved in defense, national security, and diplomacy, but we also selected a range of agencies typically seen as responsible for developing and implementing domestic policy. Examples included the departments of Defense, Energy, Justice, and State as well as the Environmental Protection Agency, the Office of Science and Technology Policy, and the Peace Corps. In the nonprofit sector, we recruited foundations, humanitarian organizations, and intergovernmental institutions. Examples included the American Red Cross, Carnegie Corporation, MacArthur Foundation, Organization of American States, United Nations Headquarters, and the World Bank.

For each participating organization, we identified, by role, two types of individuals to take part in structured interviews: a high-level human resources department representative and a high-level line manager for a border-spanning business process. Typically the human resources representative was selected first; that individual then suggested candidates who could fulfill the second role. Not all targeted individual participants had the time to be interviewed within the project's timeframe, so structured interviews were carried out with a total of 135 individuals, distributed as shown in Table 2.1.

Finally, we also sought the participation of highly knowledgeable individuals who could provide insights on emerging issues in the research from a broader set of perspectives. For this purpose, we selected 24 individuals on the basis of nominations from the project's advisory group, their established expertise in domains of interest, their contributions to relevant literature, or all of these. The advisory committee included leaders from major foreign affairs institutions, including the Council on Foreign Relations, American Enterprise-Institute, The Brookings Institution, Carnegie Endowment for International Peace, The Heritage Foundation, The Nixon Center, and the U.S. Institute of Peace, as well as RAND.

Procedures

Structured interviews were used to explore first the effects of globalization and the resulting needs for new competencies. Interviewees were next asked about how well these needs were being met—especially by post-employment development programs and other efforts intended to yield higher-level cadres of

TABLE 2.1.
Research Participants by Role and Sector

Role	Sector			
	Public	For-Profit	Non-Profit	Total
Human resources	19	21	26	66
Line management	22	21	26	69
Total	41	42	52	135

internationally capable managers and professionals. Finally, they were asked to describe current issues, problems, and prospects of globalization facing their organizations. Incorporating both closed- and open-ended items, the protocol was flexible enough to elicit rich and wide-ranging responses. Requiring about an hour, on average, to complete, these interviews were conducted during the period from October 2001 through March 2002.

Analysis Approach

We based our findings on analyses of both quantitative and qualitative data. Where interview responses were appropriate for standardized coding, they were treated quantitatively both for descriptive purposes and for purposes of assessing the extent to which systematic differences arise as a function of sector or role. Either chi-squared tests or analyses of variance were employed, depending on whether the responses were categorical in nature or represented five-point scale ratings.

RESULTS

Study results are organized into sections that parallel the key research objectives. Within sections, quantitative findings are typically presented first, followed by a discussion of qualitative data. In the tables below, we present frequency data as percentages for ease of comparison across items, but we also indicate the total number on which these percentages are based. Where averages are provided, we also indicate the number of responses they reflect. Second, we present qualitative responses to interview questions. Qualitative material is usually summarized by sector in relation to the questions under discussion. When respondents are quoted, they are chiefly identified only by sector to preserve confidentiality.

Effects of Globalization

Globalization, as defined above, refers to the increasing interdependencies that develop from growing types and numbers of interactions that span national, as well as sectoral, boundaries. One key research objective had to do with learning whether and how globalization trends have affected organizations like those that are the focus of this study. Table 2.2 summarizes, by sector, answers to the general question about effects of recent globalization trends. We found that interviewees in the public sector report significantly more globalization effects than their counterparts in the for-profit and non-profit sectors ($\chi^2 = 31.6$; $p < .0001$).

TABLE 2.2.
Globalization Effects by Sector (in percentages)

Response Categories	Sector		
	Public	For-Profit	Non-Profit
Few/negligible effects	2	24	6
Some/moderate effects	17	27	58
Many/major effects	81	49	36

Competencies for International Careers

The three sectors represented in this study experience significant organizational consequences attributable to globalization, ranging from effects on missions and operations to effects on internal structures and extramural partnerships. Changing human resource needs are part of the globalization picture as well.

Problem Solving, Strategic Thinking, and "People Skills" in Demand. During the interview, respondents were provided a list of 19 attributes that surfaced frequently in the project's literature review as key ingredients for successful career performance in international organizations. They include very generic knowledge, skills, and attitudes (e.g., "substantive knowledge in a technical or professional field") as well as qualities thought to play a special role in missions with a global reach (e.g., "cross-cultural competence") or in advancing toward leadership (e.g., "ability to think in policy and strategy terms"). Respondents were asked to assess the significance of these characteristics "for effective performance in an organization with missions like yours" using 5-point rating scales (where 5 means very important and 1 not important). Table 2.3 summarizes the resulting judgments by sector; it also provides the overall importance rank and mean rating for each attribute.

Among the top-ranking characteristics, skills and attitudes predominate; less importance is accorded to knowledge, whether in particular professional/technical domains or in international affairs. Qualitative data suggest this is because specialized subject matter knowledge is moving forward rapidly, whereas operating environments are constantly changing and becoming more complex. So what has been learned in the past is subject to obsolescence. This is not to say that professional/technical knowledge is viewed as unimportant but rather that it has to be continuously updated. Being able to learn and to solve problems is in the long run more important than present-day knowledge. If people have generic cognitive skills, according to a private sector represen-

TABLE 2.3.

Attributes of a Successful Career Professional in an International Organization

Attributes	Overall Rank	Means for Rated Importance			
		Overall Mean	Public Sector	For-profit Sector	Nonprofit Sector
General cognitive skills	1	4.6	4.7	4.7	4.5
Interpersonal and relationship skills	2	4.6	4.6	4.5	4.6
Ambiguity tolerance, adaptivity	3	4.5	4.5	4.5	4.4
Personal traits	4	4.4	4.5	4.3	4.4
Cross-cultural competence**	5	4.4	4.3	4.1	4.6
Ability to work in teams	6	4.3	4.3	4.3	4.4
Ability to think in policy and strategy terms***	7	4.2	4.3	3.9	4.5
Written and oral English language skills*	8	4.1	4.3	4.0	4.0
Minority sensitivity	9	4.1	4.1	3.8	4.2
Innovative, able to take risks	10	4.0	4.0	4.2	3.8
Empathy, nonjudgmental perspective**	11	4.0	4.0	3.6	4.2
Substantive knowledge in a technical or professional field*	12	3.9	3.6	3.9	4.1
Multidisciplinary orientation	13	3.8	3.8	3.9	3.7
Knowledge of international affairs, geographic area studies***	14	3.6	3.9	3.2	3.8
Competitiveness, drive ***	15	3.6	3.7	4.1	3.2
General educational breadth	16	3.6	3.6	3.5	3.7
Internet and information technology competency	17	3.5	3.5	3.5	3.5
Managerial training and experience†	18	3.4	3.2	3.3	3.6
Foreign language fluency ***	19	3.2	2.9	2.9	3.7

Notes: $n = 135$. Each attribute was rated for importance, where 5 = very important, 1 = not important, and 3 = moderately important. Annotations indicate significant differences in rated importance of attributes by sector.
†$p < .10$; *$p < .05$; **$p < .01$; ***$p < .001$.

tative, "the required technical skills can be taught." Echoing this point, a nonprofit sector interviewee added that "the true challenge is to grow people all the time."

Furthermore, although high-ranking competencies tend to emphasize skills and attitudes over knowledge, they are more or less evenly divided among characteristics that would promote effective performance in any type of organization (e.g., "interpersonal and relationship skills") and those more aligned with effective performance when organizational missions have a global reach (e.g., "ambiguity tolerance, adaptivity"). Interviewees explained that longstanding needs for generic capabilities have not diminished—if anything, they have increased. Rather, new internationally oriented competencies have been added to their prior human resource requirements.

As indicated in Table 2.3, there was reasonable congruence across sectors about the relative value of many of the attributes rated, however there were notable exceptions. First, and perhaps not surprisingly, the for-profit sector places significantly more importance on competitiveness and drive than do the other sectors. Second, the nonprofit sector attributes significantly more importance to cross-cultural competence than do the other sectors. The ability to think in policy and strategy terms is valued especially highly by the nonprofit and public sectors, as is the ability to take an empathic, nonjudgmental perspective. Finally, public sector respondents give significantly higher ratings to English language proficiency than do the others; however, nonprofit sector respondents give markedly higher ratings than other sectors do to foreign language fluency.

Qualitative data are enlightening on this point. On the one hand, serious negotiations require professional translators, yet becoming skilled in a second or third language is treated as a proxy for the kinds of knowledge and attitudes that effective international leaders are expected to learn. The following comments from participants are illustrative:

> "We are in a multicultural world; the greater language capabilities we have, the better we can relate."
>
> "You cannot work internationally without learning languages. It is critical for cultural understanding."
>
> "We get credibility when working on projects abroad if we can speak with our local counterparts. . . ."

In short, respondents strongly endorse foreign language learning as a significant contributor to the cross-cultural competency required for successful leadership of global missions. What, then, accounts for the stunningly low ratings given to foreign language fluency per se? The apparent disconnect is explained by participants' views that foreign language fluency, as developed and assessed by academic institutions, is not by itself sufficient to produce cross-cultural competency. Most university programs tend to emphasize literary (e.g., reading and writing) rather than applied (e.g., spoken social or business interaction) uses of foreign languages. But even when such programs are supplemented by studies abroad, respondents noted that students often live in expatriate quarters, take courses from U.S. university professors, and socialize chiefly with one another. Thus, while gaining fluency, they are not acquiring cross-cultural competence (Bikson & Law, 1994; Berryman et al., 1979). This may explain the great importance accorded by respondents to real-world international experience in competency development.

Challenges of Creating a Leadership Cadre

The findings presented above suggest that apart from some highly specialized qualifications, organizations are not having difficulty finding career employees with the substantive professional or technical competencies they need. Rather, what they lack are individuals who combine such competencies with managerial skills and international vision and experience—the kinds of individuals who should comprise the future leadership cadre in organizations with a global mission. Here we explore how the organizations in this study make use of such options.

Career Development Programs for Mid- and High-Level Managers. A majority of respondents reported that their organization provide many opportunities for development to entering career employees; while there are variations in the distribution of opportunities across sectors, the differences are not statistically significant. We also asked respondents about the types of education or training undertaken. Table 2.4 shows the percentage of respondents, by sector, based on their frequent use of a particular development approach.

Course-based instruction and on-the-job training are by far the most heavily used development approaches, although there are significant differences as a function of sector. For example, the for-profit and nonprofit sectors give about equal emphasis to formal classes and on-the-job training; in the public sector, formal classes dominate. In general, job rotation and internships are less widespread.

Despite the substantial initial and continuing investments made in career development, organizational representatives do not judge them to be particu-

TABLE 2.4.
Types of Post-Employment Development Frequently Offered by Sector
(in percentages)

	Sector		
Types of Development	*Public*	*For-Profit*	*Non-Profit*
Course work*	95	95	78
On-the-job training*	75	93	78
Job rotation**	42	42	20
Internships***	19	54	2

Notes: $n = 125$. $*p < .05$; $**p < .01$; $***p < .001$, with values of χ^2 ranging from 10.5 to 33.0.

larly effective in providing the international leadership they need. This lack-luster evaluation is similar across sectors and across roles as well; that is, human resource officers share this conclusion with senior line management. The qualitative data revealed that the most frequently used terms to characterize later-stage career development activities are "self-initiated" and "ad hoc." While individual development plans are often filed as a part of performance review procedures or to establish that employee training objectives were being met, these person-specific efforts are rarely linked to the organization's strategic plans and would be unlikely to yield the competencies critical to future international leadership. Furthermore, courses are the least likely approach to yield the integration of substantive and managerial skills. Thus, as one for-profit sector interviewee explained, there are enough development programs, but they don't hit the mark. Moreover, according to respondents from the nonprofit sector, there is "no culture of training" and "no passion for training" at higher career levels.

Lateral Hiring Rarely Used to Develop Global Leadership Skills.   In addition to career education and training, international organizations also engage in lateral hiring to remedy competency shortfalls at upper management levels. Overall, 45% of those interviewed reported this as a frequent practice in their organizations. Moreover, when organizations hire laterally, they tend to seek higher-level career candidates from within the same sector, with the for-profit sector conducting most of the lateral hires ($\chi^2 = 13.6$; $p < .01$).

Qualitative responses indicated that although most firms prefer to "grow from within," there are times when they have leadership positions open that they cannot fill internally. Yet when they hire senior professionals and managers laterally, they tend to hire not only from firms in the same sector but also in a very similar business domain. Experts in the field argued that it would be extremely risky to have top-level decisionmakers who are not thoroughly grounded in the industry's core business processes. Given that the public and nonprofit sectors do not nurture the skills and attitudes valued in the for-profit sector, hiring leaders in the for-profit world requires going within the industry.

Similarly, it is also difficult to fill leadership positions with candidates from outside the public sector due to salary differences (a problem government agencies share with humanitarian organizations) and also because of the very long hiring process within government agencies. As a result, strong senior candidates with international expertise are often lost to the private sector. Further, in many agencies there is often a cultural resistance to welcoming outsiders who, as one interviewee described it, "haven't put in their time."

Global Leadership Skills.   The mix of lateral hiring plus professional development approaches described earlier does not markedly improve the overall effectiveness of organizations' fulfilling their international competency

TABLE 2.5.
Extent of Shortfalls in Desired Competencies
for International Career Employees at Mid-Career Levels or Higher?
(in percentage)

	Sector		
Response Categories	Public	For-Profit	Non-Profit
Few or no competencies lacking	29	71	32
Some competencies lacking	45	20	61
Many/major competencies lacking	26	9	7

Notes: $\chi^2 = 22.1$; $p < .001$.

needs at higher structural levels. This shortage of desired competencies in the future leadership cadre for international organizations is reflected in Table 2.5. As these data suggest, all types of international organizations are experiencing shortages of needed competencies at higher professional and managerial levels. Given the continuing pressures of globalization, this should not be surprising. However, the extent of the problem varies significantly across sectors ($\chi^2 = 22.1$; $p < .001$). Over two thirds of for-profit sector respondents (71%) reported that few to none of the critical competencies required for their global missions were lacking at higher organizational levels. In contrast, only 29% of respondents in the public sector and 32% of the respondents in the nonprofit sector reported few critical competencies were lacking.

Many respondents in the nonprofit and public sectors emphasized the serious challenges of finding people with strong managerial skills in addition to professional competence and international experience. Some public sector participants called their organizations "neckless" because of the lack of a developing leadership cadre between high-level officers and line career employees.

FUTURE DIRECTIONS

The baby boom generation is nearing retirement, yet downsizing and hiring caps in the 1980s and early 1990s seriously vitiated the future leadership cadre. All sectors will be affected to some degree by these trends. However, sector-specific personnel policies and hiring constraints suggest most severe problems for the public sector. As one expert put it, government "can't afford to have more than a quarter retire, leaving only the mediocre and the young behind." According to another expert, these trends sum to "a human capital crisis for the federal government."

In general, human resource shortages at senior levels are expected to worsen because integrated substantive and managerial capabilities are already scarce in all three sectors. Furthermore, finding individuals with these capabilities who are internationally knowledgeable and experienced as well as willing to relocate to a post abroad is even more difficult. Again, the public sector will be hit hardest by this shortfall. As one federal agency interviewee noted, those who possess cultural sensitivity along with the requisite domain knowledge are in short supply for a job that is "physically risky, personally inconvenient, and for which there is no extra incentive to be there—like pay." This is so, said another expert, even though such "job-based experiences" are "clearly . . . a major factor in an individual's personal development as a leader."

In the for-profit and nonprofit sectors, international expertise is often acquired either by hiring consultants or by hiring foreign nationals. Consultants, however, cannot provide leadership, and foreign nationals may become even more difficult to hire in the future than they have been in the past. Public sector respondents also noted these difficulties, and the hurdles cited earlier only intensify the obstacles to hiring non-U.S. citizens in their organizations.

Opportunities to Build New Leadership

Against this background of negative expectations, what are the promising prospects on the leadership horizon? As a start, the dot-com downturn of the recent past enabled public and nonprofit organizations to acquire needed information technology (IT) professionals at salaries that would not have been competitive before. Respondents remarked that each new cohort of employees is more IT-savvy and more motivated to keep up with state-of-the-art IT uses. Technological advances, in turn, can leverage the workforce in many ways. In particular, it widens the eligible pool of employees—telecommuting, for instance, permits the hiring of people who are homebound or who live far away, including in other countries.

Another positive trend for the future state of human resources in international organizations is a general awakening of interest in and increasing knowledge about international affairs. Study participants say this trend had been in evidence for some time and was boosted by (but not initiated by) the events of September 11. Furthermore, both public and nonprofit sector representatives say there is strong interest in serving civic goals in the United States and in contributing to humanitarian goals abroad. As one nonprofit sector interviewee put it, people now believe they will "get more satisfaction with being parts of solutions to big problems." Thus, the most serious future problem for the public sector—a large gap in the international career cadre as the baby boom retires—could become its best hope if it is able to devise ways of attracting and retaining the types of high-caliber employees it seeks to provide leadership for its growing global missions.

Interviewees cited, as a first step in the process, more aggressive, targeted recruiting. Some federal agency respondents said they would also aim to "sell" the work, taking advantage of the improved perception of government service and renewed interest in globally challenging missions. Taking this tack may have the effect of bringing public sector agencies into closer competition for talent with major nonprofit sector organizations that have long relied on their ability to "sell" their service missions. For the effort to succeed, however, public sector interviewees said the agencies would concurrently have to exploit more fully the tools and flexibilities at their disposal to offer more competitive pay or other incentives.

Innovative Personnel Policies and Practices

Attracting the right kinds of new employees is only part of the solution to the human capital problem. Another part of the solution has to do with retaining and nurturing them so that they will, in the end, make effective contributions to international leadership in the organization. Toward this goal, organizational representatives said they would have to do a much better job of professional development at mid-career levels and beyond. According to some, they also would need to devise flexible arrangements for enabling valued employees to move in and out of their organizations, allowing them to develop viable career portfolios. The lifelong career model is no longer applicable to today's workforce, so all sectors will need to learn how to support and gain benefit from mobile careers in the future.

Implementing such changes, in turn, will demand considerable innovation on the part of human resource departments. Across all sectors, they will have to become more like strategic partners with senior decision makers if their organizations are to become better positioned to exercise international leadership in the 21st century.

CONCLUSION

Increasing globalization has created an environment that makes the exercise of international leadership significantly more complex. High-level representatives of public, for-profit, and nonprofit organizations must interact with one another across borders to arrive at negotiated decisions about issues that often blend advances in science and technology with policy questions while blurring the distinctions between foreign and domestic concerns. Moreover, globalization is not just about economics and finance; it has significant political, legal, and sociocultural dimensions—both positive and negative—that are becoming increasingly salient to international organizations.

To exercise leadership effectively in this environment, a multidimensional and well-integrated set of competencies is needed. There are some between-sector differences in the extent to which particular competencies (e.g., substantive domain knowledge, competitiveness and drive, foreign language fluency versus English language communication skills) are valued, but our interviewees agree that international leaders must have an integrated repertoire of skills that includes the following:

- Substantive depth (professional or technical knowledge) related to the organization's primary business processes.

Without this depth, leaders cannot make sound decisions about risks and opportunities and will not gain the respect and trust of those below them.

- Managerial ability, with an emphasis on teamwork and interpersonal skills.

Leaders need to work with external partners as well as colleagues within their organizations. A great deal of decision making is being pushed to lower hierarchical levels, making enterprise-wide decisions more collaborative.

- Strategic international understanding.

It is critical for leaders to have a strategic vision of where the organization is going and to place it in a global context. They also need to understand the implications of operating in different localities.

- Cross-cultural experience.

Multicultural sensitivity cannot readily be gained through academic instruction alone. Efforts to learn a second or third language provide evidence of interest in other cultures and can form a basis for understanding them. They are not, however, a substitute for real world experience.

This skill repertoire was seen as being in great demand but in short supply, with the result that our interviewees forecast major skill deficits in the international leadership cadre in the near future. These gaps will persist if there are not significant changes in America's approach to international career development across its sectors. Today's senior managers and professionals are nearing retirement, and it is not at all clear that succeeding cadres have the required competencies for leadership in this changed world. While the problem has demographic and cohort dimensions that cross sectors, it is most acute in federal agencies, where some have called the public sector workforce a "human capital crisis."

We found that the outlook for future leadership in international organizations was quite mixed; there are envisioned problems as well as promising prospects. The bad news is that these organizations currently lack the multidimensional competencies that future leadership cadres will need to carry out their global missions effectively. The good news is that contemporary demographic and cohort factors combined to create an unprecedented opportunity for international organizations to repopulate their upper ranks. Participants in this research believe that career candidates are generally more interested in and knowledgeable about international affairs than prior cohorts; they are also more willing to embrace mobile careers.

In the end, it will not be easy to respond to the challenges of 21st century leadership, mostly because of the complexity of the global environment that today's international organizations face. Further, effective responses to these challenges will have to be distributed over many types of organizations, all with different goals and missions. Organizations and nations that address these leadership challenges successfully should have a competitive advantage in the decades to come.

ACKNOWLEDGMENTS

The research reported here is part of a larger study funded chiefly by the Starr Foundation, with supplemental support from the Rockefeller Brothers Fund, the United Nations Foundation, and RAND. It was guided by an advisory committee made up of the leaders of major foreign affairs institutions: the Council on Foreign Relations, American Enterprise Institute, American International Group, Inc., The Brookings Institution, Carnegie Endowment for International Peace, Center for Strategic and International Studies, The Heritage Foundation, The Nixon Center, and the U.S. Institute of Peace, as well as RAND.

BIBLIOGRAPHY

Abramson, M. A. (2002). Toward a 21st Century Public Service. Arlington, VA: The PricewaterhouseCoopers Endowment for the Business of Government.

Arnold, J., Robertson, I. T., & Cooper, C. L. (1991). *Work Psychology*. London: Pitman Publishing.

Asch, B. J., & Warner, J. T. (1999). *Separation and Retirement Incentives in the Federal Civil Service: A Comparison of the Federal Employees Retirement System and the Civil Service Retirement System.* Santa Monica, CA: RAND, MR-986-OSD.

Bailes, A. B. (2002). Who Says It Can't Be Done? Recruiting the Next Generation of Public Servants. In *The Business of Government* (Spring, pp. 51–55). Arlington, VA: PricewaterhouseCoopers.

Berryman, S. E., Langer, P. F., Pincus, J., & Solomon, R. (1979). *Foreign Language and International Studies Specialists: The Marketplace and National Policy.* Santa Monica, CA: RAND, R-2501-NEH.

Bikson, T. K. (1994). Organizational Trends and Electronic Media. *American Archivist, 57*(1), 48–68. Also available as RAND RP-307.

Bikson, T. K., Cremonini, L., & van't Hof, C. (2002). *Best eEurope Practices: Work & Skills.* Leiden, NL: RAND Europe, Information Societies Technologies Programme (IST-2000-26224).

Bikson, T. K., & Law, S. A. (1994). *Global Preparedness and Human Resources: College and Corporate Perspectives.* Santa Monica, CA: RAND, MR-326-CPC/IET.

Bikson, T. K., & Law, S. A. (1995). Toward the Borderless Career: Corporate Hiring in the 90s. *International Educator, IV*(2), 12–15, 32–33. Also available as RAND RP-443.

Bikson, T. K., Treverton, G. F., Moini, J., & Lindstrom, G. (2003). New Challenges for International Leadership: Lessons from Organizations with Global Missions. RAND, MR-1670-IP.

Brown, L. D., Khagram, S., Moore, M., & Frumkin, P. (2000). *Globalization, NGOs and Multi-Sectoral Relations.* Cambridge, MA: The Hauser Center for Non-profit Organizations, 37.

Finegold, D. (1998). The New Learning Partnership: Sharing Responsibility for Building Competence. In S. A. Mohrman, J. R. Galbraith, E. E. Lawler III and Associates, eds., *Tomorrow's Organization: Crafting Winning Capabilities in a Dynamic World* (pp. 231–263). San Francisco: Jossey Bass.

Gardner, N. W., Desmesme, R. B., & Abramson, M. A. (2002). The Human Capital Challenge. In *The Business of Government* (Spring, pp. 27–30). Arlington, VA: PricewaterhouseCoopers.

Gates, S. M., Augustine, C. H., Benjamin, R., Bikson, T. K., Kaganoff, T., Levy, D. G., et al. (2002). *Ensuring Quality and Productivity in Higher Education: An Analysis of Assessment Practices*, ASHE-ERIC/Higher Education Report. San Francisco: Jossey-Bass.

Hendry, C. (1994). *Human Resource Strategies for International Growth.* London: Routledge.

Lawler, E. E., III. (1986). *High-Involvement Management: Participative Strategies for Improving Organizational Performance.* San Francisco: Jossey-Bass.

Levy, D. G., Benjamin, R., Bikson, T. K., Derghazarian, E., Dewar, J. A., Gates, S. M., et al. (2001a). *Strategic and Performance Planning for the Office of the Chancellor for Education and Professional Development in the Department of Defense.* Santa Monica, CA: RAND, MR-1234-OSD.

Levy, D. G., Thie, H. J., Robbert, A. A., Naftel, S., Cannon, C., Ehrenberg, R., et al. (2001b). *Characterizing the Future Defense Workforce*, RAND, MR-1304-OSD.

Light, P. (1999). *The New Public Service.* Washington, D.C.: The Brookings Institution Press.

Light, P. (2000). The Empty Government Talent Pool: The New Public Service Arrives. *Brookings Review, 18*(1), 20–23.

Light, P. (2003). *Rebuilding the Supply Chain of Foreign-Affairs Leaders*, RAND, IP-233-IP.

Lindstrom, G., Bikson, T. K., & Treverton, G. F. (2003). *Developing America's Leaders for a Globalized Environment: Lessons from Literature Across Public and Private Sectors*, RAND, MR-1627-IP.

Lobel, S. (1990). Global Leadership Competencies: Managing to a Different Drumbeat. *Human Resource Management, 29*(Spring), 39–47.

Malone, T. W., and Crowston, K. (2001). The Interdisciplinary Study of Coordination. In G. M. Olson, T. W. Malone, & J. B. Smith, eds., *Coordination Theory and Collaboration Technology* (7–50) Mahwah, NJ: Lawrence Erlbaum Associates.

McDonnell, L., Stasz, C., & Madison, R. (1983). *Federal Support for Training Foreign Language and Area Specialists: The Education and Careers of FLAS Fellowship Recipients*, Santa Monica, CA: RAND, R-3070-ED.

Morrison, A. (2000). Developing a Global Leadership Model. *Human Resource Management, 39*(Summer/Fall), 117–131.

Nye, J. S. (2002). *The Paradox of American Power: Why the World's Only Superpower Can't Go It Alone*. New York: Oxford University Press.

Nye, J., & Keohane, R. (1987). Power and Interdependence Revisited. *International Organization, 41*, 723–753.

Rainey, H. G. (2002). Competing for Talent: Special Hiring Authorities for Federal Agencies. In *The Business of Government* (Spring, pp. 56–58). Arlington, VA: PricewaterhouseCoopers.

Stasz, C. (1997). Do Employers Need the Skills They Want? Evidence from Technical Work. *Journal of Education and Work, 10*(3), 205–223. Also available as RAND RP-683.

Stasz, C. (2001). "Assessing Skills for Work: Two Perspectives," *Oxford Economic Papers, 53*(3), 385–405.

Stasz, C., Chiesa, J., & Schwabe, W. (1998). *Education and the New Economy: A Policy Planning Exercise*, Santa Monica, CA: RAND, MR-946-NCRVE/UCB.

Treverton, G. F. (1993). *Making American Foreign Policy* (casebook), Englewood Cliffs, NJ: Prentice-Hall.

Treverton, G. F. (2001a). Intelligence Crisis: What's To Be Done. *Government Executive, 33*(14), 18–25.

Treverton, G. F. (2001b). *Reshaping National Intelligence for an Age of Information*, Cambridge, MA: Cambridge University Press.

Treverton, G. F., & Bikson, T. K. (2003). *New Challenges for International Leadership: Positioning the United States for the 21st Century.* RAND, IP-233-IP.

Treverton, G. F., van Heuven, M., & Manning, A. (1999). Driving Forces of International Security. In *Towards the 21st Century: Trends in Post-Cold War International Security*, MR-1038.0, Santa Monica, CA: RAND.

Ulrich, D. W., & Greenfield, H. (1995). The Transformation of Training and Development to Development and Learning. *American Journal of Management and Development, 1*(2), 11–22.

Walker, D. (2001). *Human Capital: Meeting the Governmentwide High-Risk Challenge*. Washington, D.C.: General Accounting Office, GAO-01-257T.

Waterman, R. H., Jr., Waterman, J. A., & Collard, B. A. (1994). Toward a Career-Resilient Workforce. *Harvard Business Review, 72*, 87–95.

Wittenberg-Cox, A. (1991). Delivering Global Leaders. *International Management, 46*(February), 52–55.

II

Field Studies of Leadership in Distributed Work Settings

3

Leading Groups From a Distance: How to Mitigate Consequences of Geographic Dispersion

Jonathon N. Cummings
Duke University

ABSTRACT

What should work-group leaders make sure to do when members are geographically dispersed rather than collocated? This chapter offers a simple answer that group leaders often fail to appreciate—communicate frequently with members. Researchers have demonstrated a variety of negative consequences of geographic dispersion for work groups, such as mutual knowledge problems and work coordination difficulties. However, leaders of dispersed groups may be able to mitigate some of these consequences through increased communication with members. Empirical evidence from 129 work groups in a global organization supports this claim and suggests that frequent informal contact may be a key to leading dispersed groups.

Over the past 50 years, organizational expansion and globalization, industrial mergers and acquisitions, and scientific and technological advances have made geographically dispersed work groups more common (Clark & Fujimoto, 1991; DeSanctis & Monge, 1999; Sproull & Kiesler, 1991). From new product groups that utilize marketing, engineering, and manufacturing in different parts of the globe (Griffen & Hauser, 1992) to solely electronically mediated groups that respond to computer virus emergencies worldwide (Goodman & Wilson, 2000), it is increasingly likely that group members will spend time working at a distance from one another. However, research on the consequences of dispersed work for groups (and suggestions for mitigating them) has not kept up with the changing nature of organizations (see Armstrong & Cole, 1995; Hinds & Kiesler, 2002; and Kraut, 1994, for notable exceptions). This chapter focuses on one consequence of geographic dispersion, reduced communication, and suggests that group leaders can improve performance through ensuring frequent contact with members.

CONSEQUENCES OF GEOGRAPHIC DISPERSION

Previous researchers who have studied the effects of physical proximity, or the propensity that one person comes in contact with another person in the same place, found generally positive outcomes, such as greater information sharing, stronger interpersonal friendships, and higher work satisfaction (Conrath, 1973; Festinger, Schacter, & Back, 1950; Monge, Rothman, Eisenberg, Miller, & Kirste, 1985; Van den Bulte & Moenaert, 1998). Those who have studied the effects of geographic dispersion, or the physical distance among people, found generally negative outcomes, such as a decline in communication, mutual knowledge problems, and work coordination difficulties (Allen, 1977; Cramton, 2001; Herbsleb, Mockus, Finholt, & Grinter, 2000; Kraut, Galegher, & Egido, 1987; Zahn, 1991). It is still unclear, however, whether the consequences of geographic dispersion are due to reduced social presence (Kiesler & Cummings, 2002; Short, Williams, & Christie, 1976), weakened social impact (Latane, Liu, Nowak, & Bonevento, 1995; but see Knowles, 1999, for a clarification), or other factors that undermine the process of interacting at a distance.

In work groups, the consequences of geographic dispersion may even be more dramatic than for individuals given the coordination required to accomplish a set of tasks (Thompson, 1967). When group members are separated by physical distance, mechanisms are unlikely to be in place for managing the flow of work (Kraut & Streeter, 1995; Van de Ven, Delbecq, & Koenig, 1976). Moreover, the administrative and problem-solving communication necessary for successfully completing projects is likely to be diminished (Ebadi & Utterback, 1984; Katz & Tushman, 1979). Effective work groups depend on smooth coordination and communication among members, and geographic dispersion may obstruct the development of cohesion, trust, norms, and other important group dynamics (Forsyth, 1998).

MITIGATING CONSEQUENCES OF GEOGRAPHIC DISPERSION IN WORK GROUPS

Much of what we know about dispersed work groups comes under the rubric of "virtual teams," or groups that use communication technology to support members working in different geographic locations (Jarvenpaa & Leidner, 1999; Maznevski & Chudoba, 2000; Townsend, DeMarie, & Hendrickson, 1998). A common recommendation for overcoming distance has been to provide group access to email, videoconferencing, and groupware, all of which allow members to communicate across geography, space, and time (McGrath & Hollingshead, 1994). However, creating access to communication among members does not guarantee that it will happen, and it is uncertain whether technology truly supports the types of interactions members often need to complete their work at a distance (Olson & Olson, 2001). Another possibility for ensuring communication among members is to assign group leaders the responsibility of carrying out this particular function.

Leader Functions

While discussions of group leaders have tended to appear at the end of books on mainly collocated group research (e.g., Hackman, 1990; McGrath, 1984; and Steiner 1972), there are opportunities and challenges for leading groups at a distance. On the one hand, leaders who are in a different geographic location than members may provide members with an opportunity to feel autonomous or self-managing (Manz & Sims, 1987). This freedom could inspire group members to excel at their work. On the other hand, groups often require order and structure. As Levine and Moreland (1998) state in their review of small groups:

> To avoid motivation and coordination losses, groups must ensure that critical activities (e.g., obtaining resources, motivating members, coordinating members' actions) are carried out. A common way of meeting this challenge is to give someone responsibility for organizing and directing group activities. (p. 442)

This means, for example, that if communication is more difficult, group leaders should find a way to make it happen so that performance does not suffer. At least two kinds of communication are particularly important for many groups: intragroup and external communication.

Intragroup Communication. Frequent communication among members is one way groups can maintain strong performance through better coordination of work and problem-solving as well as enhanced flow of information and ideas around the project (e.g., Allen, 1977; Katz & Tushman, 1979; Smith et al., 1994). Intragroup communication includes both task-related content such as knowledge sharing and social-related content such as informal chat, both of which are important for performing the task well. Because leaders are often placed in charge of seeing projects through from beginning to end, the communication they have with members should be more important for performance than the communication among members alone.

> *Hypothesis 1a: Intragroup communication will be positively related to group performance.*

Hypothesis 1b: Leader intragroup communication (relative to member intragroup communication) will be positively related to group performance.

External Communication.   Frequent communication between members and people outside of the group (e.g., nongroup members, customers) is another way that groups can maintain strong performance through gathering technological and market information as well as promoting successes and managing the expectations of others (e.g., Ancona & Caldwell, 1992; Hansen, 1999; Tushman & Katz, 1980). External communication often yields a snapshot of the larger context and can occur through corporate-sponsored conferences or tapping social networks established through previous work experience. Given that the role of many group leaders is to communicate information about the project to others, the communication they have with external parties should be more important for performance than the communication between members and others.

Hypothesis 2a: External communication will be positively related to group performance.

Hypothesis 2b: Leader external communication (relative to member external communication) will be positively related to group performance.

Geographic Dispersion × Intragroup Communication.   For groups working at a distance, frequent intragroup communication is likely to matter even more than for collocated work groups. That is, if communication frequency decreases as groups become more geographically dispersed, then the importance of intragroup communication becomes greater. Leader intragroup communication should be more important for performance than member intragroup communication because the leader can ensure that members are aware of the assigned tasks and responsibilities and can encourage communication among members.

Hypothesis 3a: As geographic dispersion increases, intragroup communication will be more strongly related to group performance.

Hypothesis 3b: As geographic dispersion increases, leader intragroup communication (relative to member intragroup communication) will be more strongly related to group performance.

This chapter embraces a functional approach to leading groups in organizations, which argues that leaders should ensure, in any way possible, that necessary functions for both task accomplishment and group maintenance are adequately met (Hackman & Walton, 1986). Through focusing on one function, group communication, the field study reported below examines whether, in fact, leader communication with members is particularly beneficial for geographically dispersed work groups. Furthermore, suggestions for mitigating the consequences of geographic dispersion are proposed for leaders in organizations.

FIELD STUDY

This field study was part of a larger project on work groups in a multinational Fortune 500 telecommunications company (see Cummings, 2004, for more details). The organization employs over 100,000 individuals across 5 divisions, and the sample of work groups represents United States and Canada (63%), Latin America and South America (3%), Europe (14%), the Middle East and Africa (4%), India and China (5%), and Japan, Korea, and Malaysia (8%). Each work group had around 8 members (ranging from 4 to 12), was assigned a specific project, and had a designated leader who was part of the group. Further description of 6 example work groups in the sample can be found in Table 3.1.

A survey was developed and sent to each member of 182 work groups ($N = 957/1315$, 73% response rate). Even though at least one person responded from each group, data were only analyzed for work groups from which 40% of the members responded, including at least the leader and one other member. The 129 work groups that qualified for the sample did not differ from the unqualified 53 work groups in terms of geographic dispersion but did differ on group performance (survey response bias favored higher performing groups, which restricts variance on the dependent variable, making the statistical analyses more conservative). Aside from information provided from managers on geographic dispersion and group performance, it is unknown how respondents differed from nonrespondents.

Measures

Control Variables. Previous research on work groups suggests that task type, project size, project length, project resources, and project uncertainty may influence group communication and performance. Therefore, these variables were controlled in the analyses below (see Table 3.2 for means, standard deviations, and correlations). Projects ranged from product development (e.g., design handheld scanning device for shipping company) to service improvement (e.g., convert client platform for car phones from analog to digital) to process management (e.g., execute separation and sale of business unit to another stakeholder) to manufacturing operations (e.g., modify existing factory to support new production of pagers).

Consistent with labels used in the corporation, tasks were categorized as product development (0 = no, 1 = yes), service improvement (0 = no, 1 = yes), process management (0 = no, 1 = yes), and manufacturing operations (0 = no, 1 = yes).

TABLE 3.1.
Project Descriptions from Six Work Groups

#	Work Group Name[a]	Size	Locations (buildings)	Dispersion Index	Functions (members)	Length (mo.)	Project Description
1	Error Detection	4	Israel (1)	0.00	Engineer (3) Support (1)	10	Developed utility for detecting wiring errors on electrical boards
2	Handheld Design	10	Georgia (1) Tennessee (1) Illinois (2) Israel (3) Arizona (1)	2.03	Engineering (1) Manufacture (1) Quality (1) Proj. Mgmt (4) Cust. Srvc (1) Marketing (1) Sales (1)	25	Designed handheld scanning device for shipping company
3	Platform Conversion	9	Illinois (3)	0.85	Engineer (1) Quality (2) Proj. Mgmt (2) Marketing (2) Finance (1) Sales (1)	9	Converted client platform for car phones from analog to digital
4	Subscriber Requirements	6	China (3)	1.01	Engineer (3) Quality (1) Proj. Mgmt (2)	7	Enhanced phone system performance to meet subscriber requirements
5	Business Separation	8	Arizona (4)	1.21	Tech. Ops (1) Info Tech (6) HR (1)	4	Executed separation/ sale of business unit to another stakeholder
6	Factory Modification	9	Ireland (1) England (1)	0.64	Engineer (3) Manufacture (5) Quality (1)	8	Modified existing factory to support new production of pager

Note: Work group names are fictitious. Work groups 1, 2: product development; 3, 4: service improvement; 5: process management; 6: manufacturing operations.

Project size was the number of members in the work group. Project length was the number of months from the start of the project to the end. Project resources were measured as the availability of (a) financial, (b) personnel, and (c) equipment resources (10-pt scale; 1 = not very, 5 = average, 10 = very much, α = .80). Project uncertainty was measured with an item "On average,

TABLE 3.2.
Means, Standard Deviations, and Correlations of Main Study Variables ($N = 129$ Work Groups)

Variable	M	SD	1	2	3	4	5	6	7	8	9	10	11	12	13	14	15
1. Product development	0.25	0.43															
2. Service improvement	0.25	0.44	-.34														
3. Process management	0.25	0.43	-.33	-.34													
4. Manufacturing operations	0.25	0.43	-.33	-.34	-.33												
5. Project size	8.12	1.88	-.07	-.04	.01	.10											
6. Project length	2.54	0.63	.08	-.06	.08	-.10	.00										
7. Project resources	6.22	2.07	.28	.01	-.24	-.05	-.14	-.03									
8. Project uncertainty	5.63	2.41	.17	.13	-.20	-.10	.14	-.02	.09								
9. Geographic dispersion	0.52	0.55	.02	-.01	.16	-.17	.16	-.10	-.10	.14							
10. Overall intragroup communication	2.96	0.42	.01	.01	-.18	.16	-.22	-.16	.25	.14	-.36						
11. Overall external communication	2.02	0.44	.10	.11	-.14	-.07	-.01	-.16	.13	.20	.04	.37					
12. Leader intragroup communication	3.17	0.51	.04	.05	-.12	.02	-.04	-.09	.16	.16	-.21	.63	.31				
13. Member intragroup communication	2.92	0.46	.00	.00	-.16	.17	-.22	-.15	.25	.12	-.35	.97	.34	.43			
14. Leader external communication	2.14	0.71	.05	.12	-.15	-.02	.06	-.12	.14	.21	.02	.11	.67	.30	.05		
15. Member external communication	1.99	0.46	.11	.08	-.10	-.09	-.02	-.13	.12	.15	.06	.39	.95	.25	.39	.43	
16. Performance	1.74	0.69	.19	-.03	-.17	.01	.12	-.04	.01	.18	.10	.22	.30	.28	.19	.23	.30

Note: $r > .15, p < .10; r > .18, p < .05; r > .23, p < .01.$

39

to what extent did the project need skills or information that were stable or rapidly changing" (10-pt scale; 1 = stable, 5 = average, 10 = rapidly changing; higher value indicates greater uncertainty).

Geographic Dispersion. The number of different buildings group members resided in during the project was used to compute an entropy-based diversity index as defined by Teachman (1980). This measure takes advantage of complete data available from an HR database on building locations for each member and is consistent with findings by Allen (1977) and others that communication drops to near zero after 30 meters. The greater the dispersion of group members across different buildings, the higher the score on the index. For example, in Table 3.1, the Error Detection group has a dispersion index value of 0 because all four members were located in the same building while the Handheld Design group has a dispersion index value of 2.03 because the 10 members were spread across five buildings.

Communication Frequency. The survey included social network measures of how frequently each group member communicated with every other group member (intragroup) as well as with division employees, nondivision employees, and the customer outside of the group (external) (5-pt scale; 1 = never, 2 = monthly, 3 = weekly, 4 = daily, 5 = hourly). Overall intragroup communication consisted of the average of group member responses within the group (α = .77), and separate measures were computed for leader communication (i.e., average of leader with each member) and for group member communication (i.e., average of members not including leader). Overall external communication consisted of the average between members and those outside of the group (division members, nondivision members, customers; α = .67), and separate measures were computed for leader communication (i.e., average of leader with those outside of the group), and for group members (i.e., average of members not including leader and those outside of the group).

Communication Modality. Each group member also indicated the primary modality of communication used with every other group member: scheduled face-to-face, scheduled phone, informal face-to-face, informal phone, or email. That is, each member selected *one* of the above choices to describe the main way he or she communicated with another member. Averaging across the modalities for each group indicates the proportion of work group members who primarily used a particular communication method.

Performance. As part of an annual corporate-wide competition, work groups were rated by senior executives on seven dimensions of (1) teamwork, (2) clearly defined problem selection, (3) appropriateness of method used to solve problem, (4) innovativeness of remedies used to solve problem, (5) quality of impact from results, (6) institutionalization of solution, and (7) clarity of presentation. Each group was asked to make a 20–30 minute presentation to a panel of judges (5 to 12 senior executives) who were given specific training regarding the process. Different judges rated the participating groups at different levels of the competition, and in most cases, judges were unfamiliar with the projects before they made their ratings. A sample analysis ($N = 12$ judges and $N = 33$ groups) revealed that judges were able to reliably rate overall performance ($\alpha = .88$ across judges), and provided evidence of a halo effect whereby all seven dimensions loaded onto one factor ($\alpha = .80$ across dimensions). The 129 groups that qualified for the sample were given a ranking of 1 (lowest level, $N = 52$), 2 (middle level, $N = 59$), or 3 (highest level, $N = 18$), depending on how far they made it in the competition.

Statistical Models.   Ordinary least-squares regression analyses were used to examine two general models. First, the control variables and geographic dispersion were used to predict communication (overall as well as leader and member intragroup and external communication). Second, the control variables, geographic dispersion, and communication were used to predict performance. In particular, the dependent variable (Performance) was predicted in three steps: Step 1 (Dispersion), Step 2 (Dispersion + Communication), and Step 3 (Dispersion + Communication + Dispersion × Communication). A significant interaction when leader intragroup communication is included would provide support for the idea that increased leader communication with members is particularly beneficial for performance in dispersed groups.

RESULTS

As was found in earlier research (e.g., Allen, 1977), communication among group members decreased dramatically with distance (see Table 3.3). From the first general model, we see that geographic dispersion ($b = -.26, p < .01$) was significantly negatively associated with overall intragroup communication, though there was no relationship with overall external communication. In terms of leader and member communication, leader intragroup communication ($b = -.21, p < .05$) and member intragroup communication ($b = -.27, p < .01$) were significantly negatively associated with geographic dispersion, though leader and member external communication were not.

In the first step of the second general model predicting performance, geographic dispersion was not associated with performance (see Table 3.4). However, in the second step, overall intragroup communication ($b = .41, p < .05$) and overall external communication ($b = .30, p < .05$) were significantly

TABLE 3.3.
Regression Analyses Predicting Overall, Leader, and Member Intragroup and External Communication from Geographic Dispersion ($N = 129$)

Variables	Overall Intragroup Communication		Overall External Communication		Leader Intragroup Communication		Leader External Communication		Member Intragroup Communication		Member External Communication	
	B	SE	B	SE	B	SE	B	SE	B	SE	B	SE
Constant	3.26	0.24	1.98	0.29	3.13	0.33	1.65	0.47	3.25	0.27	1.96	0.30
Product development	−0.03	0.10	0.10	0.12	0.00	0.14	0.09	0.19	−0.05	0.11	0.10	0.12
Service improvement	−0.01	0.10	0.11	0.11	0.02	0.13	0.21	0.18	−0.03	0.11	0.09	0.12
Process management	—	—	—	—	—	—	—	—	—	—	—	—
Manufacturing operations	0.12	0.10	0.01	0.11	0.01	0.13	0.08	0.18	0.13	0.11	−0.02	0.12
Project size	−0.04*	0.02	0.00	0.02	0.00	0.02	0.02	0.03	−0.05*	0.02	0.00	0.02
Project length	−0.11*	0.05	−0.11†	0.06	−0.09	0.07	−0.12	0.10	−0.11†	0.06	−0.09	0.07
Project resources	0.04*	0.02	0.02	0.02	0.03	0.02	0.04	0.03	0.04*	0.02	0.02	0.02
Project uncertainty	0.04**	0.01	0.03†	0.02	0.04*	0.02	0.05†	0.03	0.04*	0.02	0.02	0.02
Geographic dispersion	−0.26**	0.06	0.01	0.08	−0.21*	0.09	0.00	0.12	−0.27**	0.07	0.03	0.08
df	8		8		8		8		8		8	
R^2	.29		.09		.11		.09		.26		.06	

Note: †$p < .10$, *$p < .05$, **$p < .01$; Process management is not included in the regression analyses because the four task types account for all groups in the sample; however the results do not change when it is substituted for another task type. B is the unstandardized coefficient and SE is the standard error.

TABLE 3.4.
Regression Analyses Predicting Work Group Performance ($N = 129$)

Variables	Dispersion		Communication		Dispersion × Communication	
	B	SE	B	SE	B	SE
Constant	1.23	0.45	−0.72	0.68	−0.69	0.68
Product development	0.45*	0.18	0.43*	0.18	0.39*	0.18
Service improvement	0.16	0.18	0.13	0.17	0.09	0.17
Process management	—	—	—	—	—	—
Manufacturing operations	0.24	0.18	0.18	0.17	0.17	0.17
Project size	0.03	0.03	0.05	0.03	0.04	0.03
Project length	−0.03	0.10	0.05	0.09	0.03	0.09
Project resources	−0.02	0.03	−0.04	0.03	−0.03	0.03
Project uncertainty	0.03	0.03	0.01	0.03	0.01	0.03
Geographic dispersion	0.11	0.12	0.22^t	0.12	0.26^t	0.14
Overall intragroup communication			0.41*	0.17	0.41*	0.17
Overall external communication			0.30*	0.14	0.31*	0.14
Geographic dispersion × overall intragroup communication					0.03	0.06
Geographic dispersion × overall external communication					0.10	0.07
df	8		10		12	
R^2	.09		.20		.22	
ΔR^2			.11**		.02	

Note: $^t p < .10$, $*p < .05$, $**p < .01$; Process management is not included in the regression analyses because the four task types account for all groups in the sample; however, the results do not change when it is substituted for another task type. B is the unstandardized coefficient and SE is the standard error.

positively associated with performance (in support of hypotheses 1a and 2a). The change in R^2 from the first ($R^2 = .09$) to second step ($R^2 = .20$) was significant ($p < .01$). Finally, in the third step, overall intragroup communication ($b = .41, p < .05$), and overall external communication ($b = .31, p < .05$) were significantly positively associated with performance, but the interaction of geographic dispersion and overall intragroup communication was not (which does not support hypothesis 3a). The change in R^2 from the second ($R^2 = .20$) to third step ($R^2 = .22$) was not significant. There were no significant interactions with other variables in the model.

When leader and member communication are substituted for overall communication, a slightly different story emerges. As we saw earlier, in the first step, geographic dispersion was not associated with performance (see Table 3.5). In the second step, leader intragroup communication ($b = .28, p < .05$) was significantly positively associated with performance, but member intra-

TABLE 3.5.
Regression Analyses Predicting Work Group Performance ($N = 129$)

Variables	Dispersion		Communication		Dispersion × Communication	
	B	SE	B	SE	B	SE
Constant	1.23	0.45	−0.87	0.67	−1.03	0.66
Product development	0.45*	0.18	0.43*	0.17	0.48*	0.18
Service improvement	0.16	0.18	0.12	0.17	0.09	0.17
Process management	—	—	—	—	—	—
Manufacturing operations	0.24	0.18	0.20	0.17	0.19	0.17
Size	0.03	0.03	0.04	0.03	0.04	0.03
Length	−0.03	0.10	0.05	0.09	0.06	0.09
Resources	−0.02	0.03	−0.04	0.03	−0.04	0.03
Uncertain	0.03	0.03	0.00	0.03	0.00	0.03
Geographic dispersion	0.11	0.12	0.22^t	0.12	0.24	0.15
Leader intragroup communication			0.28*	0.13	0.32*	0.13
Member intragroup communication			0.08	0.10	0.08	0.10
Leader external communication			0.21	0.17	0.24	0.17
Member external communication			0.21	0.16	0.20	0.16
Geographic dispersion × leader intragroup communication					0.15*	0.07
Geographic dispersion × member intragroup communication					−0.04	0.08
df	8		12		14	
R^2	.09		.23		.26	
ΔR^2			.14**		$.03^t$	

Note: $^t p < .10$, $^* p < .05$, $^{**} p < .01$; Process management is not included in the regression analyses because the four task types account for all groups in the sample; however, the results do not change when it is substituted for another task type. B is the unstandardized coefficient and SE is the standard error.

group communication was not (in support of hypothesis 3a but not hypothesis 3b). The change in R^2 from the first ($R^2 = .09$) to second step ($R^2 = .23$) was significant ($p < .01$). And in the third step, leader intragroup communication ($b = .32, p < .05$) and the interaction of geographic dispersion and leader intragroup communication ($b = .15, p < .05$) were significantly positively associated with performance (in support of hypothesis 3c). The change in R^2 from the second ($R^2 = .23$) to third step ($R^2 = .26$) was marginally significant ($p < .10$). There were no significant interactions with other variables in the model. The interaction plot of geographic dispersion and leader intragroup communication reveals that for highly dispersed groups, greater group leader communication was related to higher performance (see Figure 3–1).

DISCUSSION

The results from this field study point us in an interesting direction regarding the role of leader functions in dispersed groups. First, it is clear that geographic

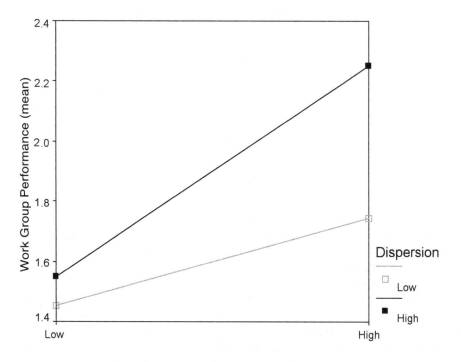

FIGURE 3–1.   Interaction plot of leader intragroup communication and geographic dispersion on work group performance ($N = 129$ work groups).

dispersion has consequences for work groups, especially in the reduction of communication among members. When members are spread across different buildings, the likelihood that they will communicate decreases considerably. However, geographic dispersion does not appear to have clear consequences for external communication. Second, and in support of the Hypotheses 1a and 2a, frequent overall intragroup and external communication are strongly related to performance, reinforcing the importance of frequent communication for all groups. In support of hypothesis 1b, leader intragroup (but not external) communication is strongly related to performance, suggesting that leader communication within the group is particularly important. Finally, in support of hypothesis 3c, group leaders can mitigate the consequences of geographic dispersion by ensuring frequent communication with members. The significant interaction of geographic dispersion and leader intragroup communication provides support for this claim.

Because the frequency measure does not reveal qualitative differences in communication used by the leader, exploratory analyses were conducted on data collected about whether the main form of communication used by the leader was scheduled or informal, and whether it occurred through face-to-face, phone, or email. The leader indicated for each group member whether the primary modality of communication was scheduled face-to-face, scheduled phone, informal face-to-face, informal phone, or email. The forced choice responses were averaged to measure the proportion of work-group members with whom the leader primarily used each communication method. A median split of dispersion (high, low) and performance (high, low) indicates that high dispersion, high performance (black bar) groups differed from high dispersion, low performance (white bar) groups by the proportion of work-group members who used scheduled phone and informal face-to-face communication (see Figure 3–2). That is, for geographically dispersed groups, significantly fewer leaders of high performing groups used scheduled phone ($t = 2.67, p < .05$) and significantly more leaders of high performing groups used informal face-to-face ($t = 3.08, p < .01$) relative to low performing groups. There was little evidence that group members relied on other forms of communication (e.g., videoconferencing, groupware, instant messenger), although because this measure did not capture the frequency of media use, these exploratory results should be interpreted with caution.

What should work-group leaders make sure to do when members are geographically dispersed rather than collocated? The empirical evidence presented above provides one simple answer—communicate frequently with members. Though the exploratory analyses suggest that informal face-to-face communication may be a key to leading dispersed groups (see Kraut & Streeter, 1995, for additional discussion), it is often not feasible for leaders to travel from one building to the next, especially when the buildings are in different states or countries. Therefore, group leaders should pick up the phone

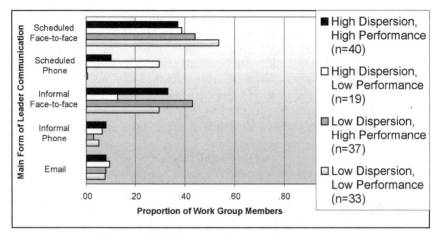

FIGURE 3–2.   Main form of leader communication by proportion of work group members for dispersion (high, low) and performance (high, low) ($N = 129$ work groups).

or send email between scheduled meetings. Even though these options were not selected as the primary mode of communication above, they would appear to be better options than waiting for a scheduled meeting to communicate.

There are several alternative explanations for why leader internal communication was beneficial for performance when groups were geographically dispersed. First, performance was evaluated roughly six months before group members completed the surveys. Although senior executives did not give detailed feedback to groups regarding their performance, all groups knew whether they advanced to the next level of the competition. Participants could have responded to the survey in a way that conformed to their intuitions about performance. Second, work groups with better performing leaders may have communicated more because of opportunities they created for themselves; thus it may not have been that communication resulted in better performance but rather that better performance resulted in more communication. However, claims about causality cannot be substantiated because the data reported here are cross-sectional in nature.

Limitations

There are also several limitations of this field study. First, the sample was chosen opportunistically; there is no documented information on how representative the work groups are in size, membership, or capabilities. Research in other companies is necessary to assess the generalizability of these results. Second, one reason for the low R^2 in the regression analyses (which ranged from .09 to .26, see Table 3.5) may be that variance was restricted on the dependent variable because only moderately to highly successful groups were examined. Including low performing groups in future studies would help further assess the extent to which leader communication makes a difference in dispersed groups. Finally, there are concerns regarding the measurement of communication and the measurement error from the self-report survey. Additional reports of communication (e.g., personal diaries, direct observation, computer records) would be preferred to validate with whom and how often communication occurs within and outside of the group.

CONCLUSION

There are several practical implications from these results for managers who design and implement dispersed work groups in organizations. First, the dispersion of members across locations should be balanced such that there are two or more members at each location. A subanalysis of the 129 groups revealed that members who had one other person in their building were significantly more likely to communicate with the group compared with members who were in a building alone ($t = 2.12$, $p < .05$). Balancing the distribution of members across locations increases the likelihood that group members (including the leader) have recurring opportunities for communication.

Second, and presumably early in the life of the group, leaders should encourage norms about communication in their groups to ensure that members feel comfortable visiting, calling, or emailing other members. Interviews with group members suggest that they established patterns of communication that persisted throughout the project (cf., Gersick, 1988), and once dispersed members stopped making frequent communication part of their routine, it dissipated. Along these same lines, it often takes extra effort to make dispersed members feel a part of the group, and the leader would be an ideal candidate to make this happen through frequent communication.

Finally, leaders should be evaluated and held accountable for frequent communication with members, and the required functions for leading collocated groups should be reinforced for dispersed groups. However, leaders should be careful to not fall into a trap of having frequent scheduled communication, given the preliminary evidence above that informal communication is particularly important in high performing groups. Leaders of dispersed groups must walk a fine line between being too overbearing and not attentive enough. In the end, making frequent communication an explicit leader function should be beneficial to dispersed groups.

ACKNOWLEDGMENTS

This research was supported by the Knowledge and Distributed Intelligence program of the National Science Foundation (#IIS-9872996).

REFERENCES

Allen, T. (1977). *Managing the flow of technology.* Cambridge, MA: MIT Press.

Ancona, D., & Caldwell, D. (1992). Bridging the boundary: External activity and performance in organizational teams. *Administrative Science Quarterly, 37,* 634–665.

Armstrong, D., & Cole, P. (1995). Managing distance and differences in geographically distributed work groups. In S. R. Jackson, M. (Ed.), *Diversity in work teams.* Washington, DC: APA.

Clark, K., & Fujimoto, T. (1991). *Product development performance: Strategy, organization and management in the world auto industry.* Boston: Harvard Business School Press.

Conrath, D. (1973). Communication environment and its relationship to organizational structure. *Management Science, 20,* 586–603.

Cramton, C. (2001). The mutual knowledge problem and its consequences in dispersed collaboration. *Organization Science, 12*(3), 346–371.

Cummings, J. N. (2004). Work groups, structural diversity, and knowledge sharing in a global organization. *Management Science, 50*(3), 352–364.

DeSanctis, G., & Monge, P. (1999). Communication processes for virtual organizations. *Organization Science, 10*(6), 693–703.

Ebadi, Y., & Utterback, J. (1984). The effects of communication on technological innovation. *Management Science, 30*(5), 572–585.

Festinger, L., Schacter, S., & Back, K. (1950). *Social pressures in informal groups.* Palo Alto, CA: Stanford University Press.

Forsyth, D. (1998). *Group dynamics.* Pacific Grove, CA: Brooks/Cole.

Gersick, C. (1988). Time and transition in work teams: Toward a new model of group development. *Academy of Management Journal, 31*(6), 9–41.

Goodman, P., & Wilson, J. (2000). Substitutes for socialization and exocentric teams. *Research on managing groups and teams, 3,* 53–77.

Griffin, A., & Hauser, J. (1992). Patterns of communication among marketing, engineering, and manufacturing. *Management Science, 38*(3), 360–373.

Hackman, R. (Ed.). (1990). *Groups that work (and those that don't): Creating conditions for effective teamwork.* San Francisco, CA: Jossey-Bass.

Hackman, R., & Walton, R. (1986). Leading groups in organizations. In P. Goodman (Ed.), *Designing effective work groups* (pp. 72–119). San Francisco: Jossey-Bass.

Hansen, M. (1999). The search-transfer problem: The role of weak ties in sharing knowledge across organization subunits. *Administrative Science Quarterly, 44,* 82–111.

Herbsleb, J., Mockus, A., Finholt, T., & Grinter, R. (2000). *Distance, dependencies, and delay in a global collaboration.* Paper presented at the Computer-Supported Cooperative Work (CSCW) December 1–6, 2000, Philadelphia, PA.

Hinds, P., & Kiesler, S. (2002). *Distributed work.* Cambridge, MA: MIT Press.

Jarvenpaa, S., & Leidner, D. (1999). Communication and trust in global virtual teams. *Organization Science, 10*(6), 791–815.

Katz, R., & Tushman, M. (1979). Communication patterns, project performance, and task characteristics: An empirical evaluation and integration in an R&D setting. *Organizational Behavior and Human Decision Processes, 23,* 139–162.

Kiesler, S., & Cummings, J. (2002). What do we know about proximity and distance in work groups? A legacy of research. In P. Hinds, & Kiesler, S. (Ed.), *Distributed work,* (pp. 57–80). Cambridge, MA: MIT Press.

Knowles, E. (1999). Distance matters more than you think! An artifact clouds interpretation of Latane, Liu, Nowak, Bonevento, and Zheng's results. *Personality and Social Psychology Bulletin, 25*(8), 1045–1048.

Kraut, R. (1994). *Research recommendations to facilitate distributed work*. Washington, DC: National Research Council.

Kraut, R., Galegher, J., Egido, C. (1987). Relationships and tasks in scientific research collaboration. *Human-Computer Interaction, 3*, 31–58.

Kraut, R., & Streeter, L. (1995). Coordination in software development. *Communications of the ACM, 38*(3), 69–81.

Latane, B., Liu, J., Nowak, A., & Bonevento, M. (1995). Distance matters: Physical space and social impact. *Personality and Social Psychology Bulletin, 21*, 795–805.

Levine, J., & Moreland, R. (1998). Small groups. In D. Gilbert, Fiske, S., & Lindzey, G. (Ed.), *The handbook of social psychology*. New York: McGraw-Hill.

Manz, C., & Sims, H. (1987). Leading workers to lead themselves: The external leadership of self-managing work teams. *Administrative Science Quarterly, 32*, 106–128.

Maznevski, M., & Chudoba, C. (2000). Bridging space over time: Global virtual team dynamics and effectiveness. *Organization Science, 11*(5), 473–492.

McGrath, J. (1984). *Groups*. Englewood Cliffs, NJ: Prentice Hall.

McGrath, J., & Hollingshead, A. (1994). *Groups interacting with technology: Ideas, evidence, issues, and an agenda*. Thousand Oaks, CA: Sage.

Monge, P., Rothman, L., Eisenberg, E., Miller, K., & Kirste, K. (1985). The dynamics of organizational proximity. *Management Science, 31*(9), 1129–1141.

Olson, G., & Olson, J. (2001). Distance matters. *Human Computer Interaction, 15*(139–179).

Short, J., Williams, E., & Christie, B. (1976). *The social psychology of telecommunications*. New York: Wiley.

Smith, K., Smith, K., Olian, J., Sims, H., O'Bannon, D., & Scully, J. (1994). Top management team demography and process. *Administrative Science Quarterly, 39*, 412–438.

Sproull, L., & Kiesler, S. (1991). *Connections: New ways of working in the networked organization*: MIT Press.

Steiner, I. (1972). *Group process and productivity*. New York: Academic Press.

Teachman, J. (1980). Analysis of population diversity. *Sociological Methods and Research, 5*, 341–362.

Thompson, J. (1967). *Organizations in action*. New York: McGraw-Hill.

Townsend, A., DeMarie, S., & Hendrickson, A. (1998). Virtual teams: Technology and the workplace of the future. *Academy of Management Executive, 12*(3), 17–29.

Tushman, M., & Katz, R. (1980). External communication and project performance: An investigation into the role of gatekeepers. *Management Science, 26*(11), 1071–1085.

Van de Ven, A., Delbecq, A., & Koenig, R. (1976). Determinants of coordination modes within organizations. *American Sociological Review, 41*, 322–338.

Van den Bulte, C., & Moenaert, R. (1998). The effects of R&D team co-location on communication patterns among R&D, marketing, and manufacturing. *Management Science, 44*(11), S1–S18.

Zahn, G. (1991). Face-to-face communication in an office setting: The effects of position, proximity, and exposure. *Communication Research, 18*(6), 737–754.

4

Designing a Tail in Two Cities: Leaders' Perspectives on Collocated and Distance Collaboration

Erin Bradner
Autodesk Inc., San Rafael, CA

Gloria Mark
University of California, Irvine

OVERVIEW

In recent years, both large and small organizations have increased their reliance on distance collaboration to accomplish work. Virtually collocated work groups are now using a wide range of technologies to engage in synchronous and asynchronous collaboration such as audioconferencing, videoconferencing, Internet chat, application sharing, and 3-dimensional media spaces. Yet as these technologies become commonplace, few longitudinal, empirical studies of distance collaboration have been reported. Although many high-quality studies of specific technology and collaboration issues exist (e.g., trust, Handy, 1995; Iacono & Weisband, 1997; Jarvenpaa & Leidner, 1998; and productivity, Bradner & Mark, 2001), few studies have focused on the experiences of leaders who manage geographically distributed teams (Haywood, 1998). The study we describe in this chapter helps to fill this gap in the literature. It reports on a 20-month collaboration among engineers that we will call the Tail Team, to preserve anonymity. This team was distributed geographically across two sites within a company we will call Airplane Incorporated. We describe experiences with technologies and distance collaboration primarily from the perspective of the team leaders. The perspective of the leaders we studied is that face-to-face interaction at the outset of the collaboration was vital to the successful collaboration of their group. The findings reported here enhance our understanding of the social ties and interdependencies that exist when a group is collocated and their role in collaboration when that same group later becomes distributed. We have focused on the attitudes and behaviors of the team leaders vis-à-vis factors leading to the success or failure of this collaboration effort.

BACKGROUND

This chapter examines leadership through studying aspects of coordination and communication in the design of the tail section of a new Airplane Incorporated airplane. This project is an interesting case of leadership at a distance for several reasons. First, the project grew out of an Airplane Incorporated initiative that called for the use of technology to coordinate with noncollocated sources of engineering manpower. When the project began, Arizona-based Aircraft Company's engineers and engineering managers were contracted to work with Airplane Incorporated engineers based in Houston, Texas, although the companies have merged now.[1] The project involved an extended period of collocation (9 months) followed by a period of distance collaboration (15 months) between engineering teams from the two organizations. Second, collaboration between the two companies involved a constellation of technologies. A premise of this study is that we can better understand the dynamics of leadership in geographically dispersed engineering teams by looking at the way each technology was appropriated by team leaders and engineers. Third, because the project involved periods of collocation and distance collaboration, tradeoffs between both can be examined. The following sections underscore some of these tradeoffs by summarizing data gathered from interviews and observations that took place over an eight-month period from April 1 to November 15, 1998.

Before we discuss details of the field study, let's examine the following question: What are some differences that leaders need to be aware of between distributed and collocated teams in order to effectively lead distributed teams? The objective of this chapter is to examine specific leadership behaviors that promote collaboration among geographically distributed teams. Implicit in this objective is the assumption that geographically distributed collaboration can change with leaders' increased awareness of the teams' challenges.

Empirical evidence suggests that this is a valid assumption. For example, the work of Maier and Sashkin (1971) strongly suggests that the leadership

---

[1]Some identifying details such as location have been changed to preserve anonymity.

approach that best promotes problem solving is one that involves open exchange of factual information among managers and subordinates. When facts are exchanged openly, leaders guide groups to a solution by consensus building rather than persuasion. Maier and Sashkin (1971) provide empirical evidence that the more a leader shares information that is relevant to a problem, the easier it is to reach consensus on that problem. Similarly, technology researchers have shown that high levels of information exchange leads to improved team outcomes (Weisband, 2002). Meanwhile, others have argued that it is harder for an electronic group to reach consensus than a group meeting face-to-face (Sproull & Kiesler, 1991), and when working at a distance, groups spend more time clarifying communication and discussing how to manage their work than those working face-to-face. Thus, whereas information exchange appears to promote positive team behaviors, we face the dilemma that information exchange is restricted when groups are distributed. Findings from management theory and human–computer interaction studies provide few clear behavioral guidelines to leaders. How can a leader of distributed teams increase consensus and productivity? Does productivity depend upon the technology used to mediate communication?

Another topic of interest to leaders of distributed teams, and around which some consensus is emerging, is trust. Not standing too close to others at a bus stop—in other words, adhering to established norms of proxemics—is one of many ways we signal to strangers that we can be trusted (Hall, 1966). Another way is through conversation. Trust and cooperation among strangers increase over time through face-to-face conversation (Kollock, 1998; Rabbie, 1991). Exactly how to promote conversation and trust when communication is not face-to-face but when it is technology-mediated, has concerned human–computer interaction researchers in recent years (Iacono & Weisband, 1997; Jensen, Garnham, Drucker, & Kollock, 2000; Muhfelder, Klein, Simon, & Luczak, 1999; Olson & Olson, 2000). Conventional wisdom might lead us to assume that people are more likely to trust others who live or work near them. If two people live next door to each other, they share the same neighborhood, parks, and socioeconomic status. They are more likely to trust each other than trust an "outsider" from another state because their interests and concerns are more closely aligned to each other's than to the outsider's. Indeed, research results support the notion that trust is higher among people who share the same geography, both in social contexts (cf. Kraut, Fish, Root, & Chalfonte, 1990; Newcomb, 1961) and in the workplace (Kraut et al., 1990).

What happens to trust among work groups when people are geographically dispersed? Iacono and Weisband (1997) have looked at trust among distributed, short-term student teams. They found that high levels of trust can be maintained in temporary teams who engage in frequent email interactions over the course of a short-term project. They argue that frequent interaction among team members fosters trust. Other researchers, such as Jensen et al. (2000), have compared the effects of communication modality on trust among teams. They tested pairs of subjects using the Prisoner's Dilemma Game. Prior studies using a similar experimental paradigm found that permitting face-to-face communication between opponents significantly increases the likelihood that a cooperative strategy will be adopted by players (Rabbie, 1991). Jensen et al. (2000) reproduced these findings and found that cooperation was significantly greater when communication was possible via voice (speakerphone) compared to when no communication was possible. Yet there is more to the story. Jensen and his colleagues also discovered that when Internet text chat was used to mediate communication, trust and cooperation increased when the text-to-speech component of chat was used. Text-to-speech is a feature that translates typed text from words on the screen to synthesized speech. When used with chat, typed messages from a sender are read aloud on a recipient's computer when they are received. This finding is interesting because it suggests that cooperation increases not only when two humans are communicating via voice but also when a computer voice is used to mediate communication!

In this chapter, we do not challenge findings such as these but rather we explore how technology and geography interact in ways that affect cohesion and trust in groups. Because building trust and consensus are two important responsibilities of group leaders, they warrant examination here. The following sections approach these topics, in addition to the related concepts of coordination and interdependencies, by drawing on empirical findings from the first author's field study of a distributed engineering team at Airplane Incorporated.

METHODOLOGY

In this study ethnographic methods were used to examine distance collaboration across the two Airplane Incorporated sites. The first author conducted 18 semistructured interviews with 10 different members of the 51-member distributed team. Multiple interviews were conducted with the team leaders. Fifteen of the 18 interviews were conducted at the Phoenix site between the 3-month period of April 1998 to June 1998. Eight one-hour meeting observations were also conducted during this time. Subsequent interviews were conducted in October of 1998 in Houston. All interviews were tape recorded and transcribed. Artifacts were collected, with permission, including Airplane Incorporated's virtual collocation plan, action item lists, and organizational charts. Specific names and identifying terms have been changed to protect the anonymity of the study participants.

Drawn from the leadership experiences we collected in interviews and observations of team meetings, several points regarding the pitfalls and promise of leadership at a distance will be presented in this chapter. Some of these experiences have specific relevance to virtual teaming at Airplane Incorporated but are also generalizable to other distributed engineering environments.

Collocation

The Tail Team worked on a section of the tail of a new Airplane Incorporated airplane including the pressure bulkhead, pivot bulkhead, APU inlet port, and tailskids. It was this section of the plane that was outsourced, or "transferred" from Houston to the Phoenix site (formerly Aircraft Company) in November of 1997. All team members were assigned to devote 100% of their time to the Tail Team project. A formal reporting structure existed in the team such that junior engineers reported to several engineering leads, who reported to two project leads. Two major phases of the project are the collocation and virtual collocation periods.

Collocation of the Phoenix engineering team at the headquarters of the Airplane Incorporated, Commercial Airplane Group in Houston occurred before work on the airplane began. The merger between Aircraft Company (alias) and Airplane Incorporated was announced in December 1996. Shortly thereafter, in January of 1997, a group of Phoenix engineers and management arrived in Houston and were assigned to the Tail Team. During the first quarter of 1997, Phoenix engineers continued to train on the Airplane Incorporated engineering process while management studied the business processes.

From May to September 1997 the collocated team researched design considerations and conceptualized the design for the tail section. During this time, engineering managers consulted with the engineers on the design and worked out the logistics of distance collaboration. This period culminated in two milestones. One was the finalization of the design concept. This was called "Firm Configuration" and occurred in mid-September 1997. The second milestone was the Design Review meeting in which the Phoenix team described the design concept, the division of labor, and how work would be coordinated between the two sites. In the month following this meeting, the majority of the Phoenix engineers and all of the managers returned to Arizona to begin the difficult work of translating the concept into formal engineering drawings. A few engineers remained until January 1998.

Virtual Collocation

Airplane Incorporated defines collaboration among geographically distributed work teams as "virtual collocation" (Mark, Grudin, & Poltrock, 1999). This term describes the collaboration between Airplane Incorporated's integrated product design teams (IPDs), which are geographically distributed. Airplane Incorporated's business process documentation defines virtual collocation as "the application of technology to achieve the advantages and avoid the disadvantages of physical collocation" during distance collaboration (Boeing, 1988).

Distribution of Labor

Local leaders were assigned to manage the work at each of the two sites, in Houston and Phoenix. The leaders were senior engineers who had been promoted to management after many (i.e., 20+) years of service. The two leaders collaborated closely to coordinate the output of the two sites. Several engineering disciplines were represented on the Tail Team. The team consisted of airframe structures specialists, electrical engineers, hydraulic and flight controls engineers, to name a few. In retrospect, one important decision agreed upon by engineering managers was to design the teams such that every Phoenix engineering discipline had a complimentary counterpart in Houston. The implications of this decision were to allow each discipline to make informed assessments of their counterpart's design decisions and progress. Other implications of the complimentary team configuration will be discussed below. In addition to engineers and managers, one administrative assistant and a computer support person were also assigned to both sites.

Schedule of Meetings

The team leads were in communication daily through telephone conferences that often involved the use of application sharing. Application sharing is a type of desktop conferencing in which two or more users see the same screen display. Their screens are synchronized, and any user can take control of the screen at any time. Weekly teleconferences among the team leaders took place over the duration of the project. In conjunction with the telephone, agendas and action items were displayed to all participants using application sharing (NetMeeting). Bimonthly meetings were also conducted. During these meetings, engineering drawings were reviewed for accuracy. These meetings, called design reviews, involved the entire complement of approximately 26 Phoenix engineers and managers along with their 25 Houston counterparts. Design reviews were teleconferences that were coordinated using a printed agenda, 3D-Groupview and action item lists.

Collaboration Technologies

A variety of technologies were used to facilitate communication and collaboration during the period of virtual collocation. This section briefly discusses how commonplace technologies, such as email and teleconferencing, were used by the team. Details about these technologies are omitted because the usage practices observed are reported in well-published accounts of these technologies (see, for example, Short, Williams, & Christie, 1976; Sproull & Kiesler, 1991). This section does, however, provide details of two technologies: Net-Meeting and 3D-Groupview. We focus attention on these technologies because leaders reported that they played a central role in the success of collaboration among the Tail Team. They receive attention also because, in the case of 3D-Groupview, no other descriptions of this technology exist in the academic literature. To avoid redundancy, further discussion of the role these technologies played in mediating leadership is discussed later.

Email was used for various purposes: to send announcements, to ask questions of experts, to coordinate schedules, to report on progress, to distribute meeting agendas, etc. Speaking broadly, the impact of email was to improve communication and tighten coordination between the Houston and Phoenix teams. Email provided a lightweight way to communicate and exchange files with remote coworkers.

In addition to email, teleconferencing was used extensively by the Tail Team. During the period of virtual collocation, weekly teleconferences acted as a surrogate for face-to-face group meetings. In addition to these group meetings, the two Team Leads used teleconferences multiple times each day to coordinate and report on progress. Individual engineers teleconferenced less, but their use was for more specific purposes, such as discussing the details of a specific engineering drawing.

At this point, the inquisitive reader may wonder how it is that the telephone—an audio-only medium—is effectively used to mediate discussions of engineering drawings because drawings are visual. The answer is that the telephone was used in conjunction with computer-aided design. CATIA is a high-end computer-aided design system used throughout Airplane Incorporated. Every design engineer on the Tail Team project had a computer dedicated to generating designs in CATIA. CATIA is a single-user application; however, the system has a built-in facility for sharing drawings between multiple users called 3D-View. 3D-View is a rendering tool that integrates geometric data from CATIA models to produce 3-dimensional images of drawings. 3D-View allows integrated structures to be visually manipulated, in other words, rotated and visually traversed on three axes. 3D-View supports cooperative work by showing designers where their models would physically overlap or in some way interfere with other designer's models after the plane is assembled. A procedure called the "Fit Check" flags all interferences and tracks the disposition of each model. The disposition is the decision an engineer makes as to who will be ultimately responsible for resolving a given interference.

3D-Groupview is an Airplane Incorporated proprietary technology that permits users at two or more locations to synchronously navigate 3-dimensional 3D-View structures. It uses TCP/IP to synchronize the screen display and send keyboard input and mouse movements to remote workstations. The Tail Team used 3D-Groupview in teleconferences conducted every other week to review the status of the project. These sessions helped resolve lingering design problems that were not resolved by individual designers through dispositioning. It also revealed new and often unanticipated problems. Further details of how 3D-Groupview revealed unanticipated problems are discussed in the next section.

LEADERS' PERSPECTIVES ON COLLOCATED AND DISTANCE COLLABORATION

On-time release of drawings is a common performance metric for engineering teams at Airplane Incorporated. In the case of Tail Team, approximately 95% of drawings were released on time. According to the Phoenix team leader, this performance was "not stellar," yet when considered in light of the merger, it was judged "for all intents and purposes . . . a success." Factors impacting this success are discussed in this section.

Dispositioning: Interdependencies in Virtual Teams Must Be Carefully Managed

Interdependencies exist in all collaborative work. However, we argue that geographic distance among team members increases the challenge of managing interdependencies. Coordination involves managing the interdependencies between the activities of two or more individuals (Malone & Crowston, 1990). To be effective, group leaders must coordinate interdependencies among group members such that inputs from different members are efficiently and appropriately combined to produce a product that is aligned with the group's shared goal. Explicit coordination among Airplane Incorporated engineers is achieved when, for example, a structural engineer appropriately passes a digital design to a stress engineer for stress analysis or when the entire design team meets to review the final integrated design and then passes it to the drawing-release team for processing. This kind of coordination is said to be explicit because it designates either a formalized hand off of work from one expert to another or a synchronous decision-making process of multiple individuals. The effectiveness of explicit coordination is often monitored through objective techniques such as performance metrics. For example, the Tail Team leaders calculated a daily percentage of engineering drawings released on time based on the total number of drawings scheduled for release. This "on-time release" metric allowed managers to objectively measure team performance and assess how well the team was coordinated. A low percentage signaled the need to troubleshoot interdependencies.

Troubleshooting coordination was accomplished largely through technology. Leaders and individual engineers used various technologies to coordinate with each other. As mentioned briefly earlier, a system called CATIA was used to produce engineering drawings. This system also tested for interferences between multiple structures (which could be built by two or more engineers). Team members viewed 3-dimensional models of the interferences through a program called 3D-View. Three types of hardwired coordination exist in 3D-View: the designer who locates an interference needs to change his or her model, the designer who designs the interfacing model needs to change his or her model, or both models need to change. 3D-View stores and tracks the dispositioning history of each model and coordinates communication between designers at the two sites. With regards to communication using the dispositioning feature in 3D-View, a Phoenix design engineer commented:

> "In terms of communication, these tools allow the designers to know which group [set of models] his or her designs are affecting and which group is interfering with us. We are allowed to select their models and say: 'Oh, this is the designer who didn't pay attention when they submitted the model.' In terms of communication, it allows us to know exactly who the responsible parties are. Especially when we are not collocated, and at such far distances, that is even more effective to us, as one big company."

The Role of Technology in Coordination

We all know from experience that simply identifying the responsible party in a conflict does not guarantee a resolution. Trust is needed. Trust reassures both parties that the other is acting in the best interest of the team. As Iacono and Weisband (1997) argue, establishing and maintaining the level of trust necessary to solve a problem requires that the involved parties engage in frequent communication. Our observations support this finding. Team members regularly used email to keep each other informed. A Phoenix design engineer explained that she often used email to prod other engineers to resolve interferences in engineering designs:

> "After you disposition, you would give it a week or so and if you still notice that the opponents haven't looked into it you would send an e-mail to remind them

basically. Exchange [e-mail] is to remind people, or tell people or ask people 'OK this is the progress we are at now and please stay informed or up-to-date with what is going on.' "

Although all of the Tail Team staff was trained on NetMeeting during the collocation period, only the two leads used it, and they used it primarily to facilitate collaborative editing of a weekly status report. NetMeeting meetings between the leads were informal meetings, customarily initiated with a telephone call from the Houston Lead to the Phoenix lead. Often the administrative assistant was brought in to the teleconference. The voice link (via telephone) was maintained as each brought up NetMeeting, enabled sharing, and cooperatively edited the status report on screen. The Team Lead explains a typical meeting:

"My counterpart and I regularly NetMeetinged the presentations that I would give up here to the program. He would assemble them, and he and I would NetMeeting them just to brush them up. That worked out very well. And it was almost instantaneous, with the T1 lines between here and Phoenix; I would hear the click (over the phone), and see the cursor move on the screen, it was that fast. That was a great tool."

The Team Leads also used NetMeeting to discuss assembly issues using digital photos. Photos were brought up in NetMeeting and the shared pointer was used to draw attention to relevant features of the image. One of the leads explained how digital photos were used in NetMeeting:

"I did call up photos on NetMeeting so we could sit there with our mice and go 'See this little area over here, well you know I'm worried that this little widget is going to interfere if we bring this duct over here . . .' and there were a couple of occasions where my counterpart and I used the digital photos to that end."

Yet, according to one leader, technology could not completely replace face-to-face interaction. In retrospect, the team leader indicated that more face-to-face time might have improved coordination:

"During parts of the program, heavy travel is warranted, when we are trying to get things up to speed. It has to be the right travel for the right people. . . . This is probably one of the things we didn't have. We had performance reviews . . . but there were no reviews where we took the individual [engineering] leads and had him sit down with his counterpart and say 'How are you doing? Where are you in the program? Show me!' If we had scheduled such things, perhaps we may have flushed out the structures problem sooner."

Face Time: Building Trust and Shared Expectations in Virtual Teams

Sociologists argue that trust diminishes as geographic distance increases between strangers (cf. Newcomb, 1961), yet do leaders of virtual teams report that unacquainted members of geographically distributed teams lack trust? In the quote immediately preceding, the team leader expressed the importance of what some engineers at Airplane Incorporated call *face time*. Airplane Incorporated team leaders have derived from experience the vital role that face-to-face communication plays in coordination, one leader explained: "There are some natural barriers to virtual teaming that could be overcome with technology [but] nothing ever replaces having the guys face-to-face in a room." This leader's conviction about the importance of face-to-face communication in sustaining trust and cohesion in collocated interaction and distributed, computer-mediated interaction is supported in the literature (Clark & Brennan, 1991; Kiesler, Siegel, & McGuire, 1984; Nardi & Whittaker, 2002). Many hypotheses exist regarding what features of face-to-face communication make it nearly irreplaceable (see Nardi & Whittaker, 2002, for a review). One hypothesis follows on our earlier discussion that in addition to being explicit, coordination can also be tacit (Wittenbaum & Stasser, 1996). Even in newly formed groups, and certainly in established groups, individuals invoke unspoken assumptions about what others in their group are likely to know and how they are likely to react to information. These assumptions smooth coordination. Over time, as one becomes familiar with an organization, individuals come to tacitly accept what to expect from colleagues in terms of how tasks are deconstructed, how responsibility is allocated, and how need is expressed. This tacit knowledge is sometimes discussed in terms of behavioral norms (Shaw, 1976) or organizational culture (Sackman, 1991). It is acquired over-time through interaction with colleagues and is often derived from subtle social cues. It is what distinguishes the "new guy in the office" from the veterans. It is also what makes coordination across geographic distance difficult to manage.

How did the Tail Team address issues of expectations and tacit coordination? Individual engineers and team leaders expressed in interviews that the extended period of collocation (six months) the Tail Team engaged in was the key to their team's ability to successfully coordinate. In short, collocation increased familiarity among collaborators with regard to domain expertise and, most importantly, norms of work. This familiarity facilitated distance communication because it helped group members align their expectations.

With respect to coordination, collocation served different purposes. First, it allowed the groups to become familiar with one another and learn the Airplane Incorporated process. According to the Team Lead, "the relocation gave everyone a chance to get acquainted first and foremost. It also gave the Aircraft Company (alias) folks a chance to study [our] business process."

This sentiment is echoed by a Phoenix engineer:

> "It helped knowing the Airplane Incorporated system and to be able to work with Airplane Incorporated people. That allowed me to see how they do business. Maybe that benefited our section because you have several people who know the system by having been up there. It makes us more effective down here and the learning curve is shorter."

In effect, the collocation period offered much more than hands-on training on the Airplane Incorporated systems. According to the leaders, it helped the Phoenix team "be able to work with the Airplane Incorporated people." Thus, although the official objective of the collocation period was training, it also served to diminish the social distance between the members of the two sites. Second, collocation also helped the Phoenix team learn the Airplane Incorporated corporate philosophy. With regard to aligning expectations such that both Airplane Incorporated and Aircraft Company engineers share norms, an Airplane Incorporated leader expressed the following in terms of work culture. He implicitly indicates that collocation, not simply formal training, leads to a transfer of work culture:

> "Can you indicate how the distance affected your schedule?"—Interviewer
>
> "I'm going to call [it] culture. Our people, our culture here, is attuned to delivering a product on time, to meeting a tight drawing schedule, to getting an airplane delivered to a customer four years down the road. Culturally it is in us. The culture change [for Phoenix engineers] is to get into the Airplane Incorporated processes where we really document and track everything. So we know when we are on track. So we can tell when we need resources to get back on track. That is something that perhaps training does not address. That's a cultural element."—Team Lead

This leader goes on to say that the period of collocation permitted cross-fertilization of knowledge and experience between the groups. These effects are explained in the following statement:

> "The time they spent up here was useful for us to give them an idea of our corporate philosophy—we shared experiences, what to do with this type of airplane—good things and bad things. A lot of sharing of knowledge and experience."

Third, specifically with regards to the two management leads, collocation engendered trust in their relationship:

> "My counterpart and I have an absolutely wonderful working relationship. He was up here all last summer and we got to know each other pretty well, working

together. It is easy to talk to someone over the phone when you have spent a good deal of time with them."

Finally, collocation extended the sphere of influence of the Houston team lead over the Phoenix team. This was accomplished through familiarity with the remote team members and knowledge of the distribution of labor at that site.

"I also know the guys who were up here working on the project over the summer and all year. I know them fairly well, so for whatever reason if my counterpart is not available, he is not my only point of contact. And I know them to the point that I can call them up and be very relaxed on the phone."

Thus, by having become familiar with the personalities and expertise of some members of the Phoenix team when they were collocated with him, the Houston team leader is able to more effectively manage the entire Phoenix group once they are remote. His remark about being more "relaxed" is revealing and strongly suggests to us that trust was established between him and the Phoenix engineers during the period of collocation, and that this trust persisted after those engineers returned to Arizona.

Floaters and Loafers: Visibility and Distance Collaboration

Airplane engineering is highly visual work. When such visual work is also collaborative, it becomes ripe with opportunity for passively and actively gaining "awareness" information about other team members. By awareness, we refer to the knowledge of others' activities, processes, attitudes, work results, and so on. Yet when work is distributed, opportunities for information exchange are reduced. Unless files are explicitly exchanged or technology like 3D-View is used, the day-to-day work of an engineer in Houston is largely invisible to engineers in Phoenix. Engineers in Houston infer what others are working on through performance metrics or reports in formal meetings. Independently, however, in Phoenix and Houston, many different three-dimensional, fully rendered designs are visible on various screens to various engineers throughout any given day. Screens are big—they accommodate detailed designs and they also accommodate small-group discussion and casual observations by passersby. Small airplane pieces, large mylar drawings, and printed schematics adorn cubical walls. Cubicals have low walls, and members of the same subgroup share aisle space in what Airplane Incorporated calls an "open bay" design. These workspaces are explicitly designed to encourage information sharing among colleagues. Thus, collocated engineers have a great deal of information available to them to use in deriving who is working on what and how far along they are toward completion.

Visibility is the quality of being observable. When an engineer is visible to a leader, the leader can actively monitor that engineer's level of involvement by noticing how frequently he attends meetings. The leader can also passively monitor things like motivation by noticing what time he arrives and leaves the office. This kind of information was not readily available to the Tail Team leaders regarding geographically remote engineers. Monitoring meeting attendance, in particular, was troublesome for the Tail Team leaders. During 3D-Groupview sessions, leaders regularly commented how difficult it was to know who was "on the other side" during these sessions. Participants failed to introduce themselves as they arrive. Also, due to lack of seating in the 3D-Groupview room in Phoenix, many engineers chose to drift in and out of meetings rather than stand. These problems compelled leaders to repeatedly stress the importance of attendance at 3D-Groupview sessions. They felt that the success of 3D-Groupview meetings was particularly due to attendance because one of the purposes of these meetings was to identify and propose solutions to interference problems between multiple drawings produced by multiple engineers. Confusion regarding who was or was not present on "the other side" and frequent stern comments such as "We aren't going to get through this if you aren't all there!" revealed leaders' frustration regarding lack of visibility into meeting attendance.

Interestingly, from the perspective of the engineers, attending 3D-Groupview sessions was not always a comfortable experience. The shared display in 3D-Groupview increased the visibility of errors in their work. Recall that the 3D-Groupview images were a three-dimensional rendering of the airplane structure. If an engineer transposed his coordinates, for example, his structure would appear unattached to the airplane model and would be "floating" in space. The color-coding of the structure would indicate what subteam the structure belonged to (i.e., electrical, hydraulic). Double-clicking the structure would show his name. Teasing occurred when the identity of the engineer responsible for a floater was identified, for example: "Uh oh, Parker! You're in trouble! It's got your name on it!" Interviews with engineers suggest that engineers were often concerned about looking and sounding "stupid" in 3D-Groupview sessions. A Phoenix engineering lead implied in the following comment that the public accountability created by 3D-Groupview caused 3D-Groupview sessions to be more formal than other teleconferences:

> "It is a lot more formal because you don't know who else is in that room. You can't see their faces and their manager is in there. When you are in the 3D-View, you don't want to sound stupid. Everybody makes mistakes, but you sort of want to be on the guarded side."

In spite of attendance problems, leaders continued to use 3D-Groupview. They valued the potential of 3D-Groupview to make invisible problems visible. This increased visibility arose from the virtual co-presence that 3D-Groupview created. During 3D-Groupview sessions, experts from the different disciplines involved in the Tail Team examined the models together. The team's ability to quickly identify problems and cooperatively construct solutions was enhanced by the detailed, shared display that 3D-Groupview provided. One informant explained how 3D-Groupview was used to this end:

> "There are a lot of good ideas that came out of the [3D-Groupview]. To say 'you know it would be a lot easier if we did this. If we put this way . . . come down on this frame and run the wire down over here and come out over there instead of over here.' Or 'Geez, this comes awfully close to the bleed duct. Are we going to have room to fit our widget in there?'—things of that ilk are really what the [3D-Groupview] sessions were for."

According to at least one informant, 3D-Groupview sessions also served to reassure the team that there would be no "surprises" at the time of assembly:

> "[3D-Groupview] also gives people more of a visual warm fuzzy that 'Yeah, this thing is going to go together as planned. There aren't going to be too many surprises when they start building this airplane,' and all of that hopefully means less errors when we build the airplane and lower cost and more profit."

Furthermore, 3D-Groupview sessions served also to increase the awareness of teaming issues. When color-coded parts appeared on screen, it often triggered discussion of resource allocation issues. For example, once when an airplane part identified as Joe's appeared on the screen, one engineer asked: "Who's going to take over when Joe leaves?" The team leader's response was: "Joe's leaving?" In this way, the airplane part on-screen acted as a proxy for Joe by increasing his visibility to the team and spurring discussion of how to address his departure. Similarly, the presence or absence of airplane parts in a 3D-Groupview model signals levels of productivity. For example, upon seeing a number of new parts on screen, a leader commented: "Look at all those frames! They're doing a lot of work!" Thus, leaders may derive evidence about productivity from what appears in the shared display.

Returning to our earlier point about passive and active monitoring, although the 3D-Groupview interface can increase the visibility of remote engineers to noncollocated leaders, some evidence exists to suggest that, in general, remote engineers are less salient to leaders. Although, it is not surprising that a leader would be less aware of noncollocated subordinates, it is important that leaders recognize this issue because our observations suggest the ramifications of this lack of awareness can be very negative. The leaders identified two failures in their distance collaboration strategy. One was revealed in a quote that appears earlier. Recall that the Houston leader indicated that if he had scheduled a face-to-face meeting among the engineers, he probably would have been able to prevent a problem with the structures' subteam from arising. He said: "If we had scheduled such things [face-to-face meetings], perhaps we may have flushed out the structures problem sooner." This leader goes on to say that the problem was later identified as a personnel issue. The structures engineer assigned to the team was loafing—he was described by other structures engineers as being "as proactive as a piece of paper." The leader explains that "he was the only person assigned to the [Tail Team] and that is why the collaboration didn't work. He was not dedicated to the project and not proactive." Interviews with this leader strongly indicate he didn't detect the failure among the structures group because he never saw them interact because they were never collocated.

CONCLUSION

It was our intent in this chapter to contribute insights into the role of collocation in distance collaboration and to examine how it affects leadership. First, we found that when team members are distributed, interdependencies must be explicitly identified to aid coordination. In the case of the Tail Team, technology helped team members make their interdependencies more clear, and it helped the team leaders to coordinate themselves as well as the entire team. In collocated teams, coordination is often accomplished through tacit communication. The period of collocation for the Tail Team helped them understand the work norms and domain expertise later, when they were distributed. Collocation helped the team align their expectations when they were distributed. Lastly, we discovered how much the lack of visibility of activities impacts team members. To some extent, technology helped to make results and even subtle information more visible. All of these points have implications for leadership of distributed teams.

Collocation was seen to be crucial for the Tail Team to get to know one another and build trust. Research suggests that the more coworkers communicate with one another, the more they like and are committed to one another (Sproull & Kiesler, 1991). We argue that collocation boosted commitment across the organizational boundaries that separated the Phoenix and Houston engineers. We do not claim to know exactly how much time (i.e., weeks or months) is necessary to build and sustain commitment.

The question of collocation is an important one because it entails a number of expensive tradeoffs including travel, office space, and possibly permanent relocation. This study suggests that although periods of collocation may be costly, the long-term benefits of improved group communication and commitment will conceivably offset the costs. It also argues that technology such as email, desktop conferencing, and videoconferencing improve coordination during periods of distance collaboration. In summary, by using technology to support distance collaboration, leaders can keep sight of their ultimate goal—highly efficient individual and group productivity. This concept is summarized in a comment made by a Phoenix LB design engineer regarding the use of 3D-Groupview:

> "Because we have meetings dedicated to look at interference, a lot of people are just so caught up just to get their part done and to meet schedule that they don't set time to look at the big picture. These meetings force you to look at the surrounding structures."

Many of the experiences reported here can be applied to analyses of other product management teams. The leaders' perceptive and details of the sociotechnical context from which they arise are a valuable resource for academicians and practitioners examining distance collaboration. For example, distant leaders must be mindful of the types of information that becomes more and less visible as their subordinates become more dispersed. We caution that the decreased visibility of the *process* of remote work may make it more difficult for leaders to detect loafing subordinates. Conversely, the increased visibility of the *product* of remote work, such as engineering drawings, may make it more difficult for hard-working subordinates to communicate the quality of their work because small errors may be magnified (e.g., floaters) when the work is presented via technologies to support distance collaboration.

We hope that the insights gained from this qualitative research can help to inform the design of new business processes and media configurations to better support leadership at a distance.

REFERENCES

Boeing. (1988). *Working together in the global marketplace.* Seattle: Boeing Corporation.

Bradner, E., & Mark, G. (2001). *Social presence in video and application sharing.* Paper presented at the Conference on Supporting Group Work (GROUP '01), Boulder, Colorado, September 30–October 1, 2001.

Clark, H., & Brennan, S. (1991). Grounding in communication. In L. Resnick, J. Levine, & S. Teasley (Eds.), *Perspectives on socially shared cognition.* Washington DC: APA Press.

Hall, E. T. (1966). *The hidden dimension.* Garden City, NY: Doubleday.

Handy, C. (1995). Trust in the virtual organization. *Harvard Business Review, 73*(3), 40–50.

Haywood, M. (1998). *Managing virtual teams: Practical techniques for high-technology project managers.* Boston: Artech House.

Iacono, C. S., & Weisband, S. (1997). *Developing trust in virtual teams.* Paper presented at the Proceedings of the Hawaii International Conference on Systems Sciences (HICS), Hawaii, January 7–10, 1997.

Jarvenpaa, S., & Leidner, D. (1998). Communication and trust in global virtual teams. *Journal of Computer-Mediated Communication, 3*(4).

Jensen, C., Garnham, S., Drucker, S., & Kollock, P. (2000). *The effect of communication modality on cooperation in online environments.* Paper presented at the Conference on Human Factors in Computing Systems (CHI '00), The Hague, Netherlands. April 1–6, 2000.

Kiesler, S., Siegel, J., & McGuire, T. (1984). Social psychological effects of computer-mediated communication. *American Psychologist, 39*, 1123–1134.

Kollock, P. (1998). Social dilemmas: The anatomy of cooperation. *Annual Review of Sociology, 24*, 183–214.

Kraut, R., Fish, R., Root, R., & Chalfonte, B. (1990). Informal communication in organizations. In S. Oskamp & S. Spacapan (Eds.), *People's reactions to technology in factories, offices, and aerospace* (p. 296). Newbury Park, CA: Sage Publications.

Maier, N., & Sashkin, M. (1971). Specific leadership behaviors that promote problem solving. *Personal Psychology, 24*, 35–44.

Malone, T. W., & Crowston, K. (1990). *What is coordination theory and how can it help design cooperative work systems?* Paper presented at the Conference on Computer Supported Cooperative Work (CSCW '90), October 7–10, 1990.

Mark, G., Grudin, J., & Poltrock, S. (1999). *Meeting at the desktop: An empirical study of virtually collocated teams.* Paper presented at the European Conference on Computer Supported Cooperative Work (ECSCW '99), Copenhagen, Denmark, September 12–16, 1999.

Muhlfelder, M., Klein, U., Simon, S., & Luczak, H. (1999). Teams without trust? Investigations in the influence of video-mediated communication in the origin of trust among cooperating persons. *Behaviour & Information Technology, 18*(5), 349–360.

Nardi, B., & Whittaker, S. (2002). The place of face to face communication in distributed work. In P. Hinds & S. Kiesler (Eds.), *Distributed work* (pp. 83–110). Cambridge, MA: MIT Press.

Newcomb, T. M. (1961). *The acquaintance process.* New York: Holt, Rinehart, and Winston.

Olson, J., & Olson, G. (2000). i2i Trust in E-Commerce. *Communications of the ACM, 43*(12), 41–44.

Rabbie, J. M. (1991). Determinants of instrumental intra-group cooperation. In R. A. Hinde & J. Groebel (Eds.), *Cooperation and prosocial behaviour* (pp. 238–262). Cambridge, UK: Cambridge University Press.

Sackman, S. A. (1991). *Cultural knowledge in organizations.* Newbury Park, CA: Sage Publications.

Shaw, M. E. (1976). *Group dynamics : The psychology of small group behavior.* (2d ed.). New York: McGraw-Hill.

Short, J., Williams, E., & Christie, B. (1976). *The social psychology of telecommunications.* New York: Wiley.

Sproull, L., & Kiesler, S. (1991). *Connections: New ways of working in the networked organization*. Cambridge, MA: MIT Press.

Weisband, S. (2002). Maintaining awareness in distributed team collaboration: Implications for leadership and performance. In P. Hinds & S. Kiesler (Eds.), *Distributed work* (pp. 311–313). Cambridge, MA: MIT Press.

Wittenbaum, G. M., & Stasser, G. (1996). Management of Information in Small Groups. In J. Nye & A. Brower (Eds.), *What's Social about Social Cognition* (pp. 3–28). Thousand Oaks, CA: Sage Publications.

5

Adaptation of Team Communication Patterns: Exploring the Effects of Leadership at a Distance, Task Urgency, and Shared Team Experience

Yan Xiao, F. Jacob Seagull, and
Colin F. Mackenzie
University of Maryland School of Medicine

Katherine J. Klein
University of Pennsylvania

Jonathan Ziegert
Drexel University

OVERVIEW

Members of trauma resuscitation teams usually work together, interacting face-to-face as they treat the patient. When the most senior member of a trauma resuscitation team (the attending surgeon) is not collocated with team members but instead interacts with the team from a distance through audio-video links, the resulting distributed team provides an opportunity to study distant leadership in a dynamic setting. In an exploratory field experiment, we compared real-life trauma resuscitation teams when the leader was collocated versus when he or she was distant. In this chapter, we first report key themes from our qualitative interviews with trauma team members who participated in the study. We then present our quantitative analyses of team communication patterns under varying conditions: (a) when the team leader was distant versus collocated; (b) when the team's task—patient treatment—was high versus low in urgency; and (c) when team members had more or less shared experience as a team. The results provide initial support for the utility of communication analysis for the study of team performance and team leadership.

In the past two decades teams have grown increasingly common—even ubiquitous—in U.S. businesses and organizations of all types. Communication technologies are changing the manner in which and the locations from which team members communicate and coordinate. In both civilian and military contexts, geographically distributed teams exploit new communication technology to support coordinated activities and to project expertise and resources over distance. Existing research on collocated, rather than geographically dispersed, teams suggests that team leaders may have a profound influence on team processes, team conflict, and team performance. Increased access to remote information and easy ways to exchange information remotely because of communication technology pose key questions for those who lead teams, supervise team leaders, and/or design training programs, work procedures, and telecommunication network: How does a leader lead a team via mediated communication at a distance, in comparison to leading in a face-to-face setting?

Several bodies of literature have been developed to understand and to devise ways to support distributed teams. A number of questions related to distributed collaborative work have been addressed to some extent, such as how face-to-face interactions are different from mediated interactions (e.g., Cohen, 1982; Kraut, Miller, & Siegal, 1996; Kuzouka et al., 2000; Olson & Olson, 2001), how properties of telecommunication channels impact on styles of distributed work (e.g., Finn, Sellen, & Wilbur, 1997; Herbsleb, Mockus, Finholt, & Grinter, 2000), and how trust is developed among distributed workers (e.g., Iacono & Weisband, 1997). Largely missing from the existing literature, however, are studies comparing the leadership and performance of action teams working in distant versus collocated conditions.

In this chapter we report the results of an exploratory experiment in which real-life emergency medical teams (trauma teams) were assigned to one of two conditions: (1) a control condition, in which the team leader, collocated with other team members, supervised, guided, and performed with the team as usual; and (2) an experimental condition in which the team leader was located at a distance, observing the team and the patient, and communicating with the team via audio and video linkages. More specifically, we first report the results of our qualitative debriefing interviews, in which we interviewed trauma team members regarding team leadership, dynamics, and performance. Second, we report the results of our quantitative analyses of intrateam communication patterns when leaders are collocated with team members versus at a distance. We conclude with a discussion of the implications of our findings for the practice and study of distant team leadership.

TEAMS AT A DISTANCE: TECHNOLOGY-MEDIATED COMMUNICATION, SHARED TEAM EXPERIENCE, AND TASK URGENCY

What happens when the leader of a team is at a distance? One body of literature to draw possible answers to this question is from the field of computer-supported cooperative work (CSCW). When a team works through medicated communication, in comparison to face-to-face, a number of changes occur in how they interact, often as a function of the medium used in communication.

Cohen (1982) reported a study comparing group communications between two conditions: face-to-face and mediated by videoconference. The videoconference condition produced more orderly turn-taking and fewer speaker exchanges that were viewed as interruptions. Face-to-face meetings were more interactive, less orderly, and less polite than videoconferences, producing more interruptions and nearly twice as many speaker exchanges as videoconferences. Cohen's findings thus suggest that that distance may foster formality in team leader's interactions and communication to team members.

More recent research suggests that face-to-face communication offers several advantages over technology-mediated (distant) communication. Building on Clark and his colleagues' grounded theory of communication (Clark & Marshall, 1981; Clark & Wilkes-Gibbs, 1986; Clark & Brennan, 1991), Fussell, Kraut, and Siegal (2000) proposed that during face-to-face communications, speakers establish a common ground for the exchange of information by establishing joint focus of attention, monitoring comprehension, and pursuing conversational efficiency. Face-to-face interaction allows the transmission of perceptual cues that facilitate the accomplishment of all three tasks. The proposal by Fussell et al. (2000) explained well the findings of several studies on interpersonal interactions in collocational settings (e.g., Bellotti & Rogers, 1997; Krauss, Garlock, Bricker, & McMahon, 1977). To provide these perceptual cues in mediated communication settings, technology solutions have been tested, such as providing a remote gesture pointer (Kuzuoka et al., 2000) and sharing workspace (Gutwin & Greenberg, 1998). These studies suggest that the impact of distant leadership will be determined by the telecommunication technology deployed in terms of perceptual cues provided.

The effects of technology-mediated (versus face-to-face) communication on team leadership and performance may depend in part on team members' shared experience and on the nature of a team's tasks (Finholt, Sproull, & Kiesler, 1990; McGrath, 1990, 1991; Valacich, George, Nunamaker, & Vogel, 1994; Weisband, Schneider, & Connolly, 1995). McGrath (1990, 1991) and his colleagues (McGrath et al., 1993; Straus & McGrath, 1994) concluded that when teams gain experience in working together, the need for communication decreases and the teams are less reliant on medium-rich models of communication (such as face-to-face meetings). In short, shared team experience may influence how and when team members communicate, and this may in turn influence team members' ability to coordinate effectively using technology-mediated rather than face-to-face communication. Furthermore, some research suggests that task urgency, or threat, may influence team communication patterns. When a team is required to perform urgent tasks—tasks that are stressful, threatening, and time-pressured—the team leader is likely to try to centralize his or her authority, ignoring team members' inputs (Driskell & Salas, 1991). At the same time, task urgency may cause team members to defer decisions to the leader (Driskell & Salas, 1991).

TEAM LEADERSHIP, HIERARCHY, AND COMMUNICATION

Much of the existing literature on teams suggests, implicitly or explicitly, that team members are of equal status and experience and that leadership functions are shared among team members (Cox & Sims, 1996; George, Easton, Nunamaker, & Northcraft, 1990; Sivasubramaniam, Murry, Avolio, & Jung, 2002; Sosik, Avolio, & Kahai, 1997). In real-life teams, however, team members often differ in experience, expertise, and status; there is a hierarchy among team members. Furthermore, many, if not most, real-life teams have one or more formal or informal team leaders. When team members vary in experience, expertise, and leadership status, multiple members of the team may enact leadership functions. Furthermore, the most experienced, expert, and senior leaders of a team may delegate leadership functions to junior leaders in an effort to give those with less experience opportunities to learn.

Communication patterns among team members may reflect differences in team members' status, experience, and expertise. For example, communication may occur solely along the gradient of experience. The most senior member may only communicate with the second most senior member and so on and so forth. At the other end of spectrum, communication may occur among team members without regard to differences in team member status, experience, and expertise; each team member may communicate with every other team member. In between these extremes lie a number of other communication patterns. For example, the team leader may communicate with every team member, but team members may not communicate with each other. Finally, communication patterns among team members may vary as a function of team members' shared experience or as a function of task urgency. That is, team communication patterns may shift as the team adapts to team members' changing tenure or to changes in the team's task characteristics. Prior communication studies (e.g., Tushman, 1979) have distinguished between horizontal or peer-to-peer communication and vertical or supervisor–subordinate communication. The ratio of communications in the two categories was assessed by centralization of communication. The centralization–decentralization dichotomy provides a first step in understanding within-team communication but may not capture diverse patterns of team communication.

In the remaining sections of this chapter, we explore hierarchy and communication patterns within trauma teams as team members provide the initial treatment—resuscitation—of patients suffering traumatic injuries. Our qualitative interviews with trauma team members illuminate the trauma team hierarchy and its effects on communication among team members. Following a presentation of key themes emerging in these interviews, we provide a quantitative analysis of team communication patterns, contrasting teams in the control-versus-experimental conditions (collocated leader versus distant leader); in conditions of high versus low task urgency; and in teams of high versus low shared experience. As part of our description of our research methods, we provide additional background information regarding trauma teams.

METHOD

Sample: Trauma Resuscitation Teams

The domain of trauma resuscitation provides an invaluable window into the performance of trauma teams. Trauma resuscitation in a dedicated facility is usually performed in a small physical area, and thus it is possible to observe all aspects of team activities. The initial phase of trauma resuscitation has also a limited duration, so it is possible to intensively study the interaction process among team members. Furthermore, it is possible to manipulate the location of a member of a team through experimental means such that distant leadership can be investigated.

During initial patient resuscitation, trauma team members must stabilize the patient's physical condition (e.g., stop bleeding, ensure that the patient has adequate oxygen), while assessing the nature of the patient's injuries. Typically a trauma center receives notification of incoming patients. The notification usually describes when the patient will arrive, how the patient is injured, and current status of the patient. Although often misleading, the notification provides a team of clinicians some ideas about what type of patient to expect and what special preparations may be needed for the patient.

Once the patient has arrived at the trauma center, initial treatment of the patient (during the first 10 to 30 minutes of resuscitation) is typically guided by a set of steps or a protocol based on expert consensus. This protocol is known as Advanced Trauma Life Support (ATLS). According to this protocol, the objectives of a trauma team should be (in order of importance and temporal sequence) "ABC": Airway, Breathing and ventilation, and blood Circulation.

Typically trauma team members take the patient's medical history, examine the patient, and obtain vital signs (e.g., heart rate and blood pressures) to assess whether the patient has immediate life-endangering injuries. Suspected injuries not directly visible are assessed through diagnostic devices, such as X-ray, computed tomography, and ultrasound machines.

In the trauma center studied, trauma teams consisted of surgical care providers (attending surgeons, surgical fellows, and surgical residents), anesthesia care providers (attending anesthesiologists, fellows, and nurse anesthetists), and trauma resuscitation unit nurses. A *resident* is a physician in one of the postgraduate years of clinical training. Once a physician has completed his or her residency, he or she may choose to get additional training by becoming a *fellow*. Fellows receive additional highly specialized training. An *attending physician* is someone who has finished all professional training and is certified to practice in certain specialties. In the center we studied, the attending surgeons have greater experience, expertise, and status than the surgical fellows, who in turn have greater experience, expertise, and status than the surgical residents.

Typically a trauma team is organized for each patient admission. The surgical members of the team taking care of a patient form a hierarchy in terms of expertise:

- The attending surgeon, the most experienced team member, is considered the person ultimately responsible for the patient's health and welfare and is referred to as the team leader.
- The surgical fellow is the second most senior member of the trauma team.
- The primary physician is a resident assigned to be in charge of the patient's admission. (The assignment was rotated among all the residents.)
- The rest of the residents in second to fourth year of their residency.

In addition to surgical members, there are one or two trauma nurses, one or two anesthesia care providers, one or two technicians, and observing medical students. (We refer to these individuals as collaborators.) The number of members in a trauma team in the studied center usually varied from four to fifteen.

The training care providers (residents and fellows) usually changed from month to month in the trauma center studied, as they started their duties at the trauma resuscitation unit (TRU) at the beginning of each month and finished at the end of each month. The attending surgery and anesthesiology physicians were in rotations and thus changed from day to day among two to four attending physicians. While taking care of patients, the training members of the team had the goal of learning. In addition to patient care knowledge and skills, the training members also learned how to work together with other members as a team in treating trauma patients.

Even though the attending surgeon is usually considered as the team leader, the team members share the overall responsibility of ensuring the welfare of the patient (Xiao & Moss, 2001). In particular, the nonsurgical members of a trauma team often lead in their respective domains of expertise.

The Field Experiment

The TRU in a major regional trauma center was outfitted with a telecommunication infrastructure. Trauma patients typically were first brought in to the TRU by helicopters or ambulances. Within the general area of the TRU, a room (the distant command center) was set up for the attending surgeon of a trauma team to work collaboratively with, but at a distance from, the rest of the team in the TRU bay. Figure 5–1 shows the workstation for the distant leader inside the distant command center. The distant leader had visual access to the rest of the team through three camera views. One of the camera views was controllable by a pan-tilt-zoom controller; another was from a tetherless head-mounted camera. The distant leader also had two-way audio communication through an infrared wireless bone-conducting headphone system.

FIGURE 5–1.   Configuration of distant leadership experiment setup.

As shown in Figure 5–1, for each of the 10 patient bays at TRU, three camera views were captured and displayed at the distant command center. The first camera had fixed lenses and was mounted from the ceiling about 10 feet away from the bay to provide overall view of the bay. The second camera was also mounted from the ceiling but had remotely controllable zoom lenses with pan and tilt control. This camera allowed the distant leader to look closely at the patient's wounds and other details. The third camera was mounted on a head harness, to be worn by one of the care providers. Coupled with the two-way audio communication system deployed, this head-mounted camera allowed better remote visual access, as well as the wearer's point of view. The video from the battery-powered, head-mounted camera was transmitted wirelessly.

The two-way audio communication system used infrared bandwidth to minimize interferences with other electromagnetic devices. Bone-conducting headphones were used so that the wearer's ear channels were not obstructed for the use of stethoscopes and for regular auditory perception (e.g., communicating with collocated team members, the patient, and listening to signals from patient monitors). The audio system, once activated, allowed hands-free operation. With such a setup, it was technically feasible to manipulate the distance from which the leader of a trauma team collaborated with the rest of the team.

Additionally, ceiling-mounted microphones and speakers were installed at each bay and were connected to the distant command center. A person sitting in the distant command center could hear all the sounds in the patient bay. He or she could also speak to everyone in the bay through the ceiling speaker and to individual team members through the two-way audio communication system.

Extensive consultation was carried out with the management clinicians of the trauma center to define field experiment procedures to ensure the standard care and the welfare of the patient. With the approval from The University of Maryland Institutional Review Board, the study participants were recruited from surgical care providers (attending surgeons, surgical fellows, and surgical residents), anesthesia care providers (attending anesthesiologists, fellows, and nurse anesthetists), and trauma resuscitation unit nurses. The subject recruitment process included a number of formal and informal meetings with impacted staff care providers (attending physicians and nurses). In these meetings, the field experiment procedures were explained and research consent packages were distributed. The training care providers (residents and fellows) were approached individually when they first started their rotation at the TRU and were similarly invited to participate in the field experiment. All staff and training care providers consented to the field experiment.

We conducted the field experiment by manipulating the location of the surgical attending physician (trauma team leader) between two conditions: distant (the leader in the distant command center) and local (the leader collocated with the rest of the team in the bay where the patient was). The experiment lasted for three months. All patient admissions between the hours of

11 A.M. and 6 P.M. on weekdays were considered as candidate experiment sessions. Due to logistical constraints such as multiple simultaneous patient admissions and extreme workload conditions, candidate sessions were assessed jointly with the attending surgeon prior to the patient arrival for their suitability as an experiment session. When a case was included for the experiment study, it was assigned to either a "distant" or "local" leadership condition according to a predetermined random table. Only the initial assessment and resuscitation of a trauma patient was included in the field experiment.

A technician was always present at the distant command center to assist the attending surgeons in using the technology involved, such as operating the camera controls and the audio communication system. To facilitate data collection, audio-video recordings were made on all audio-video communication and on patient vital signs as displayed on the bedside patient monitors. Additionally, the injury status of the patients in all studied cases was extracted from the hospital database. Information related to the identity of the patient was never collected. Figure 5–2 shows a sample video image for audio-video recordings.

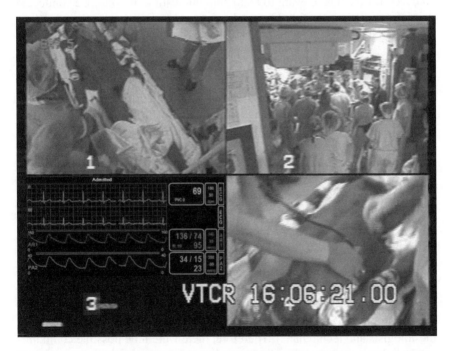

Note: Shown here are combined views from four different sources. Upper-left: the pan-tilt-zoom camera looking down the patient's gurney; Upper-right: an overview camera looking into the patient resuscitation bay; Lower-left: the screen dump of the patient monitor; and Lower-right: the view from head-mounted camera, displaying here a care provider performing auscultation to the patient's chest.

FIGURE 5–2.   Sample video images for audio-video recordings.

Shown in the figure are combined views from four different sources: (1) Upper-left: the pan-tilt-zoom camera looking down the patient's gurney; (2) Upper-right: an overview camera looking into the patient resuscitation bay; (3) Lower-left: the image of the patient monitor screen; and (4) Lower-right: the view from head-mounted camera, displaying here a care provider performing auscultation of the patient's chest.

QUALITATIVE DEBRIEFING INTERVIEWS

Within a short time (usually within hours but occasionally within a week) after the end of each field experiment session, we interviewed selected members of each trauma team, both while they viewed a videotape of the trauma resuscitation in which they participated and after viewing the videotape. We asked interviewees three broad questions: (1) What was the patient doing? (2) What was the participant doing? and (3) What was the team doing? The debriefing interviews were audiotaped and transcribed. The content of the transcripts was analyzed for themes relevant to team communication. In total, we conducted debriefing interviews with 33 attending surgeons, fellows, nurses, and residents. Three themes on team structures were identified.

Quantitative Analysis of Team Communication Patterns

Two trained research nurses observed 18 videotaped trauma resuscitations and coded communication among team members during each resuscitation. (In total, we videotaped 55 trauma resuscitations, but 37 videotapes were of poor quality—either difficult to see, difficult to hear, or both—due to equipment malfunctioning.) In total (across the 18 videotaped resuscitations), the research nurses recorded 569 communication episodes recorded between team members (excluding communications to the patient).

The trained research nurses coded every communication episode that occurred during a resuscitation. Each communication episode was coded in terms of initiator (the person who started the episode) and target (the addressee of the communication). In the current analysis, only three initiators were considered: the team leader (the attending surgeon), the senior member (the fellow), and the junior members (the residents). Targets included these three initiators plus collaborators—that is, team members who were not in the leadership hierarchy and who were typically from disciplines other than surgery (e.g., anesthesiologists and technicians). Therefore, there were nine possible communication linkages between these individuals: (1) from leader to senior member; (2) from leader to junior members; (3) from senior member to leader; (4) from junior members to leader; (5) from senior member to junior members; (6) from junior members to senior member; (7) from leader to collaborators; (8) from senior member to collaborators; and (9) from junior members to collaborators.

For each case, the percentage of communication episodes along each of the nine linkages over the total number of communication episodes was calculated. Furthermore, communication episodes originated from the team leader were coded into two types: requesting information and providing instruction.

In analyzing communication patterns observed in the resuscitations, we compared cases, first, in which the team leader was on site with the patient (local) versus cases in which the team leader was in the remote communication room (distant). Of the 18 cases, 8 were under the distant condition and 10 were collocated. Second, we compared cases that differed in task urgency. We used a measure of patient's injury status, Injury Severity Score (ISS), as a measure of task urgency. The patient in a case with an ISS score less than 5 was considered low in task urgency. A case with an ISS score equal to or higher than 5 was considered high in task urgency. Four resuscitations were high task urgency admissions and fourteen were low task urgency admissions. Finally, we compared cases that varied in shared experience among team members—that is, whether the team was at the beginning of its tenure or at the end of its tenure. We defined the first 10 days of the month as the beginning and the last 10 days of the month as the end. We omitted the cases in the middle 10 days of the month. Eight resuscitations were performed by inexperienced teams (first 10 days of the month), and eight resuscitations were performed by experienced teams (last 10 days of month), excluding two cases (from the middle of the month). Due to the small number of cases analyzed, certain significance tests were not performed.

RESULTS

In this section of the chapter, we present the results of our analyses, beginning first with the results of our qualitative debriefing interviews and then presenting our quantitative analyses of team communication patterns.

Themes from the Qualitative Debriefing Interviews

Our review of transcripts of the 33 debriefing interviews revealed that interviewees emphasized three key themes relevant to team communication patterns.

Maintaining a Hierarchical Team Structure. In the videotaped resuscitations, we observed that the attending surgeon (i.e., the team leader) primarily communicated with the surgical fellow (i.e., the intermediate leader or second in command). Both in the collocated condition and the distant condition, attending surgeons communicated infrequently with the rest of the team. Interviewees' comments supported and explained our observations: For example, a fellow noted, "I think Attendings have a tendency to talk to the Fellow first. For the most part, they may take us aside." Similarly, an attending surgeon commented, "Everything I say I say to [the fellow] and then [the fellow] tells it to the junior residents because he's supposed to be running the resuscitation with them." This attending explained that he wanted to maintain this hierarchy in the distant condition, as in the collocated condition, to maximize the fellow's opportunities to learn and to lead. While we could have provided headphones, in the distant experimental condition, to every member of the trauma team (including medical students), the attending surgeon had discouraged this plan: "That's why in that other [case] I didn't want the medical students to have the headphones because I wanted to talk to the fellow . . . I want the fellow tell the medical students what to do."

Reflecting the hierarchical communication pattern—from attending surgeon to surgical fellow to residents—a fellow commented: "I try to let [residents] make as many decisions as possible, at least come up with a plan. And if I disapprove, or disagree, we go from there."

Adaptation of Team Communication Patterns and Leadership Role Due to Task Urgency. Although a hierarchical structure appeared to be the preferred way for the studied teams to work, the interviews suggested that teams adapted their structures to task urgency. Attending surgeons emphasized that they tended to be more involved when the patient was severely injured. One attending reflected on a case just reviewed:

> After [the patient] arrived, we realized he was talking. We felt his pulses and realized he was not as ill as he sounded on transfer. So it switched from being a chief-and-attending resuscitation back to being a senior ER resident just running their plan past me.

In this segment, "chief" was the second most senior surgical member (akin to a surgical fellow) and the senior ER resident was a third-year emergency medicine resident and was a junior surgical member of the team. The two most senior members of the team had planned to be directly involved due to the anticipated seriousness of the patient's injury. The team adapted its structure to allow more training opportunity for the residents. Another attending surgeon's comments echoed this theme:

> Usually what I would do is I allow the fellow to tell me what they want to do. That way it becomes more of a teaching situation. So that if I disagree with it I can say "Well, I disagree because A, B, C, or D," so I always let the fellow give me his plan first unless the patient is so unstable, then I just say, "hey we're going to do this, this, and this."

In short, when the patient's injuries did not require urgent care, attending surgeons delegated more responsibilities to the surgical fellow and the residents. In such cases, the attending surgeon typically monitors the team's care of the patient: "I think, on this case it was a question of just overseeing and making sure that all of the appropriate decisions were made, the proper exam was performed."

In a similar vein, when a patient's injuries are not very serious or urgent, the surgical fellow monitors the team's performance, allowing the residents to direct and administer patient care, as this fellow explained:

> I usually let the admitting resident decide who he wants to do what. If I don't approve, then I will speak up. If the patient is very sick, then usually myself or the senior resident becomes more involved. Then the junior residents are less involved.

Impact of Distance on Team Members' Knowledge of Team Leader Awareness.   As noted above, the senior members of a team (i.e., the attending surgeon and surgical fellow) often monitor the team's treatment of the patient if the patient does not require urgent care or the senior team member's expertise. Interviewees commented that when the attending surgeon was in the distant condition—separated from the rest of the team—they could not tell what the attending surgeon was doing. Unable to see the attending surgeon, team members did not know where the attending surgeon's attention was focused. A fellow's comment was typical:

> When the attending surgeon's watching [from a remote location], you don't know what they're looking at so you're a little more . . . uncertain, versus, for example, the attending is sitting there in the chair a little more relaxed. So you're like "Ok, uh everything's going smooth." But you have no idea what the attending is doing or watching.

Team Communication Patterns

After viewing the tapes and reviewing the interview transcripts, we identified the four basic team communication patterns or archetypes depicted in Figure 5–3. We will use a five-member team for illustration: leader, senior members, two junior members, and a collaborator. As noted above, the collaborators are individuals who are not in the hierarchy of experience and may be from different disciplines than the other four members (e.g., anesthesiologists and technicians). In Figure 5–3, the lines between individual team members represent communication linkages. Line widths indicate different frequencies of communications.

As depicted in Figure 5–3, we observed four common communication patterns. We call the first *formal communication* (5–3a). In this type of team structures, the authority and experience hierarchy governs communication

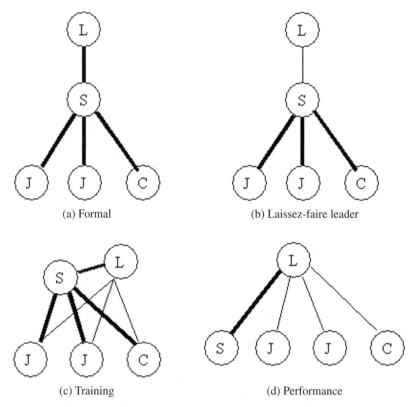

(a) Formal   (b) Laissez-faire leader

(c) Training   (d) Performance

Note: The lines represent communication linkages. Line widths indicate different frequencies of communications. L: leader; S: senior member; J: junior members; C: collaborating members.)

FIGURE 5–3.   Archetypes of team structures.

pathways. We call the second *laissez-faire leadership* (5–3b). In this type of team structure, the leader delegates to the second most senior person of the team. The role of the leader is primarily monitoring. We call the third communication pattern *training* (5–3c). In the setting studied and some other settings, a member of a team (the fellow) is being coached and trained to become an attending surgeon at the end of his or her fellowship period. The leader interacts mostly with the senior member in the training type of team structure. The leader interacts with other members of the team to help out the senior member. Finally, we call the fourth communication pattern *performance* (5–3d). Because the leader and the senior member are the most experienced members of the team, in certain conditions their direct involvement is necessary to ensure performance. In performance team structure, the communications to and from the leader are primarily with the senior member.

Figure 5.4 depicts the overall communication pattern for all 18 cases. In Figures 5–, 5–5a, and 5–5b, the percentage numbers along the communication linkages were averages across all cases. The numbers beside the arrows are the average percentages of communication episodes flowing along the corresponding arrows in proportion to the total number of episodes of a specific case. All numbers in each of the diagrams add up to 100.

Distance Versus Collocated Conditions.   Figure 5–5 summarizes the results of our comparison of communication patterns when the leader was at a distance from the team versus when the leader was collocated with the team. Numbers represent an average percentage of communications across cases in each of the two conditions. When the leader was distant, there was an increase in the influence of the senior team member (the fellow) (X^2 (8) = 23.8, $p <$ .005). The hierarchical structure of the team becomes more prevalent, with increases in communication from the leader to the senior member, and from the senior member to the junior member. Reductions in communication from the leader to the junior member and to the collaborators were also observed.

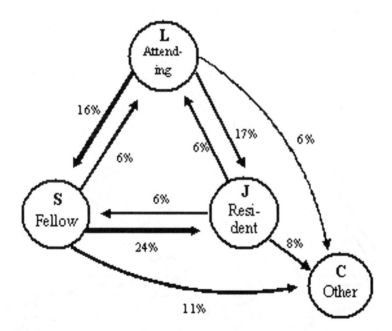

Note: The numbers beside the arrows are the average percentages of communication episodes flowing along the corresponding arrows in proportion to the total number of episodes of a specific case. All numbers in the diagram add up to 100%.

FIGURE 5–4.   Overall communication pattern.

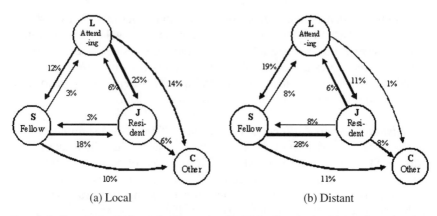

(a) Local   (b) Distant

Note: Left: Team leader (L) located with team locally; Right: Team leader (L) in a distant location, communicating with audio-video link. Numbers represent average percentage of communications across cases in each of the two conditions.

FIGURE 5–5.   The effects of team-leader location on communication.

High Versus Low Task Urgency.   When the task urgency was high (i.e., the patient injury was more severe), there was an increase in the overall number of communication episodes from the team leader to the rest of the team, from an average of 9% of episodes to an average of 15% of episodes (X^2 (8) = 14.3, $p < .10$). It also appeared that when task urgency was high, the team leader was more involved with the senior member of the team (Figure 5–6). There was an increase of communication (approximately doubling) between the senior member and the team leader, and a reduction of communication

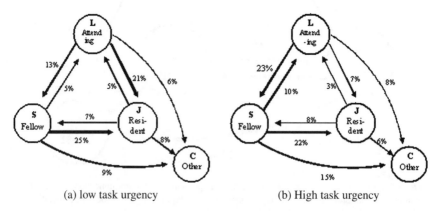

(a) low task urgency   (b) High task urgency

Note: Left: Low task urgency when patient injury severity scores (ISS) were less than or equal to 5. Right: High task urgency when ISS were greater than 5.

FIGURE 5–6.   The impact of task urgency on team structure.

from the leader to the junior member (Figure 5–7). Figure 5.7 shows the percentages of communication episodes between the team leader and the senior member, the junior member, and collaborators.

High Versus Low Team Experience. As shown in Figure 5–8, when the communication patterns were compared between the beginning of the team's tenure and the end of the team's tenure, the communication of the leader was greatly reduced, and the communication of the senior member was greatly increased (X^2 (8) = 37.3, $p < .001$). It appears that as teams became more experienced, the team leader was less involved with the rest of the team.

Leadership as Reflected by Content of Communications. When each communication episode was examined in terms of the content of the communication, further details about team leadership emerged. Figure 5–9 illustrates the differences we observed. When distant, the leaders tended to ask more questions and give fewer instructions compared to when the leaders were local. Similarly, when high task urgency cases were compared with low task urgency cases, we also observed differences in the leader's communication (Figure 5–10). When task urgency was high, the leaders tended to provide more instructions. When teams grew more experienced, the communications from the leaders tended to be questions as opposed to instructions (Figure 5–11).

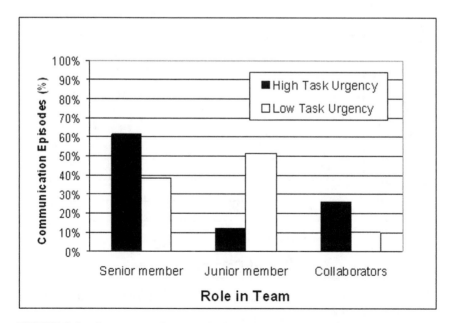

FIGURE 5–7. Percentages of communication episodes between the team leader and the senior member, the junior member, and collaborators.

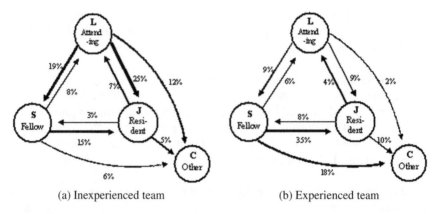

(a) Inexperienced team   (b) Experienced team

Note: Left: teams were at the beginning of their tenure (the first 10 days of formation). Right: teams were at the end of their tenure (after 20 days of formation).

FIGURE 5–8.   The impact of team experience on communication.

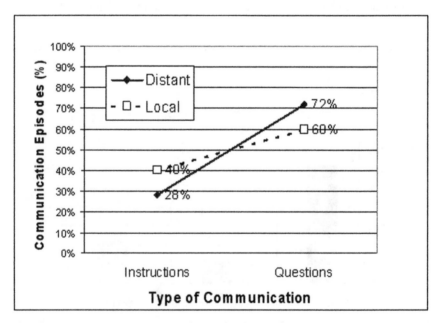

FIGURE 5–9.   Content of leader communications in distant and local conditions for instructions and questions.

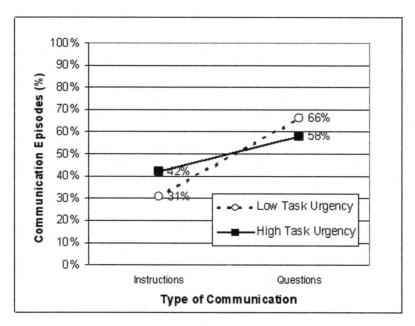

FIGURE 5–10.   Impact of task urgency on communication content.

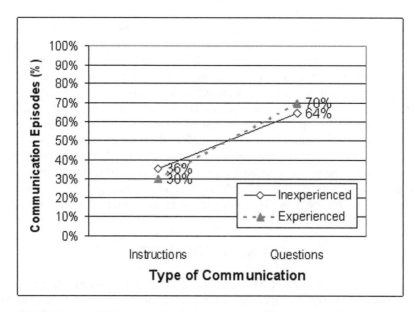

FIGURE 5–11.   The impact of team experience on leader's communication content.

CONCLUSION

In this chapter we have examined the hierarchy of leadership and team communication patterns within trauma resuscitation teams. Our qualitative and quantitative analyses reveal the apparent influence of the hierarchy of team members, the leader distance experimental manipulation, task urgency, and team experience on team verbal communication patterns. Our analysis is limited in focus, and several other aspects of team communication were not addressed (such as nonverbal communication and detailed content analysis of all verbal exchanges). However, the analysis results provided initial support to the value of the approach to team leadership.

The preliminary set of team structure archetypes, although not completely new (Bolman & Deal, 1997), should provide a starting point for future research on team communication patterns and leadership. The archetypes have direct implications for design of telecommunication systems as well. The frequencies of intrateam verbal exchanges varied in response to task urgency, team experience, and distance manipulation in the field experiment. The adaptation of team structures as uncovered by the communication analysis underscores the fluid and shared nature of team leadership, and the importance for a telecommunication system to accommodate the need of team leaders in changing the communication channels in response to contingencies.

It should be noted that the teams that we studied had two distinct goals: (1) training fellows and residents, and (2) performing life-saving procedures. In many settings, such duality of goals is not uncommon (Kozlowski, Gully, Salas, & Cannon-Bower, 1996). Adaptation of team structure in opportunistic ways is necessary when different goals are to be pursued.

Our research approach, focusing on team communication patterns, provides a useful although limited approach to the study of distant team leadership. We have not considered several important team leadership issues, such as trust and team development (Avolio, Kahai, & Dodge, 2001). Our analyses describe general communication patterns. More detailed content analyses may provide further insights into leadership processes. Lastly, due to the constraints of the setting, the field experiment was limited in terms of teams sampled and tasks studied. With increasing sophistication of technology, more expanded field experiments are possible to study teams in stressful, high-stakes, real-life environments.

ACKNOWLEDGMENTS

The research was funded by Department of Defense (contract number: DASW 01-99-K-0003). The opinions expressed here are those of the authors and do not reflect the official position of the sponsor. We wish to thank all clinicians from the University of Maryland R. Adams Cowley Shock Trauma

Center who participated in the study. The authors wish to thank Peter Hu, Jackie Moss, Becky Roys, and Paul Regnault for their contributions in data collection and analysis.

REFERENCES

Avolio, B. J., Kahai, S., & Dodge, G. E. (2001). E-leadership: Implications for theory, research, and practice. *Leadership Quarterly, 11*(4), 615–668.

Bellotti, V., & Rogers, Y. (1997). From Web press to web pressure: Multimedia representations and multimedia publishing. *In Proc. ACM CHI'97 Human Factors in Computing Systems* (pp. 279–286). March 22–27, 1997, Atlanta, Georgia.

Bolman, L. G., & Deal, T. E. (1997). *Reframing Organizations: Artistry, Choice, & Leadership* (2d ed.). San Francisco, CA: Jossey-Bass Inc.

Clark, H. H., & Brennan, S. E. (1991). Grounding in communication. In L. B. Resnick, R. M. Levine, & S. D. Teasley (Eds.). *Perspectives on socially shared cognition* (pp. 127–149). Washington, DC: APA.

Clark, H. H., & Marshall, C. E. (1981). Definite reference and mutual knowledge. In A. K. Joshi, B. L. Webber, & I. A. Sag (Eds.), *Elements of discourse understanding* (pp. 10–63). Cambridge: Cambridge University Press.

Clark, H. H., & Wilkes-Gibbs, D. (1986). Referring as a collaborative process. *Cognition, 22*, 1–39.

Cohen, K. M. (1982). Speaker interaction: Video teleconferences versus face-to-face meetings. *Proceedings of Teleconferencing and Electronic Communications* (pp. 189–199). Madison: University of Wisconsin Press.

Cox, J. F., & Sims, H. P., Jr. (1996). Leadership and team citizenship behavior: A model and measures. In M. M. Beyerlein, D. A. Johnson, & S. T. Beyerlein (Eds.), *Advances in interdisciplinary studies of work teams: Team leadership* (pp. 1–41). Greenwich, CT: JAI Press Inc.

Driskell, J. E., & Salas, E. (1991). Group decision-making under stress. *Journal of Applied Psychology, 76*, 473–478

Finholt, T., Sproull, L., & Kiesler, S. (1990). Communication and performance in ad hoc task groups. In J. Galegher, R. E. Kraut, & C. Edigo (Eds.): *Intellectual teamwork: Social and technological foundations of cooperative work* (pp. 291–325). Hillsdale, NJ: Lawrence Erlbaum Associates.

Finn, K. E., Sellen, A. J., & Wilbur, S. B. (Editors, 1997). *Video-Mediated Communication*. Mahwah, NJ: Lawrence Erlbaum Associates.

Fussell, S. R., Kraut, R. E., & Siegel, J. (2000). Coordination of communication. *Proceeding of the ACM 2000 Conference on Computer supported cooperative work* (pp. 21–30). December 2–6, 2000, Philadelphia, PA.

George, J. F., Easton, G., Nunamaker, J. F., Jr., & Northcraft, G. (1990). A study of collaborative group work with and without computer-based support. *Information Systems Research, 1*, 394–415.

Gutwin, C., & Greenberg, S. (1998). Effects of awareness support on groupware usability. In *Proc. ACM CHI'98 Human Factors in Computing Systems* (pp. 511–518). April 18–23, 1998, Los Angeles, CA.

Herbsleb, J., Mockus, A., Finholt, T., & Grinter, R. (2000). Distance, dependencies, and delay in a global collaboration. In *Proceedings of the ACM2000 Conference on Computer-Supported Cooperative Work (CSCW)* (pp. 319–23). December 2–6, 2000, Philadelphia, PA.

Iacono, S., & Weisband, S. (1997). Developing trust in virtual teams. *Proceedings of the 30th Annual Hawaii International Conference on System Sciences (HICSS)*, January 7–10, 1997, Big Island, Hawaii. pp. 412–420.

Kozlowski, S. W. J., Gully, S. M., Salas, E., & Cannon-Bower, J. A. (1996). Team leadership and development: Theory, principles, and guidelines for training leaders and teams. In M. M. Beyerlein, D. A. Johnson, & S. T. Beyerlein (Eds.), *Advances in interdisciplinary studies of work teams: Team leadership* (pp. 253–291). Greenwich, CT: JAI Press Inc.

Krauss, R. M., Garlock, C. M., Bricker, P. D., & McMahon, L. E. (1977). The role of audible and visible back-channel responses in interpersonal communication. *Journal of Personality and Social Psychology, 35*, 523–529.

Kraut, R. E., Miller, M. D., & Siegel, J. (1996). Collaboration in performance of physical tasks. *Proceedings of the ACM 1996 conference on Computer supported cooperative work* (pp. 57–66). November 16–20, 1996, Boston, MA.

Kuzuoka, H., Oyama, S., Yamazaki, K., Yamazaki, A., Mitsuishi, M., & Suzuki, K. (2000). GestureMan: A mobile robot that embodies a remote instructor's actions. *Proceeding of the ACM 2000 Conference on Computer supported cooperative work* (pp. 155–162). December 2–6, 2000, Philadelphia, PA.

McGrath, J. E. (1990). Time matters in groups. In J. Galegher, R. E. Kraut, & C. Edigo (Eds.), *Intellectual teamwork: Social and technological foundations of cooperative work* (pp. 23–61). Hillsdale, NJ: Lawrence Erlbaum Associates.

McGrath, J. E. (1991). Time, interaction, and performance (TIP): A theory of groups. *Small Group Research, 22*(2), 147–174.

McGrath, J. E., Arrow, H., Gruenfeld, D. H., Hollingshead, A. B., & O'Connor, K. M. (1993). Groups, tasks, and technology: The effects of experience and change. *Small Group Research, 24*(3), 406–420.

Olson, G., & Olson, J. (2001). Distance matters. *Human Computer Interaction, 15*, 139–179.

Sivasubramaniam, N., Murry, W. D., Avolio, B. J., & Jung, D. I. (2002). A longitudinal model of the effects of team leadership and group potency on group performance. *Group and Organization Management, 27*(1), 66–96.

Sosik, J. J., Avolio, B. J., & Kahai, S. S. (1997). Effects of leadership style and anonymity and group potency and effectiveness in a group decision support system environment. *Journal of Applied Psychology, 82*, 89–103.

Straus, S. G., & McGrath, J. E. (1994). Does the medium matter? The interaction of task type and technology on group performance and member reactions. *Journal of Applied Psychology, 79*(1), 87–97.

Tushman, M. L. (1979). Work characteristics and subunit communication structure: A contingency analysis. *Administrative Science Quarterly, 24*, 82–98.

Valacich, J. S., George, J. E., Nunamaker, J. F., Jr., & Vogel, D. R. (1994). Physical proximity effects on computer-mediated group idea generation. *Small Group Research, 25*(1), 83–104.

Weisband, S. P., Schneider. S. K., & Connolly, T. (1995).Computer mediated communication and social information: Status salience and status differences. *Academy of Management Journal, 38*(4), 1124–1151.

Xiao, Y., & Moss, J. (2001). Practice of high reliability teams: Observations in trauma resuscitation. In *Proceedings of Human Factors and Ergonomics Society 44th Annual Meeting* (pp. 395–399). October 8–12, 2001, Minneapolis, Minnesota.

III

Experiments in Remote Leadership

6

Effects of Leadership Style and Anonymity on the Discussion of an Ethical Issue in an Electronic Meeting System Context

Surinder S. Kahai
State University of New York at Binghamton

Bruce J. Avolio
University of Nebraska

OVERVIEW

A laboratory experiment that employed 42 student groups evaluated the effects of transactional versus transformational leadership styles and anonymity when groups employed an electronic meeting system (EMS) to discuss the ethical issue of copying copyrighted software. Overall participation within groups was greater under a transactional leader than under a transformational leader and also in the identified condition than in the anonymous condition. During the group discussion, transformational leadership was associated with a greater balance of arguments versus transactional leadership. Furthermore, transformational leadership induced a greater change in members' intentions to copy the software than did transactional leadership. Finally, there was an interaction effect of anonymity and leadership on postdiscussion deviation in intentions to copy within groups.

Over the last decade, a considerable amount of attention has been devoted to studying "electronic" groups, or groups that communicate via computer systems (Avolio, Kahai, & Dodge, 2000). Such groups are becoming more common in organizations, due in part to globalization, telecommuting, and the availability of easy-to-use technology such as the Internet. These groups frequently employ an electronic meeting system (EMS) to interact with team members located in the same place or remotely (Nunamaker, Briggs, Mittleman, Vogel, & Balthazard, 1997; Townsend, DeMarie, & Hendrickson, 1998).

In parallel with increasing interest in electronic groups, interest in business ethics has also grown during recent years, partly due to the ease with which privacy and intellectual property rights (such as those pertaining to software and music) can be compromised over the Internet (Stead & Gilbert, 2001; Street, Douglas, Geiger, & Martinko, 2001). In spite of the interest in both electronic groups and business ethics, little work has been done to study ethical reasoning in electronic groups (Cappel & Windsor, 2000). In this chapter, we present our study of EMS-supported groups that discussed an ethical issue.

Recent studies have found group leadership, which provides motivational support as well as guidance and structure to a group, to be an important group attribute in electronic groups (Kahai, Sosik, & Avolio, 1997; Sosik, Avolio, & Kahai, 1997). Additionally, anonymity within an electronic group has also been shown to be an important operating condition for these groups (Connolly, Jessup, & Valacich, 1990; Kahai, Avolio, & Sosik, 1998). The effects of anonymity on group process and outcomes have become increasingly relevant as virtual groups or communities in which members frequently do not disclose their identities have proliferated over the Internet (e.g., Cranor, 1999).

Motivated in part by these arguments, we examined the effects of transactional versus transformational leadership styles and anonymity on EMS-supported group interaction and the intentions of group members when they were presented with the ethical issue of copying copyrighted software. Both transformational and transactional leadership, which have been shown to influence group process and outcomes in electronic settings (Kahai, Sosik, & Avolio, 2003; Sosik et al., 1997), are considered to have an influence on ethical behavior (Gottlieb & Sanzgiri, 1996; Grundstein-Amado, 1999). Transactional leaders motivate behaviors by highlighting the rewards that followers will obtain in exchange for work performance, and then rewarding their followers based on their performance. Transformational leaders motivate behaviors by framing the issues involved in work or the work to be performed in a way that stimulates the followers and engages their intrinsic motivation to perform work. One set of questions of interest in this study is whether transformational leadership is more or less effective than transactional leadership at (a) uncovering arguments for and against copying of copyrighted software, and (b) causing a shift in intentions related to copying of copyrighted software.

Prior research indicates that anonymity may play a significant role in uncovering views of participants when they are discussing an issue (such as an ethics question) that they would normally be more inhibited to discuss in electronic mediated groups (Connolly et al., 1990; Jessup, Connolly, & Galegher,

1990; Nunamaker, Dennis, Valacich, Vogel, & George, 1991). In this study, we examined the influence of anonymity during group interactions on uncovering arguments for and against copying of copyrighted software.

GENERAL THEORETICAL MODEL

The general model for this study is based on Street et al.'s (2001) Cognitive Elaboration Model (CEM) of ethical decision making. According to CEM, an individual's *motivation* and *ability* to think about an ethical issue influence *cognitive elaboration,* that is, the effort expended by the individual in thinking about the issue. With a deeper level of processing, we would expect the individual to recognize the moral aspects of an ethical issue and carefully consider relevant moral arguments before establishing an *intention* on how to act. Conversely, when an individual performs a low level of cognitive elaboration, he or she is less likely to recognize the moral aspects of the issue at hand and is likely to rely on nonethical considerations (e.g., monetary, self-interest related) to establish an intention on how to act.

According to CEM, in addition to individual characteristics, various individual and situational characteristics influence an individual's motivation and ability to expend cognitive effort. Situational characteristics include the following attributes related to the issue at hand: level of moral intensity (Jones, 1991), personal accountability for outcomes (Tetlock, 1988), and personal relevance (Johnson & Eagly, 1989; Petty & Cacioppo, 1979).

CEM focuses on an individual thinking about an ethical issue in isolation from other individuals. However, we expect CEM to also be relevant when the individual is discussing an ethical issue in a group because even in a group situation, the level of cognitive elaboration by the individual is likely to be influenced by the individual's motivation and ability. However, there may be additional *situational* determinants of motivation and ability in a group situation. For instance, an additional situation determinant of ability in a group would be the presence of production blocking, whereby individual members are unable to produce new ideas while they are waiting for their turn to speak (Diehl & Stroebe, 1987).

Two situational determinants of motivation and ability in a group that are relevant in this study are *leadership* and *anonymity.* Leadership is considered to be an important determinant of the extent to which a group is likely to engage in a shared and systematic thought process that leads to ethical behavior (Gottlieb & Sanzgiri, 1996; Grundstein-Amado, 1999). In the context of CEM, leadership is likely to influence the motivation of group members to expend cognitive effort. For instance, both transactional and transformational leaders may influence the motivation to expend cognitive effort by highlighting the moral intensity of an issue when they articulate the magnitude of consequences of unethical behavior.

In the context of CEM, anonymity is likely to influence cognitive elaboration by members in a group by influencing members' motivation and ability to expend cognitive effort. A common view is that anonymity makes it more conducive for members to elaborate on an issue by reducing evaluation apprehension, a common barrier to participation by members of a group, (Connolly et al., 1990; Jessup et al., 1990; Nunamaker et al., 1991).

Based on the above discussion, we present in Figure 6–1 the general model of the effects of leadership and anonymity on group discussion of an ethical issue in an EMS context. Leadership and anonymity are two situational determinants of the motivation and ability of group members to cognitively elaborate on an ethical issue. Group members enter their elaborations into the EMS, which makes them available to other group members. Thus, an individual member not only has access to her or his cognitive elaborations but also has access to those of others. The pool of cognitive elaborations available to an individual member in turn influences the intentions of the member about how to act in the ethical situation at hand.

We focused on two variables that reflect cognitive elaboration within a group: *amount of participation* and *balance of arguments*. Amount of participation is the level of input provided by group members to execute the group's task. In electronic groups, providing input is akin to talking in a face-to-face situation (Kahai et al., 1998). Past research has found that simply talking about an ethical issue changes an individual's moral reasoning (Haan, 1975; Haan &

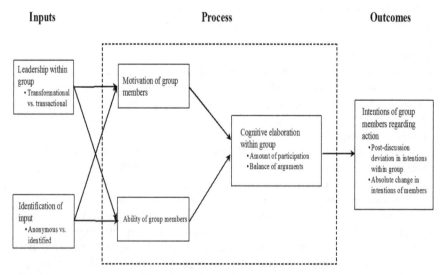

FIGURE 6–1.   General model of the effects of leadership style and anonymity on group process and outcomes for discussion of ethical issues

Block, 1968). Balance of arguments is defined as the net of arguments against unethical action and arguments for unethical action in a group discussion. While amount of participation reflects the amount of cognitive elaboration, balance of arguments reflects the orientation of cognitive elaboration within a group.

We also focused on two intention-related variables: *postdiscussion deviation in intentions* and *absolute change in intentions*. Postdiscussion deviation in intentions refers to deviation among group members in intentions to illegally copy software after the group discussion. Postdiscussion deviation in intentions to copy software is an indicator of lack of convergence among group members in their intentions to copy software after a group discussion. In the context of illegal copying of software among students who are normatively more likely to converge towards illegal copying (Cohen & Cornwell, 1989; Glass & Wood, 1996), difference in postdiscussion deviation across conditions indicates the extent to which the conditions differ in terms of moving group members away from their group norm. Absolute change in intentions refers to the absolute amount of change in group members' intentions to illegally copy software due to group discussion. It is an indicator of the extent of influence that cognitive elaboration within a group had on any participant's intention to illegally copy software.

HYPOTHESES

In this section, we develop and present hypotheses about the effects of leadership style and anonymity on group process (cognitive elaboration) and outcomes (intentions).

Effect of Leadership Style on Group Process

Transformational and transactional leaders are expected to motivate participants discussing an ethical issue at two levels. The first level pertains to motivation to expend effort discussing the issue with other participants, and the second pertains to motivation to expend effort thinking about the issue. Whereas the motivation to discuss the issue with other participants is expected to influence how much effort they put into their discussion, the motivation to think about the issue is expected to influence whether participants consider and bring forth relevant moral arguments when discussing the issue (Street et al., 2001). In the following subsections, we first discuss the effect of leadership style on participation, which reflects the effort put into the discussion. Subsequently, we discuss the effect of leadership style on the balance of arguments, which reflects the extent to which participants considered and brought forth relevant moral arguments pertaining to the ethical issue.

Effect of Leadership on Participation

Transformational leaders display inspirational motivation (IM) and promote intellectual stimulation (IS) and individualized consideration (IC). Through these behaviors, a transformational leader influences effort–accomplishment expectancies in ways that motivate participation in the discussion of an ethical issue. A transformational leader may motivate participation by promoting IS and IC. Specifically, the transformational leader may encourage group members to question and challenge each other and reframe each other's ideas (IS). The leader may also encourage participants to try to understand and show consideration for each other's opinions (IC). These behaviors motivate participants to participate by clarifying what is expected of them and increasing their confidence that, with some effort, they will meet the leader's expectations and accomplish their task successfully. Also, when participants view each other as showing understanding and support for their ideas, this positive reinforcement motivates them to participate even further.

As part of IM behaviors in a group, transformational leaders emphasize the intrinsic value of goal accomplishment and collective efficacy of the group. In the current study, the transformational leader highlighted the intrinsic value of participants' discussion by indicating that they will learn from their discussion. Such emphasis motivates effort by engaging participants' self-concepts and making their effort more meaningful (Shamir, House, & Arthur, 1993). The transformational leader also highlighted the collective efficacy of the group by indicating to the group that by working together they could arrive at a better course of action. Such behavior tends to increase participants' self-efficacy, which in turn motivates them to expend greater effort in the discussion and increase their participation by increasing their effort–accomplishment expectancies (Shamir et al., 1993).

The transactional leader motivated participation by highlighting the exchange relationships among participants, the course instructor, and the leader herself. The leader highlighted desirable outcomes that would result from a successful discussion (i.e., a long list of ideas, a feeling of satisfaction, and course credit given by the course instructor), thereby building effort–accomplishment expectancies to motivate participation. The transactional leader strengthened these expectancies and the motivation to participate by (a) clarifying what the participants were expected to do for a successful discussion (i.e., generate and exchange as many ideas as possible about the ethical issue), and (b) rewarding participants by expressing satisfaction as they progressed through the discussion.

In summary, there are both similarities and differences in the behaviors of transformational and transactional leaders described here. Both the transformational and transactional leaders linked the discussion to outcomes; the transformational leader linked the discussion to the learning that the participants were expected to achieve and the transactional leader linked the discussion to the ideas that would come out of the discussion, the feeling of satisfaction that it would generate, and the course credit that the participants would receive. However, the outcomes indicated by the transactional leader are likely to be perceived as more immediate and concrete than the outcomes indicated by the transformational leader. In the current study, participants were assigned a task of short duration. For such tasks, the more immediate and concrete the outcomes, the stronger will be their motivational effect due to two reasons. First, in the short run, the more immediate and clearer the outcomes, the more important and salient they are likely to be to participants. Second, the more immediate and clearer the outcomes, the more likely participants are to see how well they are achieving the outcomes indicated by their leader, which in turn strengthens their effort–accomplishment expectancies.

Therefore, the above discussion suggests that the amount of participation will be greater under a transactional versus a transformational leader. This is consistent with the finding of past research: in an EMS setting, transactionally led groups tend to generate a greater number of ideas than transformational groups for tasks of short duration (Kahai et al., 2003; Sosik et al., 1997). Accordingly, we hypothesize the following:

Hypothesis 1. The amount of participation will be greater under a transactional leader than under a transformational leader.

Effect of Leadership on Balance of Arguments

According to the Cognitive Elaboration Model, situational characteristics such as *moral intensity*, *personal relevance*, and *personal accountability* are likely to determine the motivation of individuals to think about an ethical issue and bring forth relevant issues when discussing the issue (Street et al., 2001). Transformational and transactional leadership can influence the perception of these situational characteristics and, thus, determine the motivation of participants to cognitively elaborate on an ethical issue.

In the current study, as part of IM behaviors, the transformational leader highlighted that not copying copyrighted software is simply the right and ethical thing to do. Specifically, the leader highlighted a better future that could result when one does not copy copyrighted software ("availability of innovative products in the market"). The leader also linked the important value of "creating a greater good for the society" that would be realized when one does not copy copyrighted software. Through these behaviors, the leader highlighted the magnitude of consequences, in other words, the sum of the harms (or benefits) when one acts unethically (or ethically), which in turn influence the perception of moral intensity of an ethical issue (Jones, 1991). The transformational leader introduced the idea that "each consumer take the responsibility for assuring that s/he lives up to the contractual agreement" thereby influencing the perception of personal accountability, which is defined as the extent to which people believe that they are uniquely responsible for a particular outcome (Street et al., 2001).

The consequences of acting ethically highlighted by the leader are likely to engage the self-concept of participants (i.e., personal desire for innovative products, doing greater good for the society, and honoring a contractual agreement), thereby making the ethical issue personally relevant to them. Thus by linking the ethical issue to participants' self-concept, the transformational leader potentially harnessed the motivational force of self-expression when participants elaborated on the issue (Shamir et al., 1993).

The transactional leader highlighted the incentives for both consumers and the producer in protecting the copyrights of software products; in other words, the producer gets a fair rate of return and continues to provide innovative products that benefit consumers when consumers pay an equitable price. Through these behaviors the leader highlighted the magnitude of consequences, potentially influencing the perception of moral intensity. Like the transformational leader, the transactional leader also introduced the idea that "each consumer take the responsibility for assuring that s/he lives up to the contractual agreement" thereby influencing the perception of personal accountability. By highlighting the consequences of acting ethically, a transactional leader may have caused participants to perceive the ethical issue at hand as personally relevant. The leader may have strengthened this perception of personal relevance by highlighting to participants that paying for software is in their own best interest and "simply the more effective transaction for consumers."

Both transformational and transactional leaders motivated participants to cognitively elaborate on the ethical issue of copying copyrighted software. However, we believe the nature of cognitive elaboration is likely to be different, thereby altering the balance of arguments across the transformational and transactional leadership conditions. By taking a value- and socially-oriented and perspective, the transformational leader probably motivated participants to rise above their own interests, obey the social contract, and follow universal ethical principles. On the other hand, by taking a utilitarian perspective in which there is a payback for your actions, the transactional leader probably motivated economic- and individual-oriented thinking in which the potential for self-interested behavior rises. In the case of the ethical issue of copying copyrighted software, self-interested behavior (i.e., copying the software) is unethical behavior.

In summary, the cognitive elaboration occurring within a group under a transformational leader is likely to be more oriented towards not copying the copyrighted software than cognitive elaboration occurring within a group under a transactional leader. Accordingly, we hypothesize the following:

> *Hypothesis 2.* The balance of arguments will be more towards not copying the copyrighted software under a transformational leader than under a transactional leader.

Effect of Anonymity on Group Process

According to our CEM-based model, one of the ways in which anonymity within a group is likely to influence cognitive elaboration is by making it more or less conducive for group members to expend cognitive effort. In the current study we focused on source anonymity, whereby participants know the members of their group but do not know who made particular comments during group discussion. Work by Kahai et al. (1998) suggests that anonymity may influence participation not by lowering inhibition to participate, as commonly claimed in the EMS literature, but by influencing the task focus exhibited by group members by turning their focus away from specific individual identities. According to Kahai et al. (1998) this effect of source anonymity on participation is more likely to occur when the level of prediscussion agreement is low among group members on the topic of discussion. When there is disagreement among group members, participants may spend time trying to figure out who is taking what position rather than contributing their own input into the discussion. In the current study, there were differences in intentions to copy copyrighted software among members in virtually all groups. Thus, based on the above discussion, we expected the employment of source anonymity would reduce the amount of participation in groups, as summarized in the following hypothesis.

> *Hypothesis 3.* The amount of participation will be greater in the non-anonymous condition than in the anonymous condition.

Anonymity may influence the orientation of cognitive elaboration by reducing the perception of personal accountability, which, according to CEM, is likely to reduce the motivation to expend cognitive effort. The Social Identity model of Deindividuation Effects (SIDE) argues that in groups where cues about group membership are present, anonymity has a depersonalizing effect of reducing attention to individual identities (Lea & Spears, 1991; Postmes, Spears, & Lea, 1998; Reicher, 1984). In such a situation, participants' perception of personal accountability for behavior reduces and their attention shifts to the group, which in turn increases conformity to the group's norms.

As indicated earlier, participants in the current study were university students. University students generally consider the copying of copyrighted software as acceptable and normative (Cohen & Cornwell, 1989; Glass & Wood, 1996). Consequently, participants within any group are more likely to present arguments that favor (rather than those that counter) copying of software and give rise to an emergent group norm that favors copying.

In the current study, group membership cues were created through task instructions provided to all participants that they would be working in a group during their task (e.g., "start a discussion with your team members"). Participants were also introduced to other members of their group at the outset of their experimental session. In the presence of group membership cues, anonymity is likely to make the group and its emergent norm that favors the copying of software salient to participants and lead them to behave in conformance with the group's norm. Consequently, we expected that anonymity is likely to cause participants to argue more in favor of and less against the copying of copyrighted software. This is indicated in the following hypothesis.

> *Hypothesis 4.* The balance of arguments will be more towards copying the copyrighted software in the anonymous condition than in the identified condition.

Effect of Leadership Style and Anonymity on Outcomes

An imbalance in the arguments for and against the copying of copyrighted software with arguments favoring copying leads participants to converge to similar intentions to copy the software at the end of their discussion. However, a greater balance in the arguments for and against the copying of software should create greater variance in intentions to copy the software at the end of discussion. Also, a more balanced discussion is likely to introduce participants to perspectives that they had not considered earlier, resulting in a greater absolute change in their intentions to illegally copy software.

Thus, given that (a) the transformational leadership styles promotes a greater balance of arguments than the transactional leadership style, as per the discussion leading to hypothesis 2, and (b) a greater balance of arguments is likely to be associated with greater postdiscussion deviation and absolute change in intentions to copy copyrighted software, we expected the transformational leadership style to be associated with greater postdiscussion deviation and absolute change in intentions to copy copyrighted software compared to the transactional leadership style. This is summarized in the following hypotheses.

Hypothesis 5. Postdiscussion deviation in intentions to copy copyrighted software will be greater under a transformational leader than under a transactional leader.

Hypothesis 6. Absolute change in intentions to copy copyrighted software will be greater under a transformational leader than under a transactional leader.

Similarly, given that (a) nonanonymity is likely to promote a balance of arguments, and (b) a greater balance of arguments is likely to be associated with greater postdiscussion deviation and absolute change in intentions to copy copyrighted software, we expected anonymity to detract from postdiscussion deviation and absolute change in intentions to copy copyrighted software, as summarized in the following hypotheses:

Hypothesis 7. Postdiscussion deviation in intentions to copy copyrighted software will be greater in the identified condition than in the anonymous condition.

Hypothesis 8. Absolute change in intentions to copy copyrighted software will be greater in the identified condition than in the anonymous condition.

METHOD

Participants

Two hundred students enrolled in an undergraduate introductory information systems course participated in a laboratory experiment for course credit. Subjects were randomly assigned to 42 ad hoc groups, 32 of which consisted of five members each and the rest consisted of four members each.

Overview of Experimental Session and Task

Subjects used Ventana Corporation's GroupSystems in a Decision Room setting (Dennis, George, Jessup, Nunamaker, & Vogel, 1988). A facilitator greeted the participants as they entered the Decision Room and then randomly assigned them to terminals designated for their group. Before the start of the experimental session, the facilitator introduced participants to other members of their group and their leader. Each experimental session lasted for approximately 90 minutes and consisted of three phases. During phase I, which lasted approximately 15 minutes, participants used the Electronic Brainstorming System (EBS) tool in GroupSystems in order to get acquainted with it. During phase II, participants used the Idea Organizer (IO) and the EBS tools to comment on and discuss the software-copying scenario presented below. In phase III, participants answered a questionnaire pertaining to their IO and EBS sessions in phase II.

In Phase II, each group commented on and discussed following ethical scenario.

> Your roommate just purchased a new software package at a price of $250. The software would enable you to complete your MIS assignments. Having the software on your computer will eliminate the need to go to public computer facilities on campus. The software is not copy protected (i.e., it can easily be copied), however it is copyrighted (i.e., the producer has the exclusive legal right to make copies).
>
>   If your roommate said it was okay to copy, would you copy the software?

A group's task was made up of three parts. Participants began by using the IO tool for 10 minutes to privately indicate whether they would copy the software and to state supporting arguments. Subsequently, participants used the EBS tool for 20 minutes to discuss the issue with group members by presenting and arguing for their positions. In accord with common usage of the EBS tool, only electronic discussion was permitted (Jessup & Tansik, 1991; Valacich, Dennis, & Connolly, 1994). Finally, participants used the IO tool for 10 minutes to privately indicate whether they would copy the software and to state supporting arguments. Since anonymity was manipulated during group discussion, anonymity's effects examined in this study pertain to group discussion.

Research Design

The current study employed a 2 (identified/anonymous discussion) × 2 (transactional/transformational leadership) factorial design. The experimental groups were randomly assigned across the anonymity and leadership conditions. The EBS tool was configured to tag comments with the author's name only in the identified condition. Depending on the anonymity condition, participants were informed that their comments were anonymous or not anonymous from other group members and the leader.

Female confederates led the task exhibiting transactional or transformational leadership. Introductory messages and scripts representing transactional and transformational leadership styles were created based on a comprehensive training program (Bass & Avolio, 1994). Before participants discussed the software-copying scenario, the EBS displayed the introductory message from their leader. During the discussion, the confederates typed eight scripted comments into the EBS at assigned times, which were constant across conditions.

Examination of the EBS transcripts showed that the leaders followed their instructions. Manipulation checks confirmed the success of our manipulations.

The introductory messages of the transactional and transformational leaders had a common beginning but differed otherwise. The common beginning highlighted that software can be recognized as property, and that it is up to the consumer to take responsibility for upholding the contractual agreement with the producer regarding certain rights and privileges for use and distribution that come with purchasing the software. Beyond this common beginning, the transactional leader's introductory message conveyed to participants that there are clear economic benefits for consumers and producers when consumers comply with software copyright laws. The transformational leader's introductory message conveyed to participants that honoring copyright protection of software is simply the right and ethical thing to do.

The transactional leader's comments during the discussion emphasized what the group was expected to do and the rewards (e.g., feelings of satisfaction, course credit) it would receive upon achieving their expected outcomes, and expressed satisfaction with the group's progress. The transformational leader's comments during the discussion emphasized understanding and appreciating different needs and viewpoints within the group, stimulating each other's efforts to be creative by questioning assumptions, reframing problems, and approaching traditional situations in new ways. The leader also provided meaning and challenge to participants' discussion while motivating them to work together on an important issue.

Measures

The study's dependent variables were two group process and two group variables. The group process variables studied were (a) amount of participation and (b) balance of arguments. Obtaining measures of these variables involved parsing the coding of EMS transcripts of group discussion using the scheme provided in appendix A. This scheme is based on a synthesis of various cognitive frameworks used by individuals when considering ethical scenarios (McDonald & Pak, 1996). Transcripts of subject groups were parsed and coded by two raters who were blind to the study's conditions and hypotheses. Each rater coded a different subset consisting of half of all the transcripts. Coders were trained in the use of the coding scheme until they demonstrated adequate parsing and coding reliability before they began coding the transcripts.

Based on Kahai, Avolio, and Sosik (1998), various participation indicators were obtained from each group's EMS transcript: number of words, number of characters, number of comment blocks, and number of parsed comments. A comment block is defined as a block of text (a maximum of five lines) entered by a participant during each system iteration (Valacich, Dennis, & Nunamaker, 1992). A parsed comment is defined as a separate idea uttered by a participant (Connolly et al., 1990; Jessup et al., 1990; Valacich et al., 1992). Each of the participation indicators was standardized. The standardized indicators were summed to obtain the amount of participation within each group.

Balance of arguments was obtained by subtracting the number of arguments in favor of copying from the number of arguments against copying. The number of arguments in favor of or against copying was obtained from the parsing and coding of transcripts.

The two outcome variables studied were (a) postdiscussion deviation within group in intentions to copy and (b) absolute change in one's intention to copy. Postdiscussion intention to copy the software was obtained by the EMS after discussion as a response to the question "Will you copy the software?" to which participants could respond on a 5-point scale (1 = definitely not, 2 = probably not, 3 = don't know, 4 = probably yes, 5 = definitely yes). The standard deviation of responses within any group was employed as an indicator of postdiscussion deviation. Absolute intention change was obtained by calculating the absolute value of the difference concerning participants' intentions to copy the software obtained through the EMS pre- and post-discussion. Unlike postdiscussion deviation, which is a group level measure, absolute intention change is an individual level measure.

Analysis

An analysis of variance (ANOVA) was employed to test the study's hypotheses. All hypothesis tests involved the following independent variables: Leadership (transactional versus transformational leadership style), Anonymity (identified versus anonymous discussion), and Leadership × Anonymity. With the exception of hypotheses 6 and 8, performed with individual level data about intentions to copy software, all hypothesis tests were performed with group level data and included group size as a covariate. Additional variables employed in the analyses for the different hypotheses are noted below.

To test hypotheses 1 and 3 about the effects of leadership and anonymity on participation, the following additional independent variables were employed for control purposes: Prediscussion deviation within group (computed similarly to postdiscussion deviation but employing intentions to copy software before group discussion) and Anonymity × Prediscussion Deviation because they have been shown to affect participation in an EMS context (Kahai et al., 1998). To test hypotheses 2 and 4 about the effects of leadership and anonymity on balance of arguments, the "within group" average of the prediscussion intentions to copy the software (hereafter simply referred to as average prediscussion intentions) was employed as an additional covariate. Average prediscussion intentions, indicative of the how the group as a whole is inclined towards copying the software, can influence the incidence of arguments for or against the copying of software. It was employed in the analysis to control for its effects on balance of arguments.

To test hypotheses 5 and 7 about the effects of leadership and anonymity on postdiscussion deviation, prediscussion deviation within group and average prediscussion intentions were employed as additional covariates. Prediscussion deviation within group was employed to control for prediscussion deviation's potential to influence postdiscussion deviation. The variable "average prediscussion intentions" was employed to control for its effect on postdiscussion deviation; average prediscussion intentions, which reflect a group's initial orientation, may influence postdiscussion deviation in intentions via its effect on balance of arguments.

To test hypotheses 6 and 8 about the effects of leadership and anonymity on absolute change in intentions, the absolute difference between a group member's prediscussion intention and average prediscussion intention within the group was employed as a covariate in order to control for the effect of normative pressure on a member due to the member having intentions different from the intentions of the group as a whole.

RESULTS

Tables 6.1 and 6.2 present means, standard deviations, sample size, and Pearson product–moment correlations among the measures for the manipulation checks and dependent variables.

Manipulation Checks

Individual-level perceptions pertaining to anonymity and leadership manipulations were employed for manipulation checks. Three questionnaire items assessed whether participants believed that other members of their group will be able to trace their comments to them, whether their leader will be able to trace their comments to them, and whether the experimenters will be able to trace their comments to them. Perceptions of anonymity were significantly stronger in the anonymous condition than in the identified condition ($M = 3.33$ vs. 2.49; $F(1,198) = 37.64$, $p < .01$). Perceptions that the leader's introductory message conveyed that honoring copyright protection of software is simply the right thing and ethical thing to do were significantly higher in the transformational condition than in the transactional condition ($M = 3.89$ vs. 3.73; $F(1,198) = 4.08$, $p = .04$). Perceptions that the leader's introductory message conveyed that there are clear economic benefits for consumers and producers when consumers comply with software copyright laws were significantly higher in the transactional condition than in the transformational condition ($M = 3.83$ vs. 3.40; $F(1,198) = 7.26$, $p < .01$).

TABLE 6.1.
Means, Standard Deviations, Sample Size, and Correlations Among Measures for Manipulation Checks

Variable	M	SD	n	1	2	3	4	5	6	7	8
Perceived anonymity	2.89	1.05	200	**.85**							
Perceived transformational nature of introductory message	3.73	1.13	200	.03	—						
Perceived transactional nature of introductory message	3.62	1.15	200	-.05	.27	—					
Perceived intellectual stimulation by leader	3.30	0.83	200	.01	.14	.01	**.81**				
Perceived individualized consideration by leader	3.23	0.81	200	-.07	.10	-.02	.71	**.88**			
Perceived inspirational motivation by leader	3.39	0.69	200	-.06	.09	-.00	.72	.83	.77		
Perceived clarification of goals and contingencies by leader	3.11	0.84	200	.01	-.04	-.00	.08	.13	.23	.70	
Perceived contingent rewarding by leader	3.66	0.90	200	-.02	.02	.12	.30	.31	.43	.34	**.78**

Note. Boldfaced diagonal elements are Cronbach's alphas for multi-item scales. Underlined correlations are significant at $p \leq .05$.

TABLE 6.2.
Means, Standard Deviations, Sample Size, and Correlations
Among Measures for Dependent Variables

Variable	M	SD	n	1	2	3	4
1. Participation	0.00	3.64	42	.93			
2. Balance of arguments	−18.36	9.00	42	−.45	—		
3. Postdiscussion deviation	0.96	0.50	42	.16	.53	—	
4. Absolute intention change	0.24	0.47	200	NA	NA	NA	—

Note. Underlined correlations are significant at $p \leq .05$. Diagonal elements represent Cronbach's alpha.

Based on responses to items measuring transactional and transformational leadership from the MLQ Form 5X (Bass & Avolio, 1996), perceptions of leader (a) clarifying goals and reward contingencies and (b) providing contingent rewards during discussion were significantly greater in the transactional versus transformational leadership condition (clarifying: $M = 3.52$ vs. 2.71; $F(1,198) = 59.30, p < .01$; contingent rewarding: $M = 3.89$ vs. 3.43; $F(1,198) = 13.53, p < .01$). Perceptions of leader displaying intellectual stimulation, individualized consideration, and inspirational motivation during discussion were significantly greater in the transformational leadership condition than in the transactional condition (intellectual stimulation: $M = 3.61$ vs. 2.98; $F(1,198) = 33.46, p < .01$; individualized consideration: $M = 3.59$ vs. 2.87; $F(1,198) = 48.22, p < .01$; inspirational motivation: $M = 3.65$ vs. 3.13; $F(1,198) = 31.91, p < .01$). These results indicate that our manipulations were successful.

Process and Outcome Effects

Table 6.3 provides descriptive statistics for the study's dependent variables in each of the cells in the study's design. Table 6.4 shows summary ANOVA results for the study's hypotheses.

Hypothesis 1 was supported. Participation was greater in the transactional leadership condition than in the transformational leadership condition ($M = 0.96$ vs. –0.96; $F(1,35) = 6.51, p < .02$). Results supported hypothesis 2, which predicted a greater balance of arguments in the transformational leadership condition relative to the transactional leadership condition ($M = -14.10$ vs. –22.62; $F(1,36) = 12.03, p < .01$). Hypothesis 3 was also supported. Participation was greater in the identified condition than in the anonymous condition ($M = 0.71$ vs. –0.79; $F(1,35) = 5.53, p < .03$). Hypothesis 4, which predicted that the balance of arguments will decrease with anonymity, was not supported ($M = -19.59$ vs. –17.00; $F(1,36) = 0.04, p = .84$).

There was no significant difference in the postdiscussion deviation in intentions to copy copyrighted software across the two leadership conditions,

TABLE 6.3.
Cell Means, Standard Deviations, and Sizes for Dependent Variables

Variable	Identified			Anonymous		
	M	SD	n	M	SD	n
Participation						
Transactional leadership	1.64	4.06	11	−0.21	4.34	10
Transformational leadership	−0.21	3.49	11	−1.77	1.63	10
Balance of arguments						
Transactional leadership	−24.64	10.11	11	20.40	6.92	10
Transformational leadership	−14.55	9.09	11	−13.60	4.45	10
Postdiscussion deviation						
Transactional leadership	0.77	0.49	11	0.95	0.41	10
Transformational leadership	1.07	0.69	11	1.06	0.33	10
Absolute intention change						
Transactional leadership	0.21	0.49	53	0.15	0.36	47
Transformational leadership	0.29	0.50	52	0.31	0.51	48

thereby not supporting hypothesis 5 ($M = 1.07$ in transformational vs. 0.85 in transactional; $F(1,35) = 0.20$, $p = .65$). Hypothesis 6, which predicted a greater absolute change in intentions to copy copyrighted software under the transformational leader than under the transactional leader, was supported ($M = 0.30$ vs. 0.18; $F(1,195) = 4.12$, $p < .05$). Hypothesis 7 was not supported. Postdiscussion deviation in intentions to copy copyrighted software were not significantly different across the anonymous and identified conditions ($M = 1.00$ vs. .92; $F(1,35) = .25$, $p = .62$). Hypothesis 8 was also not supported. There was no significant difference in absolute change in intentions to copy copyrighted software across the anonymous and identified conditions ($M = 0.23$ vs. 0.25; $F(1,195) = 0.07$, $p = .79$).

Additional Results

A significant effect of Leadership × Anonymity was observed on postdiscussion deviation in intentions to copy copyrighted software ($F(1,35) = 5.35$, $p < .03$), suggesting that the effect of anonymity on postdiscussion deviation varied across the leadership conditions.

DISCUSSION

In this study we set out to examine how different conditions of leadership and anonymity affected the discussion of an ethical issue in an EMS setting. Our results generally support our model's predictions of the effects of transactional

TABLE 6.4.
Analysis of Variance Results

	Effects											
	Leadership			Anonymity			Leadership × Anonymity		
Variables	F	df	p	F	df	p	F	df	p
Hypotheses 1–4 (Group Process)									
Participation	6.51	(1,35)	<.02	5.53	(1,35)	<.03	0.71	(1,35)	.40
Balance of arguments	12.03	(1,36)	<.01	0.89	(1,36)	.35	0.63	(1,36)	.43
Hypotheses 5–8 (Group Outcomes)									
Postdiscussion deviation	0.20	(1,35)	.65	0.25	(1,35)	.62	5.35	(1,35)	<.03
Absolute intention change	4.12	(1,195)	<.05	0.07	(1,195)	.79	0.37	(1,195)	.54

versus transformational leadership in an EMS setting. Three of the four expected effects of leadership were observed. Greater participation was observed under the transactional leader than under the transformational leader. A greater balance of arguments was observed and greater absolute change in intentions to copy copyrighted software were observed under the transformational leader than under the transactional leader. Though we expected greater postdiscussion deviation in intentions to copy copyrighted software in the transformational leadership condition relative to the transactional leadership condition, leadership did not affect postdiscussion deviation.

The effect of leadership on the balance of arguments suggests that transformational leadership was able to sway the thinking of participants away from copying copyrighted software. We had expected that transformational leadership would promote ethical thinking in which one rises above one's self-interest, obeys the social contract, and follows universal ethical principles. We had also expected that though transactional leadership would promote a utilitarian perspective, this perspective is likely to encourage self-interested behavior. Additional analysis provides some support for these ideas. This analysis was performed on arguments in the coding categories identified in appendix A. The ANOVA model used to analyze the effects on balance of arguments was employed to analyze the arguments in various categories.

Results indicate that participants made more deontological arguments against copying, arguments where one views copying as wrong in itself (e.g., "I would not copy the software because it is not the right thing to do"), in the transformational condition than in the transactional leadership condition ($M = 2.00$ vs. $.62$, $SD = 2.35$ and $.80$, $n = 21$ for both conditions, $p < .02$). However, participants made more neutralization arguments in favor copying the software in the transactional leadership condition than in the transformational leadership condition ($M = 17.00$ vs. 12.76, $SD = 6.55$ and 3.05, $n = 21$ for both conditions, $p < .02$). Neutralization arguments include arguments whereby individuals feel that the norms they are violating do not apply to their particular instance, such as "I would copy the software because I don't intend to keep it after the semester is over." Also, participants made marginally more self-interest based arguments in favor of copying in the transactional leadership condition than in the transformational leadership condition ($M = 7.38$ vs. 4.95, $SD = 3.83$ and 4.82, $n = 21$ for both conditions, $p < .08$). Self-interest based arguments are those that promote personal interest or satisfaction, such as "I would copy the software because it would make it easy for me to complete my assignments."

A greater balance of arguments (as opposed to more arguments in favor of copying) in the transformational leadership condition relative to the transactional leadership was expected to sway some of the participants away from the norm of copying copyrighted software and cause a greater postdiscussion deviation in intentions to copy the software. Even though there was a greater balance of arguments in the transformational leadership condition than in the transactional leadership condition, there was no effect of leadership on postdiscussion deviation in intentions to copy copyrighted software. One possible explanation for this may be that given the tendency of students to favor copying copyrighted software, the student participants did not perceive the arguments against copying to be as compelling as the arguments in favor of copying due to which a greater balance of arguments in the transformational leadership condition did not translate into a greater postdiscussion deviation in intentions to copy the software.

Results provide limited support for our model's predictions of the effects of anonymity. Only one of the four expected effects of anonymity were observed. As expected, participation was higher in the identified condition relative to the anonymous condition. This result supports the findings of a past study by Kahai et al. (1998), which runs counter to popular thinking about the effect of anonymity on the level of participation in electronic groups. No effects of anonymity on the balance of arguments, postdiscussion deviation in intentions to copy the software, and absolute change in intentions were observed. However, anonymity interacted with leadership to influence postdiscussion deviation in intentions to copy the software.

Why did anonymity not affect the balance of arguments? In the presence of group membership cues, anonymity was expected to lead to reduced salience of individual identities and increase the salience of the group. Increased salience of the group was expected to lead to a greater effect of the norm of copying software associated with students and, in turn, this was expected to lead to a lower balance of arguments. It is possible that the group did not become salient. This may be due to participants not perceiving group membership cues or the norm of copying software that is associated with students. When the group is not salient, individuals behave as individual members and the cover of anonymity may be used for disengagement or desertion (Postmes et al., 1998).

Anonymity was expected to cause a change in participants' intentions to copy copyrighted software as well as a change in postdiscussion deviation in intentions to copy by reducing the balance of arguments. The lack of anonymity's effect on the balance of arguments may explain the lack of its effect on participants' intentions. However, it may not be possible to attribute the lack of anonymity's effect on postdiscussion deviation in intentions to the lack of anonymity's effect on the balance of arguments; an interaction effect of leadership and anonymity on postdiscussion deviation in intentions to copy was observed even though there was no such effect on the balance of arguments. Examination of cell means in Table 6–3 indicates that the effect of anonymity on postdiscussion deviation in intentions to copy copyrighted software was greater in the transactional leadership condition compared to the transformational leadership condition. This seems to suggest that transformational leadership is able to sway participants away from the group norm irrespective of the level of anonymity whereas participants need the cover of anonymity under transactional leadership to move away from the group norm.

CONCLUSION

When leading from a distance, leaders may rely on electronic interaction with their followers. Our study shows that leadership in text-based electronic interactions indeed does make a difference. Furthermore, its effects may interact with the features of technology, such as anonymity. It is interesting to note that using computer-mediated technology to study leadership effects represents one of the purest examinations of these effects. Specifically, in this study, leadership was manipulated only with behaviors that define transformational and transactional leadership. And through this "pure" manipulation of leadership, absent all of the other facets of a leader, such as demographics, impression management, nonverbal cues, etc., we found that transactional leadership led to greater participation and transformational leadership led to a more balanced discussion and greater change in intentions.

It is also interesting to note that the leadership manipulation in this study was a relatively "weak" manipulation because the leaders were not members of their groups and were merely there to facilitate the group process. Furthermore, they had no credibility established from prior interactions. We expect that when the leader is a member of the group, has credibility established from prior interactions, and facilitates both the process and the content of group interaction, the effects of leadership on group process and outcomes are likely to be more profound.

Limitations

Several limitations of the present study suggest additional avenues to be explored in future research. First, the study was conducted using ad hoc student groups. Future research should attempt to replicate and extend these findings using intact organizational groups with a history of prior interaction and expectations of future interactions. It is likely, that "intact" groups with significant history show different effects than what we observed here. For instance, Pinsonneault, Barki, Gallupe, and Hoppen (1999) reported that members of groups with history appeared to hold back ideas during electronic brainstorming based on the assumption that other members of the group already knew what they would say. Members of established groups may mistakenly assume that they understand each other better than is actually the case.

Second, group members interacted with each other for a relatively short period of time. Future longitudinal research should examine whether the present study's results are reproduced over longer periods of time because of the potential of group processes to change (Walther, 1995). Studies that examine computer-mediated groups and leadership within them over longer periods of time will be necessary to uncover the dynamic relationship between the use of technology features, leadership, and interaction among group members.

Third, the practical implications of our study are limited to the type of task in which participants had to discuss an ethical issue, and they were not required to make a collective decision. Future studies should look at tasks in which participants have to make a collective decision for an ethical issue. We believe that the type of task would determine the efficacy of one style of leadership over another (Sosik et al., 1997). Furthermore, this study's results are restricted to the effects of attempts of both leaders to promote ethical behavior. Future studies should extend their examination of effects of leadership to leadership attempts that promote unethical behavior or are neutral.

Finally, the groups in the current study interacted via a single communication system that allowed text messages only. Group members working at a distance from one another may use several communication systems, some rich and some lean, to support their work. Future studies should examine the effects when combinations of communication systems are used.

Directions for Future Studies

We believe that this study and our previous studies (e.g., Kahai et al., 1997; Sosik et al., 1997; Sosik, Kahai, & Avolio, 1998) indicate that exploring the effects of leadership and its interaction with features of electronic communication technologies, such as anonymity, is a promising area for future studies. The effect of leadership and its interaction with technology features will likely depend on variety of factors such as the nature of the technology, the culture and values in which the group and technology are embedded, the type of issue or problem being discussed, the risks or costs associated with a failed decision, and the group's expectation of working together over time. All of these issues together and in different combinations are worth pursuing in future research.

A key aspect of leadership is building identification with a goal, mission, vision or cause (Avolio, 1999). A challenge for leaders who must now lead from a distance is to consider how to use technology to enhance the identification of their followers with the group. In the current setting, there was some evidence indicating that the transformational leaders got followers to stop and think deeper about the ethical issue. By getting followers to think more deeply about their own views and self concept, such leaders are able to connect the followers self concept to the collective concept of the group (Shamir et al., 1993).

We believe this study provides a foundation for understanding how leadership style and anonymity influence group process and outcomes in computer-mediated discussions of ethical issues. Due to increasing interest in the use of electronic communication media in organizations around the world, continued research is warranted.

Appendix A

Coding Scheme Categories

Ideas expressed in transcripts were coded into the following categories:

TESTIMONY

Statements citing testimonial facts from the problem description or data about the computer situation on students' campus WITHOUT arguing for or against copying of software (e.g., The software is not copy protected).

Preferences for Action

Expressions of preferred action (e.g., I would copy the software).

ARGUMENTS AGAINST COPYING THE SOFTWARE

Arguments may fall into the following categories.

Utlitarian

Arguments in which the principal concern is to act so as to produce the greatest ratio of good over bad for everyone (e.g., I would not copy the software because we all would lose from it).

Self-Interest Arguments Against Copying the Software

Argument based on the concern that it is not in the best interest of the individual or group to copy the software (e.g., I would not copy the software because I would not be able to get support from the software company if I had any problems).

Deontological Arguments Against Copying the Software

Arguments based on the principal that an action is either right or wrong regardless of consequence. (e.g., I would not copy the software because it is not the right thing to do).

Duty.   Arguments that involve consideration of whether an action is consistent or inconsistent with any prescribed rules of duty, such as those of a member of the MIS student organization, or those of an American citizen (e.g., I would not copy the software because it is against my duty as a member of the MIS association to promote software piracy).

Justice.   Arguments based on whether there has been a just distribution of benefits and burdens among all those concerned, despite their age, sex, religion, interests, income, personal characteristics, social or occupational position (e.g., I would not copy because that would deprive the software producer a fair return for her/his efforts).

Legal.   Arguments based on whether an action is legal or not (e.g., I would not copy the software because it is illegal to do so).

Religious/Philosophical/Ethical Conviction.   Arguments based on one's religious/philosophical conviction (e.g., I would not copy because that it is against my religion.)

ARGUMENTS FOR COPYING THE SOFTWARE

Arguments may fall into the following categories.

Self-Interest Arguments for Copying the Software

Arguments in which the principal concern is to promote personal interests or satisfaction (e.g., I would copy the software because it would make it easy for me to complete my assignments).

Light of Day.   Arguments based on whether the action will see the light of day or if it does, what are the possible consequences (e.g., I would copy because there is a very little chance of getting caught).

Neutralization.   Arguments whereby an individual feels that the norms they are violating do not apply to their particular instance (e.g., I would copy because I do not intend to keep the software after the course.)

Appeal to Higher Loyalties.   Arguments whereby individuals propose that the norm violation action is required in order to achieve a higher order ideal or value (e.g., I would copy the software because my copying will ultimately help the New York economy).

ARGUMENTS FOR NEUTRAL STANCE

For example, I don't know whether I would or would not copy the software because I have never been in a situation like this before.

Nonspecific Pressure

Statements applying pressure on actions and decisions but not toward a particular decision (Let us get done now).

Procedures

Statements about rules and procedures to be followed by the group (e.g., Let us first state the reasons behind our preferences).

Counter Statements

Statements that counter assertions in the other categories. These include testimony, arguments of various types, preferences for action, nonspecific pressure, procedures, expressions of agreement (e.g., There are 200 and not 100 public computers on campus).

Expression of Agreement

Statements that express agreement with assertions in the other categories. These include testimony, arguments of various types, preferences for action, nonspecific pressure, procedures, counterstatements (e.g., I agree with you that there are 100 public computers on campus).

Questions

Statements that pose a question or question assertions in the other categories. These include testimony, arguments of various types, preferences for action, nonspecific pressure, procedures, counter statement, expression of agreement (e.g., Is there any other way for us to get the software easily without violating any laws?).

Leader Directed Comments

Statements directed at the leader (e.g., Leader, what are we supposed to do now?).

No Code

Statements that do not state a preference for action or an argument one way or the other. These statements do not appear to have any relevance to the debate and don't fit any other category.

REFERENCES

Avolio, B. J. (1999). *Full leadership development: Building the vital forces in organizations*. Thousand Oaks, CA: Sage Publications.

Avolio, B. J., Kahai, S., & Dodge, G. E. (2000). E-leadership; Implications for theory, research, and practice. *The Leadership Quarterly, 11*(4), 615–668.

Bass, B. M., & Avolio, B. J. (1994). *Improving organizational effectiveness through transformational leadership*. Thousand Oaks, CA: Sage Publications.

Bass, B. M., & Avolio, B. J. (1996). *Multifactor leadership questionnaire manual*. Palo Alto, CA: Mindgarden.

Cappel, J. J., & Windsor, J. C. (2000). Ethical decision making: A comparison of computer-supported and face-to-face group. *Journal of Business Ethics, 28*(2), 95–107.

Cohen, E., & Cornwell, L. (1989). College students believe piracy is acceptable. *CIS Educator's Forum*, 2–5.

Connolly, T., Jessup, L., & Valacich, J. (1990). Effects of anonymity and evaluative tone on idea generation in computer-mediated groups. *Management Science, 36*(6), 689–703.

Cranor, L. F. (1999). Internet privacy. *Communications of the ACM, 42*(2), 28–31.

Dennis, A., George, J., Jessup, L., Nunamaker, J., & Vogel, D. (1988). Information technology to support electronic meetings. *MIS Quarterly, 12*(4), 591–624.

Diehl, M., & Stroebe, W. (1987). Productivity loss in brainstorming groups: Toward the solution of a riddle. *Journal of Personality and Social Psychology, 53*(3), 497–509.

Glass, R. S., & Wood, W. A. (1996). Situational determinants of software piracy: An equity theory perspective. *Journal of Business Ethics, 15*, 1189–1198.

Gottlieb, J. Z., & Sanzgiri, J. (1996). Towards an ethical dimension of decision making in organizations. *Journal of Business Ethics, 15*(12), 1275–1285.

Grundstein-Amado, R. (1999). Bilateral transformation leadership: An approach for fostering ethical conduct in public service organizations. *Administration & Society, 31*(2), 247–260.

Haan, N. (1975). Hypothetical and actual moral reasoning in a situation of civil disobedience. *Journal of Personality and Social Psychology, 32*, 255–270.

Haan, N. S. B., & Block, J. (1968). Moral reasoning of young adults: Political-social behavior, family background, and personality correlates. *Journal of Personality and Social Psychology, 10*, 183–201.

Jessup, L. M., Connolly, T., & Galegher, J. (1990). The effects of anonymity on GDSS group process with an idea-generating task. *MIS Quarterly, 14*(3), 313–321.

Jessup, L., & Tansik, D. (1991). Decision making in an automated environment: The effects of anonymity and proximity on group process and outcome with a GDSS. *Decision Sciences, 22*(2), 266–279.

Johnson, B. T., & Eagly, A. H. (1989). Effects of involvement on persuasion: A meta-analysis. *Psychological Bulletin, 106*(2), 290–314.

Jones, T. M. (1991). Ethical decision making by individuals in organizations: An issue-contingent model. *The Academy of Management Review, 16*(2), 366–395.

Kahai, S., Avolio, B., & Sosik, J. (1998). Effects of source and participant anonymity and difference in initial opinions in an EMS context. *Decision Sciences, 29*(2), 427–460.

Kahai, S., Sosik, J., & Avolio, B. (1997). Effects of leadership style and problem structure on work group process and outcomes in an electronic meeting system environment. *Personnel Psychology, 50*(1), 121–146.

Kahai, S., Sosik, J., & Avolio, B. (2003). Effects of leadership style, anonymity, and rewards on creativity-relevant processes and outcomes in an electronic meeting system context. *Leadership Quarterly, 14*(4–5), 499–524.

Lea, M., & Spears, R. (1991). Computer-mediated communication, de-individuation and group decision-making. *International Journal of Man-Machine Studies, 34*(2), 283–301.

McDonald, G., & Pak, P. C. (1996). It's all fair in love, war, and business: Cognitive philosophies in ethical decision making. *Journal of Business Ethics, 15*(9), 973–996.

Nunamaker, J. F., Briggs, R. O., Mittleman, D. D., Vogel, D. R., & Balthazard, P. A. (1997). Lessons from a dozen years of group support systems research: A discussion of lab and field findings. *Journal of Management Information Systems, 13*(3), 163–207.

Nunamaker, J. F., Dennis, A. R., Valacich, J. S., Vogel, D. R., & George, J. F. (1991). Electronic meeting systems to support group work: Theory and practice at Arizona. *Communications of the ACM, 34*(7), 40–61.

Petty, R. E., & Cacioppo, J. T. (1979). Issue-involvement can increase or decrease persuasion by enhancing message-relevant cognitive responses. *Journal of Personality and Social Psychology, 37*, 1915–1926.

Pinsonneault, A., Barki, H., Gallupe, R. B., & Hoppen, N. (1999). The illusion of electronic brainstorming productivity: Theoretical and empirical issues. *Information Systems Research, 10*(4), 378–380.

Postmes, T., Spears, R., & Lea, M. (1998). Breaching or building social boundaries? SIDE-effects of computer-mediated communication. *Communication Research, 25*(6), 689–715.

Reicher, S. D. (1984). Social influence in the crowd: Attitudinal and behavioral effects of deindividuation in conditions of high and low group salience. *British Journal of Social Psychology, 23*(4), 341–350.

Shamir, B., House, R., & Arthur, M. (1993). The motivational effects of charismatic leadership: A self-concept based theory. *Organization Science, 4*(4), 1–17.

Sosik, J., Avolio, B., & Kahai, S. (1997). Effects of leadership style and anonymity on group potency and effectiveness in a GDSS environment. *The Journal of Applied Psychology, 82*(1), 89–103.

Sosik, J., Kahai, S., & Avolio, B. (1998). Transformational leadership and dimensions of creativity: Motivating idea generation in computer-mediated groups. *Creativity Research Journal, 11*(2), 111–121.

Stead, B., & Gilbert, J. (2001). Ethical issues in electronic commerce. *Journal of Business Ethics, 34* (2), 75–85.

Street, M., Douglas, S., Geiger, S., & Martinko, M. (2001). The impact of cognitive expenditure on the ehtical decision-making process: The cognitive elaboration model. *Organizational Behavior and Human Decision Processes, 86*(2), 256–277.

Tetlock, P. W. (1988). Accountability and complexity of thought. *Journal of Personality and Social Psychology, 45*, 74–83.

Townsend, A., DeMarie, S., & Hendrickson, A. (1998). Virtual teams: Technology and the workplace of the future. *Academy of Management Executive, 12*(3), 17–29.

Valacich, J. S., Dennis, A. R., & Connolly, T. (1994). Idea generation in computer-based groups: A new ending to an old story. *Organizational Behavior and Human Decision Processes, 57*(3), 448–467.

Valacich, J., Dennis, A., & Nunamaker, J. (1992). Anonymity and group size effects in an EMS environment. *Small Group Research, 23*(1), 49–73.

Walther, J. B. (1995). Relational aspects of computer-mediated communication: Experimental observations over time. *Organization Science, 6*(2), 186–203.

7

The Mediating Effects of Leadership and Interaction Style in Face-to-Face and Virtual Teams

Pierre A. Balthazard, David A. Waldman, and Leanne E. Atwater
Arizona State University

OVERVIEW

The virtual team has been touted to represent a new and growing organization form, mostly as organizations move toward team-based work units, an increasingly global business environment, and networked technologies (e.g., Jarvenpaa & Ives, 1994). We define virtual teams (VTs) as geographically dispersed groups who are dependent on electronic communication to work with others at a distance. Virtual teams have also been referred to as computer-mediated groups or electronic groups. We use the term virtual team to convey the idea that communication can be conducted anywhere within and beyond the organization. The team members possess relevant knowledge and typically work interdependently to accomplish tasks. Oftentimes, the members have different areas of expertise and may work in different functional areas (Duarte & Snyder, 1999; Lipnack & Stamps, 1997; Townsend, DeMarie, & Hendrickson, 1998). Virtual teams can give organizations increased flexibility and responsiveness, permitting them to rapidly form geographically dispersed and disparate experts into a virtual team that can work on an urgent project. When finished, the team can be disbanded and members re-deployed to other projects; members may also serve on multiple virtual teams simultaneously.

In the task reviewed in this chapter, 42 face-to-face teams (FtFTs) and 47 VTs performed an identical team-based task. Results showed that FtFTs scored higher on cohesion, solution acceptance, and group synergy than did VTs. Face-to-face teams were also more likely to demonstrate higher levels of leadership and a constructive interaction style, while VTs more often demonstrated lower levels of leadership and a defensive style.

The impact of media type (FtFT versus VT) on contextual outcomes also tended to be mediated by leadership and interaction style. That is, the effects of media type on cohesion and solution acceptance were largely a result of the mediational effect of leadership and a constructive interaction style. We discuss our results in terms of the need to take into account leadership and interaction style when considering the effects of teams working at a distance.

Much of the growth in virtual teams is attributable to the expanded use of the Internet in business organizations and related technological advances. The Internet's infrastructure enables organizations to reliably and inexpensively communicate and work internally, as well as externally with business partners and customers through applications such as email, web sites, intranets, and extranets, many of which can be configured to function as groupware (Coleman, 1997). However, the virtual organization can present such managerial challenges such as ambiguous roles for its members, lack of cohesion or teamwork behavior, and performance problems (DeSanctis & Poole, 1997).

The purpose of the present research is twofold. First, we will add to a growing body of literature comparing the effectiveness of VTs to more traditional, face-to-face teams (FtFTs). Second, we will test the extent to which the effect of electronic group media on performance outcomes may be mediated by leadership and interaction styles among group members. As shown in Figure 7–1, the model follows a traditional input-process-output conceptualization of group effectiveness (e.g., Guzzo & Dickson, 1996), with a focus on media.

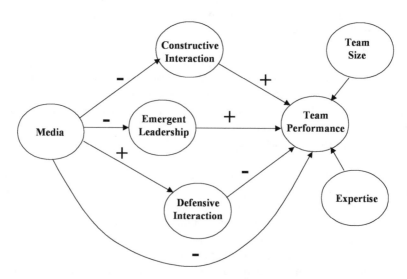

FIGURE 7–1.   A model of the hypothesized relationships between electronic media, emergent leadership, group interactions styles, and team performance.

Leadership has been shown to improve group outcomes in both FtFTs and VTs. Specifically, transformational leadership which encourages individuals to contribute ideas, has been shown to be advantageous to group processes and outcomes (Lowe, Kroeck, & Sivasubramaniam, 1996). In this study, we examine the degree to which leadership emergence or the amount of leadership demonstrated in the team is relevant to group outcomes.

Interaction style has been shown to have a substantial effect on the ability of face-to-face teams to achieve solution quality and solution acceptance (Cooke & Szumal, 1993; Hirokawa, 1985; Hirokawa & Gouran, 1989; Watson & Michaelsen 1988). Interaction style is best understood as a characterization of the communication patterns in which a group engages as it deals with the inherent conflicts of task orientation and maintenance of member relationships. Differing styles may affect team performance and group dynamics by facilitating or hindering the exchange of information among group members.

The Effectiveness of Virtual and Face-to-Face Teams

Much of the popular literature has questioned the effectiveness of virtual teams, as compared to their face-to-face counterparts. For example Duarte and Snyder (1999) argued that virtual teams may not be appropriate when issues are either highly emotional or ambiguous, or when the team is newly formed or short lived. Other work has provided anecdotal evidence of the relative ineffectiveness of virtual teams (e.g., Melymuka, 1997; Tan, Wei, Huang, & Ng, 2000).

More systematic research has also cast doubt on the effectiveness of VTs. Warkentin, Sayeed, and Hightower (1997) provided evidence that FtFTs obtain a higher degree of cohesion, have members who are more satisfied with the decision process followed by their respective teams, and have members who are more satisfied with their team's outcomes. Warkentin et al. (1997) attributed their findings to communication problems in virtual teams. Specifically, they pointed to how virtual teams are unable to duplicate the normal "give and take" of face-to-face team discussions, how VT discussions may appear to lack focus or be out of context because of multiple team members "talking" at once, and how team members who type more slowly or edit more thoroughly may find their comments become irrelevant before being sent. Such observations are in line with Hightower and Sayeed (1996) who found that VTs exchanged information less effectively than FtFTs. The problem was only accentuated by the lack of eye contact and other social context clues (e.g., head nods and voice inflections) that served to regulate the flow of group dialogue (McGrath, 1990).

Along similar lines, researchers have reported a general tendency for less overall communication in virtual teams (Hiltz, Johnson, & Turoff, 1986; Siegel, Dubrovsky, Kiesler, & McGuire, 1986), a phenomenon labeled information suppression by Hollingshead (1996). There is also evidence of less inhibition in virtual teams and a greater expression of personal opinions, unfortunately, including personal insults and profanity (Siegel et al., 1986; Weisband, 1992). In addition, although there may be some equalization of member participation (e.g., Weisband, 1992), the information suppression effect coupled with "free riding" tendencies (i.e., "hiding" behind one's computer screen) may make it difficult for virtual teams to achieve cohesion and ultimate acceptance of group decisions on the part of its members. Indeed, Lea and Spears (1991) found that VTs produced more polarized decisions than did FtFTs. There also seem to be mixed results on performance in VTs. For example, Straus and McGrath (1994) found that FtFTs were more productive than VTs on a variety of tasks, although the quality of the group's outcome was only better on what they termed judgment tasks, as opposed to idea-generation or intellective tasks. Likewise, Hedlund, Ilgen, and Hollenbeck (1998) found that FtFTs displayed higher decision accuracy than VTs. We therefore hypothesize that

> *H1:* Face-to-face team members will be more cohesive, more accepting of the group's decision, and perform better than will virtual teams.

The Role of Leadership

Very few experimental studies have examined the effects of leadership in VTs. Most of this research has looked at the impact of assigned or elected leaders on group processes or outcomes rather than measuring the amount or type of leadership that was present in the group (e.g., George, Easton, Nunamaker, & Northcraft, 1990; Hiltz, Johnson, & Turoff, 1991). Moreover, a review of studies of leadership in VTs found that very few measured leader style (Avolio, Kahai, & Dodge, 2000). Shamir (1997) suggested that leadership in VTs may be shared by virtual team members as they interact with one another and not the domain of just one assigned, elected, or emergent individual.

In this study, we believed that it was important to measure the degree of leadership, specifically transformational leadership, in two ways: For the team member who emerged as the leader, we measured his or her level of transformational leadership, and we also measured the team's average level of transformational leadership by all its members.

Earlier research demonstrated that within FtFTs, transformational leaders were likely to increase group performance in part because they overcame social loafing among group members (Kahai, Sosik, & Avolio, 2000; Shepperd, 1993). Transformational leaders are expected to show enthusiasm and confidence, promote understanding and appreciation for differing views, and intellectually stimulate group members to reexamine critical assumptions and look at problems in new ways (Bass & Avolio, 1994). Shamir and How-ell (1999) suggested that transformational leadership was also necessary in a virtual team context to infuse shared values and a sense of unified purpose or common identity.

Despite the apparent importance of transformational leadership in both face-to-face and virtual settings, little evidence exists suggesting which of these media is most likely to foster leader emergence. Sosik, Avolio, and Ka-hai (1997) examined the effects of transformational leadership on group po-tency (the group's belief that it can be effective) in a group support system, which is a virtual setting where members are collocated. They found that transformational leadership was associated with higher levels of potency than transactional leadership. Avolio et al. (2000) proposed that VTs with trans-formational leaders would have higher levels of trust, team potency, and per-formance. We extend this proposition to FtFTs as well. That is, transforma-tional leadership should enhance group cohesion and help the group perform even beyond its best individual member. However, because VTs may lack the richness of social cues present in FtFTs (e.g., facial expression, tone of voice), we expect that there will be less leadership displayed in VTs as compared to FtFTs. In addition, there is research to suggest that members in a virtual team setting may be less able to utilize the impression management strategies so essential to the formation of transformational leadership (Gardner & Avolio, 1998). We therefore hypothesize:

> *H2:* The degree of transformational leadership will be positively asso-ciated with team cohesion, member acceptance of the group's decision, and measures of task performance.

> *H3:* FtFTs will demonstrate higher levels of transformational leadership and produce leaders with higher levels of transformational leadership than virtual teams.

The Role of Group Interaction Styles

A team's interaction style can affect its performance. Watson and Michaelsen (1988) identified positive and negative behaviors as components of group interaction style. They found that groups of behaviors (expectations of per-formance and integration, leadership, and cohesiveness) contributed to team performance on an intellective task whereas one group of negative behaviors (e.g., noninvolvement and withholding of information) detracted from team performance.

Similarly, Cooke and Szumal (1994) and others (e.g., Hoffman, 1979; Maier, 1967) showed that group interaction styles were either composed of constructive or defensive behaviors. The constructive interaction style was characterized by a balanced concern for personal and group outcomes, cooperation, creativity, free exchange of information, and respect for others' perspectives. Defensive styles included passive and aggressive behaviors. Passive behaviors included limited information sharing, questioning, and impartiality. Aggressive behaviors encouraged members to approach tasks in forceful ways to protect their status and security. Empirical support for the distinctions between these behavioral styles was provided by the results of principal components analyses presented elsewhere (e.g., Cooke & Rousseau, 1988; Cooke & Szumal, 1993; Xenikou & Furnham, 1996).

Research looking at the impact of group interaction style on performance in FtFTs revealed that predominantly constructive groups were likely to produce solutions that were superior in quality and acceptance to those produced by defensive groups (Cooke & Szumal, 1994).

Group interaction style was theorized to affect performance because it could impede or enhance team members' abilities to bring their unique knowledge and skills to bear on the task, thus affecting the extent to which they developed and considered alternative strategies for approaching the task (Hackman & Morris, 1975). This is particularly critical for groups with heterogeneous levels of expertise, as communication by the most expert group members was positively correlated with group performance. For example, Zalesny (1990) found that the most accurate member in interacting groups did not influence performance unless he or she was assertive and confident—traits presumably more highly fostered in constructive groups. These arguments suggest the following hypothesis:

> *H4:* A team's interaction style will be positively associated with group cohesion, member acceptance of the group's decision, and measures of task performance.
>
> *H4a:* A constructive interaction style will be positively associated with group cohesion, member acceptance of the group's decision, and measures of task performance.
>
> *H4b:* A defensive interaction style will be negatively associated with group cohesion, member acceptance of the group's decision, and measures of task performance.

Media in Relation to Interaction Styles

Of particular interest to us is an understanding of how a predominant interaction style materializes in the team. For example, how does one team develop a predominantly constructive style, but another team develops a predominantly defensive style? We propose that the media in which team members interact (i.e., face to face or electronically) may have an important influence on the interaction style that materializes within a group. We expect that a face-to-face discussion is more likely to engender the constructive interaction style. One reason may be the relatively more free exchange of information in FtFTs. Another reason may be that face-to-face contact and the use nonverbal cues and tone of voice to communicate will help members develop respect for the perspectives and needs of others in the group. In contrast, VTs, because they lack the richness of face-to-face communication, may be less likely to foster empathy and concern, and may be more likely to suppress information and indulge in personal insults and profanity (Hollingshead, 1996; Siegel et al., 1986; Weisband, 1992). In addition, the electronic medium is likely to reduce the thoroughness of discussion and produce a less intensely critical decision-making process (Sambamurthy, Poole, & Kelly, 1993).

It follows that VTs are more likely than FtFTs to interact with a defensive style. In a review of the literature, McGrath and Hollingshead (1994) concluded that computer-mediated groups tended to be characterized by less interaction and exchange, as compared to face-to-face groups. Moreover, the lack of personal inhibition in VTs, coupled with increased tendencies of uninhibited communication, could cause more aggressive behaviors. We therefore hypothesize:

> *H5:* Media type will be associated with team interaction styles.
>
> *H5a:* FtFTs will demonstrate constructive interaction styles than will VTs.
>
> *H5b:* VTs will demonstrate defensive interaction styles than will FtFTs.

Mediational Effects

In addition to the main effects proposed above, we expect mediational effects (Baron & Kenny, 1986; Judd & Kenny, 1981; Kenny, Kashy, & Bolger, 1998). That is, leadership and interaction style may both mediate the relationship between media type and team outcomes. Prior work looking at VTs and FtFTs did not directly address the link between interaction styles and team performance. We propose that the relationship between media and outcomes are largely dependent on the fact that media type influences the emergence of leadership and the adoption of an interaction type rather than media having a direct effect on outcomes. Stated alternatively, media type may ultimately affect team outcomes through its influence on leadership and interaction styles. Specifically:

> *H6:* Transformational leadership will mediate the effect of media type on group cohesion, member acceptance of the group's decision, and measures of task performance.
>
> *H7:* Interaction style will mediate the effect of media type on group cohesion, member acceptance of the group's decision, and measures of task performance.

H7a: Constructive interaction styles will mediate the effect of media type on group cohesion, member acceptance of the group's decision, and measures of task performance.

H7b: Defensive interaction styles will mediate the effect of media type on group cohesion, member acceptance of the group's decision, and measures of task performance.

METHOD

Participants

Group interaction style, leadership, task and contextual performance data were collected from 339 members of 89 groups who had completed the "Ethical Decision Challenge" (Balthazard, 2000; Cooke, 1994), a structured problem-solving exercise used for management development and team building in classroom and corporate settings. Subjects were MBA and senior undergraduate students in multiple Management Information Systems course sections that required a semester-long systems development group project. The exercise, completed with these systems development groups at the team-building stage of their projects, was performed for course credit. There were 25 three-member teams (28%), 56 four-member teams (63%), and 8 five-member teams (9%). All participants were assumed to be highly computer literate.

Task and Technology

The "Ethical Decision Challenge" required participants to rank ten biomedical and behavioral research practices—all of which involved human subjects—in terms of their relative permissibility and acceptability (Balthazard, 2000; Cooke, 1994). This provided participants with an opportunity to practice their skills in both ethical analysis and group decision making. Solutions to the "Ethical Decision Challenge" were developed first on an individual basis and then as a group. Individual and team solutions were then compared to experts' solution based on the decisions of over 800 Institutional Review Board (IRB) members who were responsible for reviewing proposals for research involving human subjects. Comparisons between individual solutions and the experts' solution indicated how well participants exercised their knowledge, experience, and skills with respect to ethical analysis and complex problem solving. Comparisons between participants' individual scores and their team's score indicated whether they were able to achieve synergy by fully using and building on their collective knowledge and skills (see Cooke & Kernaghan, 1987). In other words, if group synergy were achieved, the team's score was expected to be better than any individual score. Participants in certain course sections (42 teams, 149 subjects, traditional classrooms) completed the paper version of the exercise with a face-to-face discussion, while participants in other course sections (47 teams, 190 subjects, computer-supported classrooms) completed an Internet version of the exercise with a computer-mediated discussion.

In both scenarios, participants were introduced to the "Challenge" during a regular 90-minute class meeting. Each participant was given 10 minutes to read the situation and challenge either in booklet form or on the web. Each participant was then given 10 minutes to rank 10 items (e.g., permissibility and acceptability of 10 behaviors). Those in paper-based (i.e., face-to-face) teams indicated their ranking on an answer form provided within the booklet. Those in computer-mediated (i.e., virtual) teams submitted their personal solution via an interactive web form.

Groups were then given 35 minutes to discuss the problem and provide the best possible consensus ranking of the items—a ranking with which *all* group members agreed. Computer-mediated team members were asked to select dispersed computers within the large classroom and to avoid verbal communication and nonverbal cues with anyone (regardless of team membership). They were told that this type of communication would disqualify their participation and cause their team members to forfeit class credit for the exercise. All of their discussion was to take place in writing within the "chat" feature of a web-based communication tool. Each team was provided with its own password-protected "chat" software.

Conversely, face-to-face participants huddled around a table with their team members. They were provided with a micro-cassette tape recorder and asked to record the conversation. Although the recorders could allow for content analysis by the researchers (similar to the text byproduct of the chat system), they were used to create a more formal task environment with some similarities to the computer-based groups, namely physical setup and the creation of a "witness" to the conversation.

Upon achieving a consensus solution, the team's appointed secretary either registered the ranking with the facilitator (face-to-face) or submitted a web form (virtual). Lastly, each member independently completed three questionnaires: (1) the Group Styles Inventory questionnaire in which team members assessed the group's interaction style, (2) a transformational leadership questionnaire in which all team members assessed the leadership exhibited by each individual member, and (3) a group process questionnaire that assessed group cohesion and the participant's acceptance of the consensus solution. The questionnaires were answered after completing the group consensus ranking exercise but before receiving feedback on the "experts' rank" or the quality of their own (and their team's) solution.

Measures

Transformational Leadership. To assess the level of transformational leadership (TFL) in the group and the emergent leader, participants assessed each peer team member by answering eight questions that describe behaviors usually exhibited by leaders. These items were taken from a short form of the Multifactor Leadership Questionnaire (Bass & Avolio, 1990). Specifically, items were chosen that were judged by the researchers to be potentially relevant to a 35-minute problem-solving task. These items generally tapped into inspirational leadership and intellectual stimulation factors. Each participant answered by indicating the extent to which each of the following items described the behavior of each member, using a 5-point response scale ranging from *not at all* (1) to *a very great extent* (5). Sample items included "Seek out differing perspectives when solving the problem," "Display a sense of power and confidence," and "Suggest new ways of looking at how to solve the problem."

The answers to these items were averaged to form a single measure of TFL for each participant (Cronbach alpha = .90). The formation of a single measure was in line with previous research that has typically identified an overall TFL factor, rather than distinct subfactors (e.g., Podsakoff, MacKenzie, Moorman, & Fetter, 1990). The individual with the highest leadership measure for each team was deemed to be the emergent leader on that team. Further, the overall level of transformational leadership within each team was computed by averaging the scores obtained for each individual member. The standard deviation of theses scores also provided an indication of the distribution of leadership within the team. (Justification for aggregation of our measures is discussed below.)

Group Interaction Styles. To assess a group's interaction style, participants answered 48 questions that focused on the ways in which members of a group interact with one another and approach their task during a meeting or specific problem-solving session. The items were a subset of the Group Styles Inventory described in Cooke and Szumal (1994). Participants completed the questionnaire by indicating the extent to which each item described the style of their group using a 5-point response scale ranging from *not at all* (1) to *a very great extent* (5). The answers to 24 items that assessed the constructive interaction style were summed to form a single measure (Cronbach alpha = .94). Sample items included: "To what extent did the group set goals and work toward them?" "Were conflicts and differences used constructively (to generate better ideas)?" and "Was the group helpful in crystallizing your ideas?"

Another 24 items that assessed the defensive interaction style were also summed to form a single measure (alpha = .91). Following Cooke and Szumal (1994), half of the defensive items assessed aggressive behaviors, including

"To what extent did some members seem more interested in 'winning the point' than in solving the problem?" and "Did the discussion seem to turn into a contest?" The other half assessed passive behaviors, including "To what extent were members evasive when decisiveness was needed?" and "Did people stay detached (and never fully come together as a team)?" The overall level of constructive and defensive interaction styles within each team was then computed by averaging the scores of individual members.

Measures of Task Performance. Two measures of solution quality were derived for each team. The first, "Team Error," was calculated by summing the absolute values of the numerical differences between the team rank for each item and the rank suggested by the institutional review board (IRB) experts (Cooke, 1994; McGrath, 1984). Since it is an error score, a lower score (ideally 0) indicates better performance. Second, "Synergy" was operationalized by subtracting the lowest of its individual members' error scores from the team's error score (see Szumal, 2000). A synergistic team should perform beyond the capabilities of its "best" member prior to the team interaction. Low error scores (Team Error) along with significant gain over best member scores (Synergy) reflect effective performance; in contrast, high team error scores with no gain or synergy (and often loss) reflect poor team performance.

Measures of Contextual Performance. Two contextual measures of performance were derived for each team: "Cohesion" and "Solution Acceptance." Cohesion was measured by asking participants on the posttask questionnaire to rate nine phrases that dealt with group atmosphere and satisfaction with the group (Cook, 1981; O'Reilly, Caldwell, & Barnett, 1989). Respondents were asked to indicate their level of agreement with such items as (1) members appeared to feel that they were really part of the group; (2) the group members really helped each other out; and (3) some people showed no respect for the others (reverse coded). Responses to each of these items, ranging from *strongly disagree* (1) to *strongly agree* (5), were summed for each team member (alpha = .85). High scores reflect a high degree of group cohesion.

Member acceptance of the group's decision (solution acceptance) was measured by three additional questions included in the group interaction questionnaire. Respondents were asked to report the extent to which they (1) had any reservations about any of the decisions reached by the group (reverse coded); (2) believed that the team had developed a solution that was better than their own initial solution; and (3) felt comfortable defending the group's solution. The questions were adapted from the work of Cooke and Lafferty (1988). Responses to each of these items, ranging from *not at all* (1) to *to a very great extent* (5), were summed for each team member (alpha = .72). High scores on this scale therefore reflect a high degree of solution acceptance.

The overall levels of cohesion and member acceptance of the group's decision (solution acceptance) within each team then were computed by averaging the scale scores of individual members.

Control Variables. We included two control variables in our analyses, "Team Size" and "Expertise." Even though almost two-thirds of the groups were composed of four-person teams, we thought that smaller teams might perform better than larger teams (Barry & Stewart, 1997). The "expertise" measure represents the average of the absolute difference between individual solutions and the expert's solution (measured prior to the team's interaction). We reversed the sign on this error score to produce an expertise measure. Thus, an ideal expertise score is 0, denoting consistency between the participants' solutions and the expert's solution. At the group level of analysis, higher expertise (average of individual's expertise) indicates teams with better *potential* for performance.

Level of Analysis and Reliability

Justification for aggregating member's reports on the various scales is summarized in Table 7.1. Interrater reliability and agreement was assessed for appropriate measures by means of the eta-squared statistic, a series of one-way analyses of variance (ANOVAs) with group membership as the independent variable and the measure to be aggregated as the dependent variable), and tests based on the multiple-item estimator $r_{wg(j)}$ for scales with moderately skewed distributions (see James, Demaree, & Wolf, 1984, 1993; Lindell & Brandt, 1999; Lindell, Brandt, & Whitney, 1999).

TABLE 7.1.
Tests of Inter-Rater Reliability and Agreement

	Indices of Agreement		
	Eta[a]	*Anova*[b]	$R_{wg(i)}$
Interaction Style	(% var.)[a]		
Constructive	43	1.92*	0.87
Defensive	44	2.06*	0.81
Outcomes			
Cohesion	58	2.27*	0.93
Solution Acceptance	50	2.31*	0.87

[a]The percent of variance explained by group membership.
[b]F-ratio indicating variance in responses between groups is significant in relation to total variance.
*$p < .01$

The $r_{wg(j)}$ estimates of interrater consistency and consensus, along with the η^2 and F statistics, support the statistical aggregation of individual responses to the group level for our analyses.

RESULTS

Means, standard deviations, t values, and the reliability of each scale are presented in Table 7.2. In support of H1, FtFTs scored higher on cohesion, solution acceptance, and synergy. There was, however, no difference between media types for team error. The results testing group means for FtFTs and VTs are presented in Table 7.2. Face-to-face team members reported significantly more leadership in their groups than did members from virtual teams, although there were no differences in leadership variance. The measure for leadership emergence was significantly higher in FtFTs than in VTs. Furthermore, FtFTs scored significantly higher on constructive style whereas VT's scored significantly higher on the defensive style. Thus, H3, H5a, and H5b were supported. Finally, Table 7.2 shows, via the expertise score (average of individual performance prior to interaction), that a priori FtFTs and VTs had the same task performance potential.

We tested H2, H4a, and H4b with correlation analyses, segregating the data by media type. The results of these analyses are presented in Table 7.3. In partial support of H2, leadership is positively and significantly related with

TABLE 7.2.
Group-level Means, Standard Deviations, t-test for Equality of Means, and
Reliability of Scales (Cronbach alpha)[a]

Measures	FtFTs		VTs		Scale	
	Mean	SD	Mean	SD	t^b	?
Expertise (indiv. Error $\times$ -1)	-23.58	4.36	-23.10	4.01	-0.67	n/a
Emergent leader	4.03	0.59	3.80	0.61	1.82*	0.90
Average leadership	3.54	0.45	3.16	0.47	3.98**	0.90
Variance in leadership	0.58	0.29	0.63	0.29	-0.89	0.90
Team error	19.80	5.22	20.47	5.25	-0.78	n/a
Synergy	-2.28	4.00	-4.53	4.67	3.12**	n/a
Solution acceptance	3.72	0.49	3.44	0.63	2.92**	0.72
Cohesion	4.40	0.38	4.01	0.53	4.40**	0.85
Constructive style	3.99	0.40	3.62	0.45	5.06**	0.94
Defensive style	2.07	0.52	2.21	0.39	$-1.90*$	0.91

[a]$n = 89$ teams; 42 FtFTs and 47 VTs.
[b]1-tail t-test, 87 degrees of freedom.
*$p < .05$; **$p < .01$.

TABLE 7.3.
Group-Level Correlations by Media Type

		1	2	3	4	5	6	7	8
Emergent leader	FtFTs								
	VTs								
Average leadership	FtFTs	.86**							
	VTs	.79**							
Variance in leadership	FtFTs	.55**	.15						
	VTs	.39**	-.13						
Constructive style	FtFTs	.34*	.48**	-.15					
	VTs	.39**	.65**	-.13					
Defensive style	FtFTs	-.30*	-.24*	.25*	-.62**				
	VTs	.08	-.28*	.33**	-.25*				
Team error	FtFTs	.09	-.04	.38**	-.19*	.25*			
	VTs	.01	.02	.12	.14	.03			
Synergy	FtFTs	-.14	-.17	-.20***	.22*	-.22*	-.58**		
	VTs	.17	.08	-.05	-.07	-.02	-.58**		
Cohesion	FtFTs	.20***	.49**	-.38**	.66**	-.67**	-.21***	.22	
	VTs	.28	.25*	.29*	.36**	-.31**	.09	-.03	
Solution acceptance	FtFTs	.43**	.50**	-.05	.47**	-.60**	-.27*	.11	.57**
	VTs	.16	.41**	-.12	.46**	-.45**	-.01	.15	.48**

*p < .05; **p < .01; ***p < .10.

cohesion and solution acceptance in both media types. However, neither the emergent or average leadership measures are related with team error or team synergy, in either media type. These relationships generally hold for the emerging leader measures, although there is a loss of variance and significance in some instances. In partial support of H4a, constructive interaction style is positively and significantly related to solution acceptance and cohesion in both media types, but is not significantly related to team error or synergy in virtual teams. In FtFTs, constructive interaction style is negatively related to team errors and positively related to team synergy. Defensive interaction style is negatively related to cohesion, solution acceptance, and synergy in both media types but is not related to team error or team synergy in virtual teams. In FtFTs, defensive interaction style is positively related to team errors and negatively related to team synergy.

In short, the higher the constructive style, the greater the cohesion and solution acceptance; the higher the defensive style, the lower the cohesion and solution acceptance. Furthermore, in FtFTs a constructive style leads to fewer team errors and more team synergy whereas a defensive style leads to more team errors and less team synergy. Thus, although there is strong support for H4a and H4b in FtFTs, there is only partial support for these hypotheses in virtual teams. That is, there is overall support for the general hypothesis that interaction style will predict both task and contextual performance in FtFTs, but interaction style will only predict contextual performance in VTs.

Unanswered questions are how does media type affect the way leadership emerges in a group or how group interaction materializes in a group, and what variable best explains group outcomes? For example, does media type really explain synergy or solution acceptance, or is a more complex model required to explain the phenomenon? A multiple regression that includes media type, leadership, and group interaction may provide a better indication of the magnitude of the relative impact of media, leadership, and interaction styles on performance outcomes than simple correlations.

We used a four-step regression model. In the first step we included team size and expertise as control variables. In the second step we added the dichotomous media variable to the equation. In the third step we added transformational leadership (TFL) and variance in leadership into the equation. In the last step we added both interaction styles simultaneously (as per Watson & Michaelson, 1988). Analyses were repeated for each task and contextual outcome measure as dependent variables. The regression analyses are presented in Table 7.4.

Not surprisingly, we find that expertise is the most powerful predictor (inhibitor) of the team error measure ($\beta = -.69, p < .01$). That is, in "content full" tasks like the Ethical Decision Challenge, the quality of the team solution is related to the amount of expertise available in the team (e.g., greater expertise will decrease team errors). We also find that expertise may have a marginal role to play in predicting group cohesion). The negative beta suggests

TABLE 7.4.
4-Step Regression Analyses

Models	Team Error	Team Synergy	Group Cohesion	Solution Acceptance
Step 1				
Team Size	−.01	−.09	−.27**	−.22*
Expertise	−.69**	−.04	−.26*	−.12
R^2	.48	.01	.13	.06
F	−35.75**	0.50	6.24**	2.45+
Step 2				
Team Size	−.02	−.04	−.12	−.15
Expertise	−.70**	.07	−.20*	−.09
Media[a]	−.04	−.11	−.30*	−.12
R^2 Change	−.00	.01	.07	.01
F Change	−0.14	0.68	6.58*	0.92
Step 3				
Team Size	−.03	−.04	−.10	−.13
Expertise	−.68**	−.04	−.21*	−.12
Media	−.02	−.08	−.22*	−.01
TF Leadership[b]	−.06	−.05	−.34**	.41**
Variance in Leadership	−.10	−.13	−.17	−.30*
R^2 Change	.01	.01	.09	.14
F Change	0.62	0.50	4.74*	6.97**
Step 4				
Team Size	−.03	−.03	−.02	−.01
Expertise	−.68**	.03	−.15	−.04
Media	−.02	−.08	−.15	−.08
TF Leadership	−.08	.05	−.10	−.10
Variance in Leadership	−.12	−.09	.08	−.03
Constructive Style	.01	−.07	.29**	.39**
Defensive Style	−.03	−.17	−.34**	−.45**
R^2 Change	.00	.02	.18	.31
F Change	0.06	0.91	0.87	25.32**

**p < .01; *p < .05; + p < .10.

[a]Note: For Media, FtFTs = "0" and VTs = "1".

[b]Note: The score of emergent leader used for TF Leadership.

that teams with more expertise have a more difficult time becoming a cohesive unit. Team size did not have a significant effect on our solution quality or contextual outcome measures.

Both FtFTs ($\beta = -.30$, $p < .05$) and transformational leadership ($\beta = .34$, $p < .01$) have a significant role in explaining group cohesion; however, after interaction styles are included in the model, the media and leadership effects disappear. A constructive style promotes group cohesion ($\beta = .29, p < .01$) and a defensive style inhibits group cohesion ($\beta = -.34, p < .01$).

Leadership and variance in leadership have a significant role in explaining solution acceptance ($\beta = .41, p < .01; \beta = -.30, p < .05$, respectively). That is, teams exhibiting greater leadership and less leadership variability achieve greater solution acceptance. However, as before, when group interaction styles are adding in the final step of the regression, solution acceptance is enhanced by a constructive style ($\beta = .39, p < .01$) and inhibited by a defensive style ($\beta = -.45, p < .01$).

Overall, the multiple regression results provide some support for hypotheses H2, H4a, and H4b, particularly with respect to the impact of leadership and interaction styles on contextual outcomes. It also indicated that team error is best predicted by the available expertise in the group and that team synergy cannot be explained properly by the set of variables in our models.

These data suggest a mediating role for leadership and interaction styles. That is, media type may contribute to solution acceptance and group cohesion only through its effect on leadership and interaction style. In other words, the effect of media type on solution acceptance and cohesion tends to dissipate when either leadership or interaction style is taken into account.

A regression procedure for examining mediation (Baron & Kenny, 1986) was used to test H6, H7a, and H7b. The procedure involves estimating three separate regression equations, and the following conditions must be met in each equation respectively: (a) the independent variable must predict the mediator, (b) the independent variable must predict the dependent variable, and (c) the mediator must predict the dependent variable. Furthermore, in order to support mediation, the effect of the independent variable on the dependent variable must decrease in magnitude when the mediator is included in the regression equation. This procedure was repeated for cohesion and solution acceptance for leadership and both constructive and defensive interaction styles.

Mediational effects were found for leadership, and for both constructive and defensive styles with respect to cohesion and solution acceptance. To achieve this conclusion for leadership, four conditions must have been met. First, media type must predict leadership ($\beta = -.39, p < .01$), our mediator variable. Second, media type must predict the dependent variables. This holds for cohesion ($\beta = -.38, p < .01$) and solution acceptance ($\beta = -.24, p < .01$). Third, leadership must predict cohesion ($\beta = .44, p < .01$) and solution acceptance ($\beta = .47, p < .01$) and, lastly, the effect of the media type on the dependent variable must decrease in magnitude when leadership is included in the regression equation. This holds for cohesion ($\beta = -.23, p < .05$) and solution acceptance ($\beta = .01$, ns). Recall that media type is coded as a dichotomous variable where FtFTs are coded as 0 and VTs are coded as 1. This may generate negative standardized betas in the multiple regressions since VTs exhibit less leadership than FtFTs. Furthermore, VTs have lower solution acceptance and less group cohesion than FtFTs.

To achieve the mediational conclusion for the interaction styles, the same four conditions must have been met. First, media type must predict constructive styles ($\beta = -.39, p < .01$) and defensive styles ($\beta = .17, p < .05$), our mediator variables. Second, media type must predict the various dependent variables. This outcome was obtained and described above. Third, the interaction style must predict the dependent variables. With respect to the constructive style, this holds for cohesion ($\beta = .54, p < .01$) and solution acceptance ($\beta = .51, p < .01$). With respect to the defensive style, this also holds for cohesion ($\beta = -.46, p < .01$) and solution acceptance ($\beta = -.53, p < .01$). Lastly, the effect of the media type on the dependent variable must decrease in magnitude when the interactive style is included in the regression equation. For the constructive style, this holds for cohesion ($\beta = -.20, p < .05$) and solution acceptance ($\beta = -.05$, ns). For the defensive style, this also holds for cohesion ($\beta = -.31, p < .01$) and solution acceptance ($\beta = -.16, p < .05$). Again, negative standardized betas may occur in the multiple regressions because VTs are less likely to be constructive than FtFTs, although they are more likely to be defensive, and VTs have lower solution acceptance and less group cohesion than FtFTs.

Overall, our interpretation of these results suggests that the relationship between media type and contextual performance can best be understood based on the mediational effects of leadership and interaction style. That is, FtFTs exhibit more leadership, which in turn accounts for more variance in group cohesion and solution acceptance than media type alone. Alternatively, FtFTs also promote a constructive interaction style, which in turn accounts for more variance in group cohesion and solution acceptance than media type alone. Similarly, VTs inhibit leadership and promote a defensive interaction style, which in turn accounts for more variance in cohesion and solution acceptance than media type alone.

DISCUSSION

Our results suggest a number of important conclusions. First, the development of transformational leadership and a dominant group interaction style appears to be at least somewhat dependent on media type. As compared to VTs, FtFTs have a greater tendency to facilitate the emergence of leadership and to develop a constructive style. In contrast, VTs inhibit leadership and have a greater tendency to develop a defensive style.

Second, FtFTs were more successful on performance dimensions, especially those that deal with group processes. Specifically, they displayed higher synergy, group cohesion, and solution acceptance than did VTs. These findings suggest that the more serious impact of VTs on group performance may occur over the long term as a result of poor cohesion.

Third, while media type was related to leadership, interaction style, and outcomes, the mediational analyses suggested that, in fact, media type might contribute to outcomes only through its effect on leadership and interaction style. In other words, the effect of media type on contextual outcomes tends to dissipate when leadership and interaction type are taken into account. This finding is especially interesting in light of how others have proposed more direct effects of media type on outcomes. For example, Straus and McGrath (1994) found FtFTs to be more cohesive than VTs. The present findings would suggest a more informed explanation for the relationship between media type and cohesion.

These results are provocative for organizations adopting VTs in that they imply that steps need to be taken to help VTs exhibit leadership and adopt constructive interaction styles before they embark on team tasks. This may suggest that initial face-to-face meetings are warranted before the VT proceeds. It may also suggest that team-building exercises should precede team performance tasks. But without any intervention and left to their own devices to complete a task, virtual teams may suffer from a lack of leadership and the development of a defensive interaction style.

We should note, however, that our study involved a short-duration, consensus-type task that has its pros and cons. On the positive side, our research is somewhat unique in that a large number of FtFTs and VTs performed systematically the identical task in the same time frame and provided feedback by answering validated instruments, whereas much extant research in virtual teams has been either anecdotal and/or limited in the number of teams examined (e.g., Maznevski & Chudoba, 2000; Melymuka, 1997; Tan et al., 2000). On the other hand, VTs may fare better when members have a longer time period to get acquainted. Some have argued that VTs are inappropriate when the team is newly formed or short lived (Duarte & Snyder, 1999; Walther, 1994, 1996). A second limitation of our study was that these teams were not real work groups but rather student groups assembled for a semester. Although grades were dependent on their team performance, the risks of poor performance were not as great as might have been in an actual work setting. This context may represent the reason for our relatively weak findings involving objective performance measures.

Finally, we recognize the common methods problem that exists when correlating leadership and interaction style measures with our process measures of performance. Specifically, all of these measures were obtained from a common source (i.e., the student participants) after the completion of their group activities. We re-analyzed the data by randomly selecting from each team's data a subset of team members for process performance measures and a distinct subset for the group interaction style and leadership measures. Although our findings are essentially the same, the increase in variability and decrease in power, and the presence of several three-member teams that cannot be split into two multi-member subsets, have forced us to accept the limited threat to our findings due to common methods. However, this problem should not affect the conclusions drawn from the mediational analyses. That is, the common methods that existed between our mediator variables (i.e., leadership and interaction type) and our process performance outcomes (i.e., cohesion and solution acceptance) should have no bearing on whether media type loses its effect when the mediator variables are included in regression equations. Moreover, most of the relationships examined in this study were either not affected by common methods or were involved variables collected at different time intervals following the group task.

CONCLUSION

The present study suggests that additional research is warranted comparing behaviors of FtFTs to those of geographically or temporally dispersed VTs and examining the effects of leadership and group interaction styles. Further research is needed to establish whether our results hold true in a field design with computer-supported groups working on actual (as opposed to simulation-based) problem-solving tasks. This would help capture the motivational element that is somewhat missing from the present study. It may also yield insights into the relative strengths of the effects of leadership and interaction styles on real-world virtual teams.

Additional studies may wish to investigate task effects and substitute any number of appropriate tasks for the problem-solving task used here. The nature of the task—as well as the background of the subjects—also has to be considered to ascertain whether these same relationships hold when group members are familiar with and have expertise relevant to the problem (e.g., in a content-full simulation with higher levels of expertise). Issues of synchronization (co-action) and time pressure may also influence the relationships. Thus, future research could attempt to include asynchronous VTs, although comparisons with synchronous FtFTs would be inherently more tenuous. Furthermore, subsequent studies might incorporate independent variables other than media type, such as aggregates of individual personality.

Another avenue of research is to investigate the types of interventions or training best used to diminish the effects of a lack of leadership or defensive interaction styles and enhance the positive interaction in a virtual setting. As noted earlier, VTs are on the increase, a trend that will only expand in the future. A task for management researchers is to better understand the dynamics of such groups and to find mechanisms to make them as effective as possible.

ACKNOWLEDGMENTS

The authors wish to thank Human Synergistics/Center for Applied Research, Inc., and Knowledge Instruments, LLC, for permission to adapt their Ethical Decision Challenge and Group Style Inventory instruments. We also thank Dr. Robert A. Cooke for helpful insights relating to the psychometric properties of the instruments.

REFERENCES

Avolio, B., Kahai, S., & Dodge, G. (2000). E-leadership: Implications for theory, research and Practice. *Leadership Quarterly, 11*, 4, 615–668.

Balthazard, P. A. (2000). *Ethical decision challenge—Internet edition* (adapted from R. A. Cooke). Arlington Heights IL: Human Synergistics/Center for Applied Research.

Baron, R., & Kenny, D. (1986). The moderator-mediator variable distinction in social psychological research: Conceptual, strategic, and statistical considerations, *Journal of Personality and Social Psychology, 51*, 1173–1182.

Barry, B., & Stewart, G. L. (1997). Composition, process, and performance in self-managed groups: The role of personality. *Journal of Applied Psychology, 82*, 62–78

Bass, B. M., & Avolio, B. A. (1990). *The multifactor leadership questionnaire*. Palo Alto, CA: Consulting Psychologists Press.

Bass, B. M., & Avolio, B. A. (1994). *Improving organizational effectiveness through transformational leadership*. Thousands Oaks, CA: Sage.

Coleman, D. (1997). *Groupware: The changing environment*. Englewood Cliffs: Prentice-Hall.

Cook, J. D. (1981). *The experience of work: A compendium and review of 249 measures and their use*. New York: Academic Press.

Cooke, R. A. (1994). *Ethical decision challenge*. Plymouth, MI: Human Synergistics.

Cooke, R. A., & Kernaghan, J. A. (1987). Estimating the difference between group versus individual performance on problem-solving task. *Group and Organization Studies, 12*, 319–342.

Cooke, R. A., & Lafferty, J. C. (1988). *Group styles inventory*. Plymouth, MI: Human Synergistics.

Cooke, R. A., & Rousseau, D. M. (1988). Behavioral norms and expectations. *Group and Organization Studies, 13*, 245–273.

Cooke, R. A., & Szumal, J. L. (1993). Measuring normative beliefs and shared behavioral expectations in organizations: the reliability and validity of the organizational culture inventory. *Psychological Reports, 72*, 1299–1330.

Cooke, R. A., & Szumal, J. L. (1994). The impact of group interaction styles on problem-solving effectiveness. *Journal of Applied Behavioral Science, 30*, 415–437.

DeSanctis, G., & Poole, M. S. (1997). Transitions in teamwork in new organizational forms. In B. Markovsky, M. J. Lovaglia, L. Troyer, & E. J. Lawler (Eds.), *Advances in Group Processes* (157–176). Greenwich, CT: JAI Press.

Duarte, D. L., & Snyder, N. T. (1999). *Mastering virtual teams*. San Francisco: Jossey-Bass.

Gardner, W. L., & Avolio, B. J. (1998). The charismatic relationship: A dramaturgical perspective. *Academy of Management Review, 23*, 32–58

George, J., Easton, G., Nunmaker, J., & Northcraft, G. (1990). A study of collaborative group work with and without computer-based support. *Information Systems Research, 1*, 394–415.

Guzzo, R. A., & Dickson, M. W. (1996). Teams in organizations: Recent research on performance and effectiveness. *Annual Review of Psychology, 47*, 307–338.

Hackman, J. R., & Morris, C. G. (1975). Group tasks, group interaction process, and group performance effectiveness: A review and proposed integration. *Advances in Experimental Social Psychology, 8*, 45–99.

Hedlund, J., Ilgen, D. R., & Hollenbeck, J. R. (1998). Decision accuracy in computer-mediated versus face-to-face decision-making teams. *Organizational Behavior and Human Decision Processes, 76*(1), 30–47.

Hightower, R. T., & Sayeed, L. (1996). Effects of pre-discussion information character-istics on computer mediated group discussion. *Information Systems Research, 7*, 451–465.

Hiltz, S. R., Johnson, K., & Turoff, M. (1986). Experiments in group decision making: Communication process and outcome in face-to-face versus computerized confer-ences. *Human Communication Research, 13*, 225–252.

Hiltz, S. R., Johnson, K., & Turoff, M. (1991). Group decision support: The effects of des-ignated human leaders and statistical feedback in computerized conferences. *Journal of Management Information Systems, 8*(2), 81–108.

Hirokawa, R. (1985). Discussion procedures and decision-making performance: A test of a functional perspective. *Human Communication Research, 12*, 203–224.

Hirokawa, R., & Gouran, D. S. (1989). Facilitation of group communication: A critique of prior research and an agenda for future research. *Management Communication Quar-terly, 3*(1), 71–92.

Hoffman, L. R. (1979). Applying experimental research on group problem solving to orga-nizations. *Journal of Applied Behavioral Science, 15*, 375–391.

Hollingshead, A. B. (1996). Information suppression and status persistence in group deci-sion making: the effects of communication media. *Human Communication Research, 23*, 193–219.

James, L. R., Demaree, R. G., & Wolf, G. (1984). Estimating within-group inter-rater reli-ability with and without response bias. *Journal of Applied Psychology, 69*, 85–98.

James, L. R., Demaree, R. G., & Wolf, G. (1993). $R_{(wg)}$—An assessment of within-group inter-rater agreement. *Journal of Applied Psychology, 78*, 306–309.

Jarvenpaa, S., & Ives, B. (1994). The global network organization of the future: Informa-tion management opportunities and challenges, *Journal of Management Information Systems, 10*(4), 25–57.

Judd, C. M., & Kenny, D. A. (1981). Process analysis: Estimating mediation in treatment evaluations. *Evaluation Review, 5*, 602–629.

Kahai, S., Sosik, J., & Avolio, B. (2000). Effects of leadership style, anonymity, and rewards in an electronic meeting system environment. Working paper, Center for Leadership Studies, Binghamton University.

Kenny, D. A., Kashy, D. A., & Bolger, N. (1998). Data analysis in social psychology. In D. T. Gilbert, S. T., Fiske, & G. Lindzey (Eds). *The Handbook of Social Psychology* (4th ed., Vol. 1, pp. 233–265). New York: McGraw-Hill.

Lea, M., & Spears, R. (1991). Computer-mediated communication, de-individuation, and group decision-making. *International Journal of Man-Machine Studies, 34*, 283–301.

Lindell, M. K., & Brandt, D. J. (1999). Assessing inter-rater agreement on the job relevance of a test: A comparison of the CVI, T, (rWG(J)), and r*(WG(J)) indexes. *Journal of Applied Psychology, 84*, 640–647.

Lindell, M. K., Brandt, D. J., & Whitney, D. J. (1999). A revised index of inter-rater agree-ment for multi-item ratings of a single target. *Applied Psychological Measurement, 23*, 127–135.

Lipnack, J., & Stamps, J. (1997). *Virtual teams: Reaching across space, time, and organi-zations with technology*. New York: John Wiley & Sons.

Lowe, K. B., Kroeck, K. G., & Sivasubramaniam, N. (1996). Effectiveness correlates of transformational and transactional leadership: A meta-analytic review of the MLG literature. *Leadership Quarterly, 7*, 385–425.

Maier, N. R. F. (1967). Assets and liabilities in group problem-solving: The need for an integrative function. *Psychological Review, 74*, 239–249.

Maznevski, M. L., & Chudoba, K. M. (2000). Bridging space over time: global virtual team dynamics and effectiveness. *Organization Science, 11*(5), 473–492.

McGrath, J. E. (1984). *Groups: Interaction and performance.* Englewood Cliffs: Prentice-Hall, Inc.

McGrath, J. E. (1990). Time matters in groups. In J. Galegher, R. E. Kraut, & C. Egido (Eds.), *Intellectual teamwork: Social and technological foundations of cooperative work.* Hillsdale, NJ: Lawrence Erlbaum Associates.

McGrath, J. E., & Hollingshead, A. B. (1994). *Groups interacting with technology.* Thousand Oaks, CA: Sage.

Melymuka, K. (1997). Virtual realities. *Computerworld, 31*(17), 70–72.

O'Reilly, C., Caldwell, D., & Barnett, W. (1989). Work group demography, social integration, and turnover. *Administrative Sciences Quarterly, 34*, 21–37.

Podsakoff, P. M., MacKenzie, S. B., Moorman, R. H., & Fetter, R. (1990). Transformational leader behaviors and their effects on followers' trust in leader, satisfaction, and organizational citizenship behaviors. *Leadership Quarterly, 1*, 107–142.

Sambamurthy, V., Poole, M. S., & Kelly, J. (1993). The effects of variations in GDSS capabilities on decision making processes in groups. *Small Group Research, 24*(4), 523–546.

Shamir, B. (1997). Leadership in boundaryless organizations: Disposable or indisposable? Unpublished manuscript, Hebrew University.

Shamir, B., & Howell, J. M. (1999). Organizational and contextual influences on the emergence and effectiveness of charismatic leadership. *Leadership Quarterly, 10*, 257–283.

Sheppard, J. (1993). Productivity loss in performance groups: A motivation analysis. *Psychological Bulletin, 113*, 67–81.

Siegel, J., Dubrovsky, V., Kiesler, S., & McGuire, T. W. (1986). Group processes in computer-mediated communication. *Organizational Behavior and Human Decision Processes, 37*, 157–187.

Sosik, J., Avolio, B., & Kahai, S. (1997). Effects of leadership style and anonymity and group potency and effectiveness in a group decision support system environment. *Journal of Applied Psychology, 82*, 89–103.

Straus, S. G., & McGrath, J. E. (1994). Does the medium matter? The interaction of task type and technology on group performance and member reactions. *Journal of Applied Psychology, 79*(1), 87–97.

Szumal, J. L. (2000). How to use group problem solving simulations to improve teamwork. In M. Silberman (Ed.) *Team and organization development sourcebook.* New York: McGraw Hill.

Tan, B. C. Y., Wei, K. K., Huang, W. W., & Ng, G. N. (2000). A dialogue technique to enhance electronic communication in virtual teams. *IEEE Transactions on Professional Communication, 43*, 153–165.

Townsend, A., DeMarie, S., & Hendrickson, A. (1998). Virtual teams: Technology and the workplace of the future. *Academy of Management Executive, 12*(3), 17–29.

Wagner, J. A., III. (1995). Studies of individualism-collectivism: Effects on cooperation in groups. *Academy of Management Journal, 38*, 152–172.

Walther, J. B. (1994). Anticipated ongoing interaction versus channel effects on relational communication in computer-mediated interaction. *Human Communication Research, 20*, 473–501.

Walther, J. B. (1996). Computer-mediated communication: Impersonal, interpersonal, and hyperpersonal interaction. *Communication Research, 23*, 1–43.

Warkentin, M. E., Sayeed, L., & Hightower, R. (1997). Virtual teams versus face-to-face teams. An exploratory study of a web based conference system. *Decision Sciences. 14*(4), 29–64.

Watson, W. E., & Michaelsen, L. K. (1988). Group interaction behaviors that affect group performance on an intellective task. *Group and Organization Studies, 13*, 495–516.

Weisband, S. (1992). Group discussion and first advocacy effects in computer-mediated and face-to-face decision-making groups. *Organizational Behavior and Human Decision Processes, 53*, 352–380.

Xenihou, A., & Furnham, A. (1996). A correlational and factor analytic study of four questionnaire measures of organizational culture. *Human Relations, 49*, 349–371.

Zalesny, M. D. (1990). Rater confidence and social influence in performance appraisals. *Journal of Applied Psychology, 75*, 274–289.

8

Social Engineering in Distributed Decision-Making Teams: Some Implications for Leadership at a Distance

Garold Stasser
Miami University

Maria Augustinova
Université René Descartes, Paris, France

OVERVIEW

One aspect of leadership is team management including the mobilization and deployment of members' task-relevant resources. Team management frequently involves social engineering, the activity of introducing planned interventions that are designed to change team structure and process—typically, with the goal of increasing the quality of process and productivity (Stasser & Birchmeier, 2003). In this chapter, we discuss ways in which electronic communication offers many possibilities for social engineering. We show that teams adjust their communication strategies and styles of interaction and explore some of the social engineering implications of this and other research for improving communication performance. Implications for leadership at a distance are then discussed.

When the team task is physical and the members have immediate feedback about each other's actions, management of team resources may be relatively simple. If the job is getting a couch from the third floor of a building to a moving van, the leader's job consists largely of getting the strongest members of the team focused on the task at the same time and providing benefits that are sufficient to justify the expenditure of effort and time. In contrast, when the team task is cognitive and feedback about what others are doing is delayed or unavailable, deployment of members' resources and efforts is more difficult to orchestrate. For example, consider the task of deciding a matter of corporate policy that will satisfy multiple stakeholders and environmental constraints when the primary mode of communication is email. In this case, success depends on getting the right information to the right people at the right time. However, as participants sort through what they know and decide what to say to whom, information about others' actions and contributions may be incomplete and delayed. The distribution of the process over time and place and the vagueness of task parameters make it difficult to coordinate effectively.

Because electronic media has an enormous capacity to store and distribute information, the problem of getting the right information to the right people seems trivial. If everyone tells everyone else everything that seems relevant, then the right people (whoever they are) will know what they need to know (whatever that may be) to take informed action. This simplistic view of the information transfer problem ignores many systemic problems such as the limited capacity of the human component of communication networks. Given the cognitive limitations of human actors, timing is critical. What we were told last week or even yesterday may be useful for solving a current problem, but it is often displaced by more recently acquired information. Moreover, the presumption that simply encouraging information exchange will be productive ignores the kudzu problem. Kudzu first arrived in the United States in 1876 as part of Japan's contribution at the Centennial Exposition in Philadelphia, Pennsylvania. In the ensuing decades, its use was promoted in the United States as ornamental plants in landscaping, food for foraging livestock, groundcover for erosion control, and a source for herbal treatments. It thrived in the geography and climate of the southeastern United States and quickly began to crowd out other valuable flora. It simply grows too well and too fast and is amazingly resistant to common herbicides (see the University of Alabama, Center for Public Television and Radio website for an entertaining history of kudzu in the United States: www.cptr.ua.edu/kudzu).

Like kudzu, some information, due to its wide distribution and intuitive appeal, simply survives too well in the fertile soil of group communication. For example, the discussions of face-to-face problem-solving and decision-making groups are dominated by information that is shared among members before they meet. This domination tends to crowd out the consideration of unique information that individuals bring to the discussion (Larson, Christensen, Abbott, & Frantz, 1996; Stasser, Taylor, & Hanna, 1989b; Stasser & Titus, 1985, 1987; Stewart & Stasser, 1995). Additionally, when widely shared and uniquely held information emerges in face-to-face discussion, the widely shared information has a survival advantage. It is more likely to be repeated later in discussion (Larson et al., 1996; Stasser et al., 1989b) and more likely to be remembered by members after the group disbands (Stewart & Stasser, 1995). Finally, commonly known information tends to be viewed as more credible and important than unique information (Kameda, Ohtsubo, & Take-zawa, 1997; Postmes, Spears, & Cihangir, 2001; Wittenbaum, Hubbell, & Zuckerman, 1999).

Electronic communication is just as susceptible, and potentially more susceptible, to the kudzu problem. Several studies have shown that computer-mediated discussions contain less information than face-to-face discussions while the relative dominance of common information remains (e.g., Dennis, 1996; Hollingshead, 1996; Straus, 1996). Other studies have shown that even when electronic groups successfully exchanged unique information, it had little impact on their final decisions (e.g., Dennis, 1996; McLeod, Baron, Marti, & Koon, 1997). Clearly, problems of promoting effective information pooling do not disappear when people communicate electronically.

ELECTRONIC COMMUNICATION
AND SOCIAL ENGINEERING

Notwithstanding the less-than-stellar effectiveness of electronic decision-making groups in these studies, electronic communication does offer many possibilities for social engineering. First, electronic communication can be designed to filter out irrelevant social cues and accentuate cues that are critical for effective communication. For example, one way of facilitating the exchange of unique information is to assign members expert roles that signal the kinds of unique information that they can contribute. In face-to-face groups, making expertise known increased the exchange of unique information and increased the repetition of unique items (Stasser, Stewart, & Wittenbaum, 1995; Stasser, Vaughan, & Stewart, 2000). Additionally, Stewart and Stasser (1995) found that expert roles increased the recall of unique information both during and after discussion. However, these effects have been modest, partly because members did not strongly adhere to their expert roles (Stasser et al., 2000). It seems plausible that expert roles may have a stronger effect in distributed teams if electronic communication filters out other social cues that may obscure or dilute the expert designation (Siegel, Dubrovsky, Kiesler, & McGuire, 1986; Spears & Lea, 1994). If members are identified primarily by their expertise in computer-mediated interaction, they may enact their expert roles more effectively in much the same way that local group norms seem to flourish in computer-mediated interaction (Postmes et al., 2001; Postmes, Spears, & Lea, 1998).

A second social engineering advantage afforded by electronic communication is the ease of storing and summarizing communication. Beyond simply providing a record of who said what, this record provides a useful training tool. None of the studies of face-to-face decision-making groups trained members in effective communication. Most were one-shot studies in that groups made one decision, and none provided feedback about their communication effectiveness. Nonetheless, Moreland, Argote, and Krishnan (1996) showed that teams that were trained together could learn to coordinate their activities. In their studies, teams who were trained together to construct kit radios developed more complete transactive memories (Wegner, 1986). That is, they learned who was good at doing what and allocated responsibilities for subtasks accordingly. In the same way, repeated experience working with similar tasks may permit decision-making teams to learn who has what kinds of information and shape their communication content accordingly. Of course, such training can be implemented in face-to-face groups but electronic media permits one to store and summarize the content of communication easily and to present the summary for participants' review and reflection. In this way, systematic omissions in communication may become evident and team members can adjust their communication strategies accordingly.

A third social engineering possibility in electronic communications is the potential to shape social interaction. An important distinction in the decision-making process is the degree to which communications are characterized by a preference-driven or an information-driven style. Hastie, Penrod, and Pennington (1983), in their seminal study of the civil jury, noted that about one third of their juries exhibited a verdict-driven style characterized by early and frequent polling and selective consideration of evidence as necessary to address and eliminate differences of opinion. Another third of their juries exhibited an evidence-driven style characterized by systematic review of the evidence in an effort to construct a plausible story before trying to reach a consensus on the verdict. In the remaining third of the juries, neither style seemed to dominate. Preference-driven interaction often offers a quick way to reach a consensus, particularly if members' preferences converge on a consensual choice. The danger in preference-driven communication is that relevant information may be overlooked, leading to suboptimal decisions. This risk is particularly high when members have diverse perspectives and information. Moreover, Stasser and Birchmeier (2003) concluded that preference-driven communications are very susceptible to the kudzu problem.

The factors that determine which style of interaction will dominate are not well understood although the literature provides some strong hints. Tasks that appear to have demonstrable solutions seem to promote more information-driven interaction (Kaplan, 1987; Laughlin & Ellis, 1986; Stasser & Stewart, 1992). Encouraging early commitment to a position seems to promote preference-driven discussions (Sawyer, Houlette, & Yeagley, 2006; Janis, 1972). Norms regarding the importance of "getting along" (consensus, cohesion) versus "being right" (accuracy) may also shift the focus of communication (Postmes, Spears, & Cihangir, 2001). Indeed, Postmes, Spears, and Lea (1998) suggested that the transmission of norms may be very efficient in electronic groups under certain conditions: strong identification with the group and anonymity of members during the interaction. Thus, decision-making groups

that feel strongly interdependent may be very responsive to procedural interventions that encourage either preference- or information-driven styles.

TEAM METAKNOWLEDGE AND COMMUNICATION FEEDBACK

To assess the ability of teams to adjust their communication strategies based
on experience, we observed information flow in hierarchically organized
teams who communicated via computers in a simulated military situational assessment task. The Situation Assessment Simulation (SAS) presented seven-
person teams a military scenario that required the team to communicate
20 items of diagnostic information (see Figure 8–1). Teams received two different types of feedback. In one condition, teams learned only whether they
made a correct decision after each episode (*no communication feedback*)
whereas in another condition they also learned what information reached the
commander before a decision was made (*communication feedback*). That is, in
the communication feedback condition, teams learned not only whether they
made the correct decision but also what information the commander had when
deciding. Teams also received different levels of metaknowledge, or, knowledge about how task-relevant information is distributed among team members (Larson & Christensen, 1993). In the *limited metaknowledge* condition,

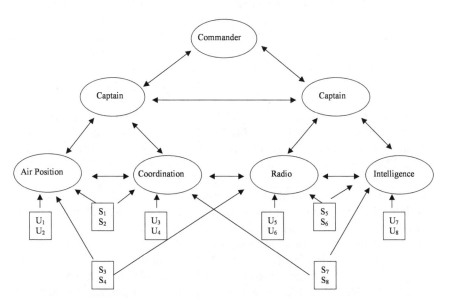

FIGURE 8–1.   Communication links and access to information in the Situational Assessment Task (SAS).

each member knew which of the 20 items he or she could and could not access. In the *elaborated metaknowledge* condition, members also knew what information other team members could and could not access.

We hypothesized that when teams learned what information reached the commander, they would adjust their communication strategies over time to correct or, at least diminish, information biases. Moreover, to be successful, a team had to get information to the commander in a limited time. Much of this information (16 of the 20 cues) had to be assessed by the four members at the bottom of hierarchy and communicated, via the captains, to the commander. When metaknowledge was limited, we hypothesized that teams would evidence the bias observed in earlier work on face-to-face groups, and that partially shared information would be communicated more frequently and reach the commander more often than unique information. In contrast, more elaborated metaknowledge of how access to information was distributed among team members is expected to reverse this bias so that unique information would be more likely to be communicated than partially shared information. This hypothesis assumes that team members identify strongly with their roles and accept primary responsibility for items that only they can access.

Particularly relevant to the present discussion is the distribution of information depicted in Figure 8–1. Eight items of *partially shared* information were available to two members (S_1, S_2, . . . , S_8); and eight items of *unique* information were available to only one member (U_1, U_2, . . . , U_8). An additional four items of *common* information were available to all members and are not shown in Figure 8–1, the eight partially-shared and eight unique items. To be considered by the commander, the eight partially-shared and eight unique items had to be accessed by the four members at the bottom of the hierarchy and transmitted through the communication network before a final decision was required. Strict time limits were imposed for reacting to each episode. In the research discussed here, teams completed 32 episodes of the situation assessment task.

Figure 8–2 gives the mean number of unique and partially shared items that reached the commander over the last 8 of the 32 trials. The left two pairs of bars give the results for groups that did not receive communication feedback. These results supported the predictions regarding the effects of information distribution knowledge on communication of partially shared and unshared information. When the distribution of information access was limited, partially shared information was communicated more often than unique information. As a result, partially shared information was more likely to reach the commander than unique information. Thus, with limited metaknowledge and no communication feedback, partially shared items were about 50% more likely to reach the commander than were unique items over the last 8 episodes. In short, the kudzu problem was evident in the communication patterns of these teams. Partially shared items, due to their redundant access across mem-

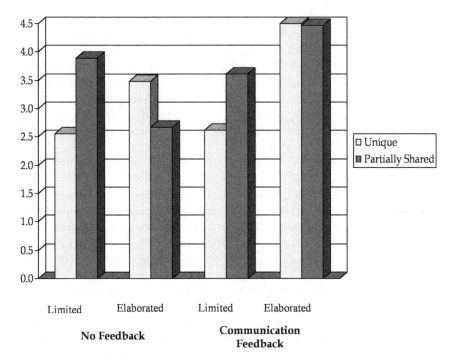

FIGURE 8–2. Mean numbers of unique and partially shared information reaching the commander over the last 8 of 32 episodes by metaknowledge and communication feedback.

bers, took root more readily and crowded out unique information as communication flowed up the team hierarchy.

In contrast, when members had elaborated metaknowledge about information access (i.e., who could access what), the pattern was reversed in that unique items were more likely to reach the commander than were partially shared items. This result is contrary to the usual information distribution effect observed in face-to-face groups. When team roles were accentuated by making apparent what each member could uniquely contribute, members not only eliminated the structural sampling advantage that partially shared information enjoys but also overcompensated by focusing their communications on unique items. This effect is strikingly different than the modest effects typically observed for role assignments in face-to-face groups (cf. Stasser et al., 2000). Because the SAS task is different in many ways than the typical decision task used in studies of face-to-face decision-making teams, this unusually strong adherence to roles could be due to several factors. First, the military overtones of the task may have primed members to accept roles more readily.

Second, the filtering of social cues afforded by computer-mediated communication may have facilitated the enactment of roles. Third, it may be that the military scenario in the SAS task and the performance interdependence among team members underscored their group identity. This is consistent with the SIDE model of Postmes and his colleagues (Postmes et al., 1998; Postmes, Spears, Sakhel, & de Groot, 2001), who found that anonymity in electronic groups fostered the development and adherence to group norms when group identity was salient. Moreover, members knew little about each other except for the different positions that they occupied in the team. Thus, these electronically linked members, more than in face-to-face groups, may have been sensitive to role demands.

In the communication feedback condition (see the right two pairs of bars in Figure 8–2), teams were told what information reached the commander before a decision was rendered. Interestingly, the results revealed that communication feedback was not uniformly effective in shaping communications. Communication feedback did not eliminate the kudzu problem when members had limited metaknowledge. In this condition, teams received complete summaries of the information reaching the commander after each episode but did not know how access to information was distributed across team members. Here we found that partially shared items continued to be overrepresented in the information reaching the commander. In contrast, communication feedback with elaborated metaknowledge resulted in nearly equal numbers of partially shared and unique items reaching the commander over the last 8 episodes.

In sum, communication feedback was efficacious when members also had elaborated metaknowledge. Without this knowledge, feedback had little systematic effect. Moreover, the combination of communication feedback and elaborated metaknowledge resulted in more information (both unique and partially shared) reaching the commander after the team had gained experience. By avoiding redundancy in communication and the resulting bottlenecks as information flowed up the hierarchy, teams in this condition were able to communicate more efficiently.

The finding that communication feedback by itself did not reduce the bias favoring partially shared over unshared items (i.e., reduce the kudzu problem) was not anticipated. When members knew little about how access to information was distributed across the team, they were seemingly unable to implement a strategy that allowed them to address the disproportionate omission of unique items. Nonetheless, there is evidence that they detected a problem. When they received communication feedback but had limited metaknowledge, requests from one team member to another for specific items of information increased by threefold over episodes, and the number of these requests was 60% higher in the last 16 episodes than in any of the other conditions. Unfortunately, such requests, which typically flowed down the hierarchy, were very inefficient ways of getting information in the SAS task. They not only used up valuable time given the time pressure of the task but also interfered with the upward flow of information.

Several social engineering implications follow from this study. First, when information is not uniformly available to all members, increasing the number of members who have access to particular items may increase the likelihood that they will be successfully transmitted through a communication network. Thus, when task knowledge permits an assessment of the relative value of different domains of information, leaders should include members who have access to, or are experts in, in these domains. Second, if common information (like kudzu) thrives, make sure that important domains of information have multiple entry points in a communication network. Third, if team members know who can access particular types of information, members may be more likely to communicate information that is uniquely available to him or her. The implication is that when experts know that others in a team share their expertise, they may shift their contributions away from their primary domain of expertise to areas that they think will permit them to make distinctive contributions. Finally, communication feedback (debriefing) regarding the information reaching a decision maker was not sufficient by itself to ensure that teams addressed the communication biases introduced by the patterns of information access across team members. Teams seemingly need to know how information access is distributed among their members to use communication feedback effectively in developing efficient communication strategies. Of course, the use of communication feedback depends on having teams work on a series of similar problems. In some contexts, this may not be feasible or have limited value because of changes in the structure and nature of a team's task.

PREFERENCE-DRIVEN AND INFORMATION-DRIVEN COMMUNICATION

In the foregoing study, teams were constrained to communicate information by the design of the SAS software. In subsequent studies the constraint was relaxed by permitting members to send recommendations for the team's decision in addition to sending information. This added possibility allowed teams to approach their task in two different ways. On the one hand, they could continue to concentrate on getting information to the commander, using the recommendation option only as a supplement to communicating information or not using it at all. On the other hand, they could focus on accessing as much information as they could, forming opinions about the appropriate decision and forwarding their recommendations and communicating information only as they deemed necessary to support their recommendations. These two approaches parallel the two aforementioned styles of decision making that have been observed in face-to-face groups: preference driven versus information driven.

We found that our teams very quickly and uniformly adopted a preference-driven approach when they could forward recommendations. Communication of information dropped substantially and members, with few exceptions, routinely forwarded their recommendations. They did this even though it was clear that they were each basing their recommendations on relatively little information and that their recommendations could be contradicted by what they did not know. Also, it is worth noting that this reduction of information flow tended to aggravate the communication biases that were observed in the earlier study and negated the benefits of communication feedback. For example, under conditions of elaborate metaknowledge (which should have made what they did not know painfully obvious), being able to send recommendations reduced the amount of partially shared information reaching the commander by 44%. The corresponding reduction in unique information was 28%.

Perhaps team members thought that sending recommendations was an effective way of quickly communicating the gist of what they knew, and thus a functional strategy given the limited time that the team had to react. Or they may have used a variant of the "consensus implies correctness" heuristic: If all or nearly all agreed on the recommended course of action, then it must be the best choice (Chaiken & Stangor, 1987; Kameda et al., 1997; Stasser & Birchmeier, 2003). However, as already noted, team members should have been aware that each of their recommendations risked being wrong given the relatively small amount information that they each could access. Indeed, the always-present performance feedback between episodes should have made apparent the frequency with which their local knowledge was misleading. Nonetheless, the preference-driven style spread quickly in these teams. Moreover, this shift to a preference-driven style resulted from a seemingly minor change in the SAS software. These findings underscore two features of electronic teamwork. First, seemingly small changes in the electronic software can have dramatic effects on social interaction in task groups. Second, as Postmes et al. (2001) suggested, behavior in electronic groups may be highly contagious under conditions of high interdependence and relative anonymity.

Returning to the social engineering theme, several implications are suggested. One general point is that leaders have powerful ways of shaping behavior in virtual teams. Second, rather minor changes in communication and decision support software can have substantial effects on the communications styles of teams. Third, interaction and performance norms can spread rapidly in electronic teams. Of course, a leader needs to know what works and what does not. As our research showed, detrimental interaction patterns are just as easy to instill as are beneficial ones. Kudzu is again a useful metaphor. The promoters of kudzu thought it was a valuable plant for many reasons and did not anticipate that it would eventually be widely regarded as an annoying, often destructive, and virtually indestructible weed. If it is the case that electronic teams are fertile grounds for germinating and growing norms, then leaders need to plant the right seeds.

SOCIAL ENGINEERING: THE SCOPE MODEL

It would be wrong to suggest that a recipe exists for designing the optimal conditions for distributed decision-making teams. Nonetheless, there are general principles that can summarize our ideas about potentially fruitful interventions. Stasser and Birchmeier (2003) organized such principles in the SCOPE model: Social engineering, Climate, Opportunity, Procedures, and Expert roles. In their model, social engineering is the overarching concept and underscores the idea that teams and their interaction need to be designed to promote effective information pooling. A social engineering approach involves several steps: defining the areas of expertise and experience that are relevant to the decision at hand, recruiting members that collectively cover the necessary areas of knowledge, and designing their interaction to promote effective information pooling. The rest of the SCOPE model identifies areas of concern in designing effective interactions.

Climate

Decision-making climate refers to group norms and behavioral expectations that guide how the group approaches its decision-making task. Several theorists have noted that norms of interaction and task strategies often develop quickly in task-oriented groups without explicit discussion (Bettenhausen & Murnighan, 1985; Gersick, 1988; Hackman & Morris, 1975; Ridgeway; 2001). Several studies of face-to-face interactions have demonstrated how norms and strategies can be primed by seemingly minor interventions. For example, Stasser and Stewart (1992) simply told groups that consideration of all the clues in a murder mystery would identify the guilty suspect. This expectation leads to more discussion of uniquely held clues than when group were asked to identify the most likely suspect. Similarly, Postmes et al. (2001) found that critical thinking groups attributed more importance to unique information, and unique information had more effect on their decisions.

Opportunity

The SCOPE model emphasizes the role of complementary knowledge and time in affording opportunity for effective information pooling. First, group members must bring complementary areas of knowledge. Much of our discussion has presumed that members have unique information to contribute. Of course, this may not be the case in practice and is unlikely to occur if groups are composed of members who share common experiences and interests. Groups of likeminded members will probably be highly cohesive and enjoy interacting, but each member will have little to contribute that others do not already know. As already noted, part of the social engineering task is to bring diverse sets of knowledge to the groups. Diverse teams should be easier to compose in distributed rather than in face-to-face decision making specifically because membership in face-to-face groups is often constrained by who is locally available.

Second, time is a critical resource. Members must have, and feel that they have, the luxury of systematically exploring information. As collective information sampling theory suggests, initial contributions to discussion are most likely to be common information. The sampling advantage of common information will be continually reduced as discussion continues (Larson et al., 1996). Therefore, allowing teams sufficient time to complete their tasks also increases the likelihood that unique information will be brought to the group's attention.

Procedures

How electronic meetings are conducted can alter the flow of information in a team. Often minor procedural variations can make a difference. For example, Hollingshead (1996) found that requiring groups to rank order decision alternatives, as opposed to simply choosing the best option, increased the discussion of unique information and the likelihood that they would discover a hidden profile. Hollingshead reasoned that ranking required discussing all alternatives and thus avoided the tendency to focus on one or two initially popular options. Houlette, Muzzy, and Sawyer (2000) found that when members were not asked to indicate their preference before discussion, they were more likely to use unique information and discover hidden profiles. Their findings imply that one should discourage the formation of preferences before discussion and certainly not begin consideration of an issue with soliciting opinions. If members bring preferences to the conservation, leaders should request that participants postpone voicing these preferences. Once majority or popular positions are identified, discussions tend to center around these positions to the exclusion of options that have little initial support.

Computer-mediated communication seems to offer other potential benefits. For example, Dennis (1996) showed that computer-aided discussion, as compared to face-to-face discussion, resulted in more exchange of unique information. However, in spite of more complete information pooling, computer-mediated communication did not increase the quality of group decisions. Lam and Schaubroeck (2000) also found that computer-mediated discussion increased the dissemination of unique information. Moreover, and contrary to Dennis' (1996) findings, they found that computed-mediated communication improved the quality of decisions. Both studies underscore the general idea that computer-aided communication can change the flow information. However, as the aforementioned work with the SAS task illustrates, seemingly small changes in the communication software can have striking effects on the amount and kinds of information that are communicated. Whereas communication and decision-making software offers a powerful tool, it must be applied with care. The role of such technology needs to be carefully considered and more adequately studied (McGrath & Hollingshead, 1994).

Expert Roles

As already noted, making explicit the locations of information and expertise within a team alters patterns of information exchange (Stasser et al., 1995, 2000; Stewart & Stasser, 1995, Wegner, 1986, 1995). Moreover, it may be easier to instill expert roles in computer-mediated communication, particularly if participants are identified primarily by their expertise. Mutual recognition of expertise in a decision-making team offers at least two benefits. First, expert roles allow members to focus their contributions and increase the likelihood that uniquely held expert knowledge will emerge during discussion. Thus, in the social engineering approach, not only must the group be composed of members who bring complementary sets of knowledge but also the members need to be aware of the expert roles that they are expected to enact. However, as the SAS results suggest, diffusing the distinctiveness of expert roles by recruiting and identifying multiple experts may have paradoxical effects. For example, two experts may not be better than one if expert roles are salient. Each may try to avoid saying things that she thinks the other will say in an effort to make unique contributions. As a result, the core of their expertise may be unwittingly omitted from communications to other team members.

A second benefit of instilling expert roles is that information from recognized experts is credible. We already mentioned the experimental studies of face-to-face groups that demonstrate the tendency for discussions to repeat common more than unique information during discussion (Larson et al., 1996; Stasser et al, 1989b). One presumed reason for this failure to continue consideration of unique information is that its credibility remains in doubt if no other member than the communicator can attest to its accuracy (Parks & Cowlin, 1996). However, if the rest of the group knows that individuals are experts, these persons are recognized as credible sources of specific kinds of information (Stasser et al., 1995, 2000; Stewart & Stasser, 1995; see also discussions of transactive memory theory: Wegner, 1986; 1995). Thus, unique knowledge learned from a person who is a designated expert is much more likely to survive than when the expertise of the communicator is unknown or not salient.

SCOPE: Implications For Distant Leaders

SCOPE emphasizes the social engineering function of leadership. To facilitate effective decision making in distributed teams and to address the kudzu problem, leaders need to design teams and their interactions with forethought. They need to foster a *climate* that encourages problem solving, critical thinking, and consideration of diverse points of view. They need also to provide *opportunity* by composing teams with complementary and relevant expertise and by ensuring the members have the time and take the time to explore and integrate information. Because distributed teams are often linked electronically, leaders have a unique opportunity to shape communication and decision-making *procedures* by selecting or designing software judiciously. However, as we have noted, how features of communication and decision-aided software affect decision process and effectiveness are not fully understood. Finally, manipulating perceptions of the distribution of expertise in a team may be a powerful way to shape communication content.

CONCLUSION

The research on information pooling in decision teams, whether face-to-face or computer-mediated, has a consistent theme. Teams trying to reach a consensus often do not effectively pool information. The dynamics of unstructured discussion are conducive to eliciting widely shared knowledge and identifying popular decision alternatives but are not conducive to communicating unique information. Notwithstanding this theme, groups do occasionally make innovative decisions. The SCOPE model summarizes factors that are thought to promote effective process in decision-making groups. Some of the elements of the SCOPE model have strong empirical and theoretical support whereas other elements are more speculative. Notably, the relationship between group composition and metaknowledge has not been extensively studied. In particular, the SAS results suggest that emphasizing expertise in team members' electronic personalities is most helpful when members have distinctive and unique roles to play. However, highlighting expertise when expert roles are duplicated may backfire, steering experts away from contributing their shared knowledge. While these interpretations have potentially useful implications for managing distributed teams, they need to be more thoroughly evaluated.

Effective pooling of information requires that teams and their interaction be designed to combat the kudzu problem. On the one hand, simply connecting knowledgeable people and letting them communicate at will is not sufficient to overcome these problems. Unstructured communication will often fail to pool diverse knowledge effectively. On the other hand, there are several ways to promote effective information pooling, and electronic media seem will suited for implementing many of these interventions.

ACKNOWLEDGMENTS

Preparation of this chapter and the research reported herein was supported by grants from the Office of Naval Research (N00014-90-J-1790) and the National Science Foundation (BCS-0001910) and by the grant 'Aires Culturelles' from the Ministère de la Recherche (France) to the second author. The authors thank Sara Kiesler and Suzanne Weisband for their suggestions and comments on an earlier version of this chapter. Thanks to Jim Larson for suggesting the kudzu analogy.

REFERENCES

Bettenhausen, K., & Murnighan, J. K. (1975). The emergence of norms in competitive decision-making groups, *Administrative Science Quarterly, 30,* 350–372.

Chaiken, S., & Stangor, C. (1987). Attitudes and attitude change. *Annual Review of Psychology, 38,* 575–630.

Dennis, A. R. (1996). Information exchange and use in group decision making: You can lead a group to information but you can't make it think. *MIS Quarterly, 20,* 433–455.

Gersick, C. J. (1988). Time and transition in work teams: toward a new model of group development. *Academy of Management Journal, 31,* 9–41.

Hastie, R., Penrod, S. D., & Pennington, N. (1983). *Inside the jury.* Cambridge, MA: Harvard University Press.

Hackman, J. R. & Morris, C. G. (1975). Group tasks, group interaction process, and group performance effectiveness: A review and proposed integration. In L. Berkowitz (Ed.). *Advances in experimental social psychology* (Vol. 8, pp. 45–99). New York: Academic Press.

Hollingshead, A. B. (1996). The rank order effect in group decision making. *Organizational Behavior and Human Decision Processes, 68,* 181–193.

Houlette, M., Muzzy, E. L. & Sawyer, J. E. (August, 2000). Information sharing and integration in culturally diverse cross-functional groups. In J. E. Sawyer (Chair), Decision-Group Composition, Structure and Processes: Applications of The Hidden Profile Paradigm to Group and Organizational Research. Symposium presented at the Annual Meeting of Academy of Management, OB and MOC Divisions, Toronto, Ontario, Canada.

Janis, I. L. (1972). *Victims of groupthink.* Boston: Houghton Mifflin.

Kameda, T., Ohtsubo, Y., & Takezawa, M. (1997). Centrality in sociocognitive networks and social influence: An illustration in a group decision making context. *Journal of Personality and Social Psychology, 73,* 296–309.

Kaplan, M. F. (1987). The influencing process in group decision making. In C. Hendrick, et al. (Eds.). *Group processes* (pp. 189–121). Newbury Park, CA: Sage.

Lam, S. S. K., & Schaubroeck, J. (2000). Improving group decisions by better pooling information: A comparative advantage of group decision support systems. *Journal of Applied Psychology, 85*(4), 565–573.

Larson, J. R., Jr., & Christensen, C. (1993). Groups as problem-solving units: Toward a new meaning of social cognition. *British Journal of Social Psychology, 32,* 5–30.

Larson, J. R., Jr., Christensen, C., Abbott, A. S., & Franz, T. M. (1996). Diagnosing groups: Charting the flow of information in medical decision making teams. *Journal of Personality and Social Psychology, 71*, 315–330.

Laughlin, P. R., & Ellis, A. L. (1986). Demonstrability and social combination processes on mathematical intellective tasks. *Journal of Experimental Social Psychology, 22*, 177–189.

McGrath, J. E., & Hollingshead, A. B. (1994). *Groups interacting with technology: Ideas, evidence, issues and an agenda.* Thousand Oaks, CA: Sage Publications.

McLeod, P. L., Baron, R. S., Marti, M. W., & Koon, K. (1997). The eyes have it: Minority influence in face-to-face and computer-mediated group discussion. *Journal of Applied Psychology, 82*, 706–718.

Moreland, R. L., Argote, L., & Krishnan, R. (1996). Socially shared cognition at work: Transactive memory and group performance. In J. L. Nye & A. M. Bower (Eds.). *What's new about social cognition? Research on socially shared cognition in small groups.* Thousand Oaks, CA: Sage.

Parks, C. D., & Cowlin, R. A. (1996). Acceptance of uncommon information into group discussion when that information is or is not demonstrable. *Organizational Behavior and Human Decision Processes, 66*, 307–315.

Postmes, T., Spears, R., & Cihangir, S. (2001). Quality of decision making and group norms. *Journal of Personality and Social Psychology, 80*, 918–930

Postmes, T., Spears, R., & Lea, M. (1998). Breaching or building social boundaries? SIDE-effects of computer-mediated communication. *Communication Research, 25*(6), 689–715.

Postmes, T. Spears, R. Sakhel, K. & de Groot, D. (2001). Social influence in computer-mediated communication: The effects of anonymity on group behavior. *Personality and Social Psychology Bulletin, 27*, 1243–1254.

Ridgeway, C. L. (2001). Social status and group structure. In M. A. Hogg & S. Tindale (Eds.), *Blackwell handbook of social psychology: Group Processes* (pp. 352–375). Oxford, UK: Blackwell.

Sawyer, J. E. Houlette, M. A. & Yeagley, E. L. (2006). Decision performance and diversity structure: Comparing faultlines in convergent, crosscut, and racially homogenous groups. *Organizational Behavior and Human Decision Processes, 99*, 1–15.

Siegel, J., Dubrovsky, V., Kiesler, S., & McGuire, T. W. (1986). Group processes in computer-mediated communication. *Organizational Behavior and Human Decision Processes, 37*, 157–187.

Spears, R. & Lea, M. (1994). Panacea or panoptican?: The hidden power in computer-mediated communication. *Communication Research, 21*, 427–459.

Stasser, G., & Birchmeier, Z. (2003). Group creativity and collective choice. In P. Paulus & B. Nijstad (Eds.) *Group Creativity* (pp. 85–109). New York: Oxford University Press.

Stasser, G., Kerr, N. L., & Davis, J. H. (1989a). Influence processes and consensus models in decision-making groups. In P. Paulus (Ed.). *Psychology of group influence* (2nd ed., pp. 279–326). Hillsdale, NJ: Lawrence Erlbaum Associates.

Stasser, G., & Stewart, D. (1992). Discovery of hidden profiles by decision-making groups: Solving a problem versus making a judgment. *Journal of Personality and Social Psychology, 63*, 426–434.

Stasser, G., Stewart, D. D., & Wittenbaum, G. M. (1995). Expert roles and information exchange during discussion: The importance of knowing who knows what. *Journal of Experimental Social Psychology, 31*, 244–265.

Stasser, G., Taylor, L. A., & Hanna, C. (1989b). Information sampling in structured and unstructured discussions of three- and six-person groups. *Journal of Personality and Social Psychology, 57*, 67–78.

Stasser, G., & Titus, W. (1985). Pooling of unshared information in group decision making: Biased information sampling during discussion. *Journal of Personality and Social Psychology, 48*, 1467–1478.

Stasser, G., & Titus, W. (1987). Effects of information load and percentage of shared information on the dissemination of unshared information during group discussion. *Journal of Personality and Social Psychology, 53*, 81–93.

Stasser, G., Vaughan, S. I., & Stewart, D. D. (2000). Pooling unshared information: The benefits of knowing how access to information is distributed among members. *Organizational Behavior and Human Decision Processes, 82*, 102–116.

Steiner, I. D. (1972). *Group process and productivity.* New York: Academic Press.

Stewart, D. D., & Stasser, G. (1995). Expert role assignment and information sampling during collective recall and decision making. *Journal of Personality and Social Psychology, 69*, 619–628.

Straus, S. G. (1996). Getting a clue: the effects of communication media and information distribution on participation and performance in computer-mediated and face-to-face groups. *Small Group Reserach, 27*, 115–142.

Wegner, D. M. (1986). Transactive memory: A contemporary analysis of the group mind. In B. Mullen & G. Goethals (Eds.), *Theories of group behavior* (pp. 185–208). New York: Springer-Verlag.

Wegner, D. M. (1995). A computer network model of human transactive memory. *Social Cognition, 13*, 319–339.

Wittenbaum, G. M., Hubbell, A., & Zuckerman, C. (1999). Mutual enhancement: Toward an understanding of the collective preference for shared information. *Journal of Personality and Social Psychology, 77*, 967–978.

Wittenbaum, G. M., & Stasser, G. (1996). Management of information in small groups. In J. L. Nye & A. M. Bower (Eds.). *What's new about social cognition? Research on socially shared cognition in small groups.* Thousand Oaks, CA: Sage.

Wittenbaum, G. M., Stasser, G., & Merry, C. J. (1996). Tacit coordination in anticipation of small group task completion. *Journal of Experimental Social Psychology, 32*, 129–152.

IV

Leading Large-Scale
Distributed Collaborations

9

Community Effort in Online Groups: Who Does the Work and Why?

Brian Butler
University of Pittsburgh

Lee Sproull
New York University

Sara Kiesler and Robert Kraut
Carnegie Mellon University

OVERVIEW

As in any social organization, people need to invest effort in the health of their online groups. Electronic mailing list servers, such as LISTSERV and Majordomo, and other such groups need people to maintain the technology infrastructure, carry out social management tasks, and recruit new members. Members must read and contribute to discussion. Here, we ask why people do this. In many online groups, preexisting social ties and material benefits for contributions are weak or nonexistent. In this chapter, we consider how the formal leadership role, personal and community benefits, and community characteristics influence the effort members put into helping their online groups. Results from a survey of Internet mailing list owners and other members suggest that although owners, who have a formal leadership role, do more of the effortful community building work than do regular members, other members also take on some of the work. Moreover, members who value different benefits are likely to contribute to the development of an online community in different ways.

Every day millions of people log on to the Internet to talk with other people. From its earliest days, the Internet has been used for social interaction as much as for intellectual or economic purposes (Sproull & Faraj, 1995; Sproull & Kiesler, 1991). Social electronic interaction can have serious or frivolous goals. We use the phrase "social interaction" to mean interacting with other people rather than interacting with impersonal databases or programs. Much social interaction on the Internet occurs among those with preexisting social ties. Far-flung friends and family members use the Internet to sustain relationships with one another (Kraut, Mukhopadhyay, Szczypula, Kiesler, & Scherlis, 2000; Wellman, Quan, Witte, & Hampton, 2001). In these cases, family and friendship ties are the foundation for continued online interaction. Employees use corporate networks to organize work, ask for help, or exchange advice (Bell, Bobrow, Raiman, & Shirley, 1998; Constant, Kiesler, & Sproull, 1996; Finholt & Sproull, 1990). In these cases, corporate ties are the foundation for continued online interaction. Even if employees do not know one another personally, their shared employer is a real-world bond. Yet a great deal of interaction in online social groups occurs among strangers without preexisting family, friendship, or corporate ties.

Some of these online social groups resemble street corner settings or park squares where practically anyone may show up. In these settings, there is little expectation of personal commitment or sustained interaction. Other online groups exhibit some properties of long-lived social groups or communities. Some have been in existence for close to twenty years (e.g., Rheingold, 2000). They may have hundreds or even thousands of members who return to them repeatedly and feel psychological commitment both to specific members and to the group as a whole. Some larger online groups have complex internal structures, roles, and explicit conventions, whereas others seem more ad hoc and informal. The diversity of structure and form leads to interesting questions about the nature of online community. However, in all cases these groups are faced with the communal challenge of developing and maintaining their existence as an identifiable social entity.

Within the past few years some online groups have been supported by commercial ventures using paid employees. Even in these cases, volunteers do much of the community work. In the real world, volunteers may be motivated to serve a group out of a wish to make friends and have companions, or because they feel commitment to the local neighborhood, church, work organization, or cause for which they volunteer (Callero, Howard, & Piliavin, 1987; Deaux & Stark, 1996; Grube & Piliavin, 1996; Omoto & Snyder, 1995; Snyder & Omoto, 1992). In the online world, these opportunities for real-world contact and local impact may be rare or absent. What, then, explains the continued existence and vitality of online groups?

How Are Online Groups Sustained?

Technology itself provides part of the answer. The Internet offers a variety of technical tools and mechanisms to support online social interaction in groups. Centralized mailing lists, which are maintained and managed on list server software,[1] allow members to send email messages to all group members. Electronic bulletin boards such as Freenets and Usenet allow anyone with Internet access to post to a designated group location where others can read and comment on those messages. Commercial service providers like AOL support forums for their members. Other tools support real-time chat, group message archives, and links to related groups and members' individual web pages.

Tools and technical infrastructure make online group communication possible and support the group's interactions with the outside world. Social behavior sustains these groups over time. At least four kinds of social behavior are necessary. First, people must tend the tools themselves by managing software versions, keeping address files up to date, and so on. People also must recruit members to replace those who leave. They must manage social dynamics. They must participate. Without these group maintenance activities, even sophisticated tools and infrastructure will not sustain viable online groups. Indeed, Butler (1999, reported in Cummings, Butler, & Kraut, 2002a) showed that in a random sample of list servers in 1997, 16% were defunct and 33% of the remainder distributed no messages during a 130-day period.

Infrastructure administration involves installing and maintaining the basic systems that enable group communication—setting up and operating software, hardware, and telecommunications systems. This aspect of infrastructure administration typically requires special technical expertise as well as investment in (or at least trusted access to) computer systems. Infrastructure administration also involves developing and maintaining components that are unique to the needs of the particular group, such as an up-to-date content archive, group descriptions, lists of frequently asked questions (FAQs), and the list of people who have access to the group. Even in cases in which core technological systems are provided by a designated technology support staff or a commercial service, some community member typically invests substantial effort in infrastructure administration. This effort is needed to maintain the basic communication infrastructure used by group members to communicate with one another.

---

[1]A list server is an electronic mail distribution list, in which messages sent to the list are forwarded to members who have subscribed to the list. Contents are often archived. Typical list server software provides commands for people to post, read, and reply to messages and to subscribe, unsubscribe, or receive digests of messages sent to the list. LISTSERV and Majordomo are the names of two major brands of list server software. We use "list server" to refer generally to all list management software.

Technological infrastructure establishes a public space for the group. On-line public spaces, like physical public spaces, are subject to a variety of problems arising from how people use or misuse community resources (Kollock & Smith, 1996). Hence, not just technical but also social management is needed to control detrimental use and encourage appropriate use of the communication infrastructure. Social control includes letting newcomers know the norms of the group; managing disputes, discouraging use of the infrastructure to discuss topics that are outside the community's interests (i.e., off-topic messages); preventing exploitation of individual members, as through "junk email"; explicitly chastising those who engage in inappropriate behavior; and denying access to the community's communication infrastructure, usually as a last resort. Social encouragement entails promoting desirable behavior by recognizing people who contribute especially informative or supporting messages, and people who create interesting or useful group activities. Together these control and encouragement activities serve to ensure that the group does not collapse due to abuse of the public space created by the communications infrastructure, and to render the group a comfortable and enjoyable place to interact. Unlike real-world groups and neighborhoods whose members may not be able to leave easily, members can abandon online communities easily. Social management is therefore essential to the health of these groups.

External promotion is another needed community building activity. On-line groups die without new members to replace those who leave. Butler (1999) documented an annual drop-out rate of 22% in the list servers that he studied, but double this number joined each year. Someone or something must have attracted people to these online groups. Since online group interactions typically are invisible to the outside world, explicit effort must be made to attract and inform people outside about the benefits of becoming involved. People recruit new members through both word of mouth and more explicit promotion, including creating and maintaining a group-specific web site, posting references to the group on related web sites (or in other online groups), and publicizing the group in personal documents such as email signatures and personal web pages. All of these activities can increase the salience of the community among potential members.

Perhaps the most basic type of investment in an online group is active participation in the form of creating content and consuming it. At first glance, participation may not seem to be part of community building. Yet, as in real world communities, without participation, few of the beneficial characteristics of most online groups would come about. In a real-world volunteer groups, participation means showing up, talking, listening, raising money, baking cookies, serving on committees, and organizing activities. In online groups, participation means generating messages, responding to messages, organizing discussion, and offering other online activities of interest to members. If members do not create relevant content, other community building activities are largely irrelevant. Participation also means consuming content; if members do not regularly read the material that others provide, an online group will not remain viable. Group identity and personal relationships are constructed through the messages that members send and read. Attending to and reading messages are prerequisites for others to provide them. Thus, active participation by providing and consuming content plays a crucial role in sustaining an online group.

Who Does the Work?

A major challenge in sustaining an online group is inducing people to devote the time and effort needed to perform these community maintenance activities. Members who regularly read messages or provide content for others expend real time and attention doing so. People who seek to mange group interaction find that controlling and encouraging members' behavior takes time, demands attention, and in some cases exacts an emotional toll. Promoting the community and maintaining its infrastructure also requires that people take time from other activities. Thus, a key challenge in developing viable online communities involves inducing people to perform these activities.

Most software created to run an online group requires a person to take a formal leadership role, often called an owner, administrator, host, or wizard. In some cases, the role exists because setting up the technical infrastructure requires someone with high-level administrator privileges on a server. Even in cases where the core technology is administered by an outside agency, the distributed nature of online groups usually means there is a need for a formal position in community administration. As with a formal position of administrator in a traditional organization, the owner (or administrator, host, or wizard) of an online group is a role that is formally named and characterized by distinctive rights and responsibilities. The role is defined and reinforced through community structure and rules. Owners are typically assigned special email addresses, are prominently identified in the description of the community, and have special privileges. They can add or remove members from the community and, in the case of an infrastructure that provides archival capabilities, they can add or remove items from the archive. In cases of moderated groups, they can approve or reject messages or can delegate these rights to particular others.

In real-world organizations, a formal administrative role and in-role administrative behavior creates further administrative competence and psychological role identity, which encourages further commitment to the group and more role activity (Organ, 1994; Piliavin & Callero, 1991). Likewise, in online groups, competence and role identity should lead owners to engage in more community building activities than other members. Because owners typically have special access to the technical infrastructure, they are often held responsible for infrastructure management. By virtue of the legitimacy that arises from their role, owners also have an increased authority and responsibility for the social activity in the group, particularly when it involves taking action to limit undesirable behavior. Although it is not necessarily inherent in the infrastructure or facilitated by the formal role, owners' role identity and commitment to the group would lead them to promote the community externally and provide more content than other participants. It is less clear whether owners would be expected to show greater audience engagement than other involved group members. On the one hand, owners might be more vigilant in reading content than would be other members. On the other hand, to the degree that owners create content themselves, they can spend less time reading it. Taken all together, however, we expect that owners will do significantly more community building work than will other members of the community.

Why Do People Do the Work?

Whether people are formally designated leaders or not, presumably they do community-building work because they expect to derive benefits from it, either directly or through the benefits they provide the group. In real-world communities, volunteers have differing motivations for volunteer work (e.g., Omoto & Snyder, 1995). Some people seek escape, sociable interaction, self-esteem, or future employment, and others are highly altruistic and contribute in order to help a group or cause. Many people who identify with a group, feel personally gratified when the group benefits. The benefits people expect influence the types of community-building work that they do, the effort they expend, and how long they continue to do volunteer work (e.g., Deaux & Stark, 1996; Penner & Finkelstein, 1998).

Although online groups do not offer all of the potential benefits for community participation offered by real-world communities, they offer some benefits particular to the electronic domain. Prior studies of online groups suggest that people often participate as a way to gain access to otherwise obscure or inaccessible information that is relevant to their work, hobbies, health, and other topics in which they are personally interested (Galegher, Sproull, & Kiesler, 1998; Ogan, 1993; von Hippel, 2001). This information benefit may come in the form of receiving answers to specific questions or general knowledge arising from exposure to group communications. People who value information benefits should be engaged as an audience.

People also benefit from participating in social relationships (Baym, 1999; Cummings, Sproull, & Kiesler, 2002b; Galegher, Sproull, & Kiesler, 1998). Online groups can provide a place to build and maintain social ties with people already known offline as well as those first met online. Social relationships provide camaraderie and social support. Social relationships also create trust and increase the credibility of the information that the group exchanges. People who value these social benefits are likely to do the work of providing content and managing social behavior (particularly by encouraging others). They are also likely to be more engaged in reading and posting, because following others' social exchanges and online conversations can provide a basis for their own participation.

In addition to providing information and social benefits, online groups also provide opportunities for people to be visible beyond the boundaries of their local work or geographical community (Lerner & Tirole, 2000). Becoming visible may be most important for work-related online groups because in these settings visibility may have direct economic and professional payoffs. Even for those in online groups dealing with topics of personal interest, being viewed as skilled, knowledgeable, or respected may have psychic payoffs. In contrast to informational benefits that can come from the typically invisible work of audience engagement, the benefits of personal visibility accrue to those who provide content and those who do social encouragement and external promotion.

To this point we have focused on the personal benefits one expects to receive from the information, social relationships one enjoys within online group, and visibility one gains from contributing to an online group. As with voluntary associations in general, however, people also contribute because they are trying to help the group itself or a larger community of people that the online group is part of. That is, the motivation is an altruistic one in which contributors value the opportunity to benefit others. Together, expectation of these four types of benefits—informational, social, visibility, and altruistic—provide a range of motivations for why people do the work of online community building.[2]

What Contextual Factors Affect Community Building?

Although people must do community-building work in all online groups, the amount they do of different types of work may be related to the characteristics

---

[2]We initially derived these categories from items used in previous research on volunteer motivations, particularly Omoto and Snyder (1995), as well as from items more suited to online community. Omoto and Snyder's scales of volunteer motivation included personal development (e.g., making friends), esteem enhancement (e.g., escaping stress), understanding (e.g., learning more about the problem), values (e.g., helping others), and community concern (e.g., sense of obligation to the community). Our category, social benefit, overlaps with their category, personal development. Our category, information benefit, overlaps with their category, understanding; and our category, altruism, overlaps with their categories, values and community concern. Our category, visibility benefit, perhaps is especially pertinent to online communities, where contributions can make one known to hundreds or thousands of others, and perhaps less so in real-world communities, where even highly involved volunteers often toil in comparative obscurity.

of the group itself. In traditional organizations, many of the activities described above increase in importance and complexity as the number of community members increases. Larger organizations, groups, and associations require more effort to maintain. However, one of the features of online communities is that its population size does not matter in the conduct of many activities; for example, it is just as easy to post a message to a community of several thousand as to a group of several (Sproull & Kiesler, 1991). On the other hand, some maintenance work may be related to the size of the group. For example, the need for encouraging proper behavior and controlling undesirable behavior is likely to grow with the number of members in an online community.

In contrast to sheer size, the amount of activity in the group may be related significantly to other types of work that must be done. The time and attention needed to process content is likely to be higher in online groups in which the volume of activity is greater.

The type of group also may affect community-building work. Online groups organized around career and other work-related topics are in some ways the online equivalent of professional associations. Members in work-related online groups may hold membership in analogous real-world professional associations and maintain ties through these associations. In contrast, groups that focus on nonwork activities, such as hobbies, political causes, and other personal interests, are more likely to behave like clubs or informal social groups. Following this reasoning, in work-related online groups, information and visibility benefits might be more important to those who do community-maintenance work, whereas in nonwork groups, social benefits might be more important. Altruism could be important to members in both kinds of groups. Those with a strong professional identification may be highly committed to their online work-related groups. Those with a strong political, charitable, or avocation identification may be highly committed to their online nonwork-related groups.

METHOD

To examine the determinants and consequences of community-building work, we conducted an electronic survey of members in a sample of Internet list servers. We drew upon prior research conducted in 1997 that characterized topic, message volume, and membership size in a sample of 284 unmoderated, unrestricted public list servers (see Butler, 1999). The sample included work-related and nonwork groups. Groups whose focus was medical or psychological support were excluded due to the possible sensitivity of these groups to an unsolicited survey.

In the fall of 1998, we sent email surveys to a stratified sample of members drawn from the online list servers characterized by Butler in 1997. We sent a survey to the list owner for each group. In cases in which the owner could not be personally identified, we sent a survey to the designated owner address for the community. When a person owned more than one list and could be identified as such, one list was randomly selected as the target of the survey. In cases where a person was identified as an owner of multiple lists after responding, one response was randomly chosen for inclusion in the final dataset. The survey was also sent to two samples of members from each community, that is, active participants and silent participants, or "lurkers." Active participants were defined as the top 20 most active posters, selected from people who had contributed messages to the group in the time period covered by the first stage of data collection. When the number of active contributors was fewer than 20, they were all included in the sample. In addition, up to 20 members were selected from the set of members who had not contributed a message during a 130-day period, in the first stage of data collection.

The sample selection process resulted in a three-level sample of 2,992 people consisting of owners, active participants, and silent participants from 212 different lists. The survey was sent via email to all people in the initial sample. One month later a second round of surveys was sent to nonrespondents. In the two rounds, 573 surveys were not deliverable due to invalid email addresses, resulting in an effective sample of 2,419 people from 147 different lists. Significantly incomplete responses and duplication (arising primarily from owners who were sent two surveys) were removed to create a dataset comprised of responses from 385 people from 121 different lists. This sample represents 16% of the total list members and 82% of the lists sampled.

The dataset contained responses from 25 list owners (6.5%), 273 active participants (70.9%), and 87 silent participants (22.6%). Respondents were on average 41 years old. Fifty-six percent were male, 65% had some graduate school education, 69% were employed full time, and 43% had income of more than $60,000. Chi-squared tests of gender, income, occupational level, and analysis of variance (ANOVA) of respondent age indicate that, with one exception, there was no significant demographic difference across the respondent subsamples. Owners were significantly more likely to have some graduate education (84% of owners versus 61% of active participants and 70% of silent participants).

Measures

Basing their judgments on brief online descriptions of the lists, two coder rated the extent to which each list was about nonwork or work-related topics. Cronbach's alphas, measuring the reliability of the judgments, were 0.88 and 0.79 respectively. We classified each group based on its highest rating. For example, lists for a folk dance society, botany club, and environmentalist information were classified as personal and nonwork, whereas those focused on copy editing and computer-aided design systems were classified as work-related.

Survey respondents were distributed between nonwork and work-related groups in the same proportion as in the sample. Chi-squared tests indicated that there was no significant difference in the distribution of member types (owner, active participant, silent participant) across the group types (nonwork versus work). The total percentage of owners in the response set (6.5%) matched that in the sample (6.6%). However, active participants, people who contributed at least one message to the community, were a higher proportion of the response set than in the sample (71% versus 54%).

The subsamples did not differ on whether they were members of work or nonwork groups, but they did have differences with respect to size, measured in terms of the number of individuals on a list's mailing list on November 30, 1997, and content volume, measured in terms of mean number of messages posted per day. Analysis of variance shows that compared to the sample of active readers, the owner and silent participant samples were from lists that were smaller ($p < .10$) and that exchanged fewer messages ($p < .001$). Because of these sample differences, we include list size and volume as control variables in the analyses.

Group size was operationalized as the number of people on each list server's mailing list at the end of November 1997. To address nonnormality, we used a log (base 10) transformation of the list server size. Content volume was measured by calculating the mean number of messages sent to the list server each day during a 130-day observation period starting in the end of November 1997. Again, we applied a log (base 10) transformation to address nonnormality. Before taking the log, we added 0.01 to each measure to handle cases with a value of 0. (The value of 0.01 was selected to place the 0 valued cases at just beyond the lowest transformed value.)

Respondents' community-building work was measured with a survey question that asked respondents to indicate how many hours per week they spent performing activities such as reading messages, composing messages, and maintaining the mailing list and whether they cross-posted messages to other groups, mentioned their membership in their email signature file, or sent messages to other participants in order to reduce "off-topic" messages. We carried out an exploratory factor analysis to identify the structure of these items. Using standardized values for each of the items, principal component analysis of the community building activities, with Varimax rotation and pairwise exclusion of missing values, resulted in 5 factors explaining 60% of the variance. One somewhat unexpected outcome of the factor analysis was that items related to content provision loaded on a factor with infrastructure maintenance items. However, these are conceptually distinct activities, and it is likely that many people who provide content lack the technical capability to maintain a community's infrastructure. Therefore, these items were placed in separate indices. The means of each item set were then used to construct six indices of community building activity (Table 9.1).

TABLE 9.1.
Measures of Community Building Work

Index	Items*	Alpha
Content provision	How many hours per week do you spend composing and posting list msgs [messages]?	0.73
	How many hours per week do you spend corresponding in private email with list members?	
Infrastructure maintenance	How many hours per week do you spend maintaining list address files?	0.82
	How many hours per week do you spend maintaining, posting publicizing ancillary files?	
Social encouragement	Please check each of the following activities that you do: Cross-post messages from this list to other lists	0.66
	Regarding messages you post to the list or send as private email, please check if any have as their purpose to: Praise someone's informative message Praise someone's supportive message style Encourage people to tell others about the list	
Social control	Regarding messages you post to the list or send as private email, please check if any have as their purpose to: Encourage people to introduce themselves Adjudicate disputes Reduce "off-topic" messages Chastise someone's inappropriate behavior Remove someone from the list	0.73
External promotion	Please check each of the following activities you do: Maintain a web site for the list. Post links to related web sites. Identify yourself as a list server member in your sig [signature] file Give information about the list on your home page.	0.70
Audience engagement	How many hours per week do you spend reading list messages?	NA

* All items are standardized.

Similar analyses were conducted for 14 items related to motivations and expected benefits of contributing to these groups. Respondents were asked to indicate, on a 7-point scale, "How important is each of the following as a benefit you receive from participating in this listserv?" Principal component analysis of the standardized values, with Varimax rotation and pairwise exclusion of missing values, resulted in four factors explaining 64% of the variance. The means of each item set were then used to construct four measures of respondents' perceptions of the benefits to contributing to the community (see Table 9.2).

Preliminary Analysis

The correlations among the main constructs indicate that many of the items are correlated (see Table 9.3). On average, people who said they contributed to one community-building activity contributed to several. Similarly, respondents who expected one benefit from contributing to the group tend to perceive several benefits. Those who perceived that there were important benefits from participating in an online group were more likely to contribute to community building activities.

The remainder of this chapter examines these relationships in more detail and asks whether contributions, perceived benefits, and the relationships among them were different for owners of the lists (formal leaders), active posters, and lurkers of the groups, and for nonwork-related and work-related groups. To test our hypotheses, we conducted repeated measures ANOVAs with respondent role (owner or other member) and group type (nonwork- or work-related) as fixed effects, and group size and content volume as covariates.

TABLE 9.2.
Measures of Community Benefit Expectations

Index	Items*	Alpha
Visibility benefits	Career advancement or professional visibility.	NA
Information benefits	Learn more about or keep up with the topic. Get my questions answered.	0.60
Social benefits	Meet people and make friends. Have fun. Have others appreciate my participation. Gain a sense of accomplishment. Become known to list members. Build relationships with list members.	0.84
Altruistic benefits	Help other people. Think about others instead of myself. Support the real world community associated with this topic. Support this list community. Promote the topic or issue of the group.	0.77

*All items followed the prompt: "How important is each of the following as a benefit you receive from participating in this list server (1 = not at all important, 7 = extremely important)?" All values are standardized.

TABLE 9.3.
Correlations Among Measures

	1	2	3	4	5	6	7	8	9	10	11	12	13	14
1. Total time	1.00													
2. Infrastructure maintenance	.68**	1.00												
3. Social control	.29**	.28**	1.00											
4. Social encouragement	.42**	.29**	.47**	1.00										
5. External promotion	.31**	.33**	.29**	.32**	1.00									
6. Content provision	.87**	.65**	.29**	.36**	.28**	1.00								
7. Audience engagement	.39**	.11*	.12*	.16**	.06	.24**	1.00							
8. Visibility benefits	.18**	.16**	.03	.17**	.16**	.20**	.01	1.00						
9. Information benefits	.16**	.05	-.10	.13*	.00	.06	.15**	.24**	1.00					
10. Social benefits	.33**	.17**	.20**	.35**	.22**	.28**	.17**	.30**	.30**	1.00				
11. Altruistic benefits	.28**	.23**	.10	.34**	.15**	.26**	.13*	.32**	.28**	.49**	1.00			
12. Work-related group	-.06	.07	-.09	.04	-.02	-.03	-.02	.28**	.08	-.12*	.09	1.00		
13. Log (group size)	-.01	-.11	-.02	.02	-.09	-.11*	.10	.07	.20**	-.08	-.05	.17**	1.00	
14. Log (message volume + .01)	.19**	-.04	.08	.13*	-.03	.08	.13*	.06	.21**	.08	.09	-.18**	.52**	1.00
15. No. of members known outside the group	.14**	.20**	.06	.08	.07	.31**	-.01	.06	-.06	.02	.12*	.05	-.07	.01

Pairwise Ns range from 325 to 385.
$*: p < = 0.05$; $**: p < = 0.01$.

RESULTS

A premise of this research is that community building requires significant expenditures of time and effort on the part of members. The descriptive analysis presented below shows that members reported investing significant amounts of time in community-building work, with an average of almost 4 hours a week and a maximum of 31 hours (see Table 9.4).

We had reasoned that owners, in their role as formal administrators, would contribute more to community-building work than would their members. We found, however, that owners did not did not differ significantly from either silent or active participants on the total time they expended in community-building work. Owners did significantly more of the active work of infrastructure maintenance, social control, and external promotion work than did other members (see Table 9.5 and Figure 9–1). They did not differ from other members, however, in the time they devoted to reading messages and encouraging other members. By definition, owners contributed more content than silent participants ($p < .05$). However, there was no difference in the level of content provision of owners and active participants. Overall, the control variables of group type (nonwork- versus work-related) and group size were not significant. As we expected, group activity as measured by the volume of content did have a significant influence on the level of community work, with an overall significant effect ($F = 11$, $p < .001$) and a significant effect for social control, social encouragement, and content provision.

To examine the motivations of owners in comparison to other members, we carried out repeated measures analyses of the importance of community benefits to both groups. These analyses showed that owners valued different community benefits than did other members (see Table 9.6 and Figure 9–2). Owners perceived altruistic benefits to be significantly more important and information benefits to be significantly less important than did other members. This finding is as we expected and is consistent with the role identity theory and research by Piliavin and her colleagues. They suggest that in-role volunteer activity encourages an altruistic self image and commitment to the community (see, for example, Callero et al., 1987; Piliavin & Callero, 1991).

The analyses presented above suggest that owners engaged in different types and amounts of community-building work and valued different benefits than did other members. The repeated measures ANOVA results presented in Table 9.7 examine the link between benefits and community-building work. This analysis, when compared with that in Table 9.5, shows whether perceived benefits mediate the degree to which owners and other members engage in community building work. If the benefits of participation drive community building, then differences between owners and other members will be reduced when benefits are entered into the models. The analysis in Table 9.7 shows that including benefits in the model does not reduce the impact of the owner role; indeed, in comparison to active participants it is slightly strengthened. That

TABLE 9.4.
The Nature and Extent of Community-Building Work

	All Responses			Respondents Reporting Activity	
	N	Range (hrs/weeks)	Mean (hrs/weeks)	N	Mean (hrs/weeks)
Reading list messages	368	0–14	1.99	356	2.06
Composing and posting list messages	359	0–10	0.8239	291	1.02
Corresponding in private email with list members	351	0–15	0.789	255	1.08
Maintaining list address files	340	0–3	0.16	90	0.58
Maintaining, posting, and publicizing ancillary files (e.g. FAQs, "rules of the road," etc.)	340	0–7	0.22	70	1.045
Total time:	371	0–31	3.85	363	3.94

% of respondents who report having sent messages (privately or publicly) to:	*N = 384*
Praise someone's informative message	68
Encourage people to tell others about the list	25
Praise someone's supportive message style	24
Adjudicate disputes	22
Reduce "off-topic" messages	16
Encourage people to introduce themselves	13
Chastise someone's inappropriate behavior	12
Remove someone from the list	6

% of respondents who report that they:	*N = 384*
Post messages from the list to other lists	32
Post links to related web sites	22
Provide information about the list on their personal home page	16
Maintain a web site for the list	10
Identify themselves as list members in their email signature files	7

is, the analysis shows that owners invest more hours than other members in community building work, and the difference between owners and members is especially strong for nonwork-related groups. This analysis suggests that the leadership role itself accounts for some of the additional effort that owners contribute in active community building.

TABLE 9.5.
ANOVA Parameter Estimates for Community Building Activity

	Community Building Work						
	Total Time	Infrastructure Maintenance	Social Control	Social Encouragement	External Promotion	Content Provision	Audience Engagement
Intercept	7.073***	1.410***	.459+	.391	.564*	.828*	-.481
Silent participants[1]	-1.429	-.953***	-.597***	-.303	-.487**	-.436	.123
Active participants[2]	-.986	-.818***	-.510***	-.207	-.511**	-.185	.175
Work-related group	-2.090	-.908+	.352	-.076	.179	-.175	-.189
Log (size)	-.953	-.252+	-.003	-.050	-.059	-.285**	.145
Log (volume + 0.01)	1.190***	.057	.073	.135*	.010	.120+	.090
Group type × Silent participant	3.158	.982+	-.209	-.181	-.317	.434	.332
Group type × Active participant	1.975	.677	-.228	-.063	-.124	.081	.236

$N = 334$ + : $p \leq 0.1$; * $p \leq 0.05$; ** $p \leq 0.01$; *** $p \leq 0.001$.
[1] Coefficients indicate the results of comparing silent participants to owners.
[2] Coefficients indicate the results of comparing active participants to owners.

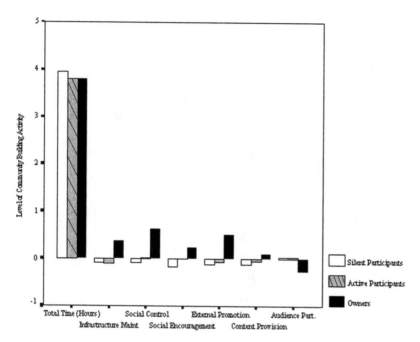

FIGURE 9–1.   Relative Levels of Community Building Work for Owners and Other Members.

TABLE 9.6.
ANOVA Parameter Estimates for Community Benefit Expectations

	Benefits from Community Participation			
	Visibility	Information	Social	Altruistic
Intercept	.258	−1.054***	.080	.974***
Silent participants[1]	−.170	.947***	.196	−.692***
Active participants[2]	.022	.870***	.345+	−.423*
Work-related group	−.749	.054	1.204***	−.099
Log (size)	−.031	.147	−.167	−.198*
Log (volume+0.01)	.127	.215*	.068	.126*
Group type ×				
Silent participants	.003	−.257	−1.554**	−.297
Group type ×				
Active participants	.040	−.299	−1.003**	−.122

$N = 343$ +: $p \le 0.1$; *$p \le 0.05$; **$p \le 0.01$; ***$p \le 0.001$
[1]Coefficients indicate the results of comparing silent participants to owners.
[2]Coefficients indicate the results of comparing active participants to owners.

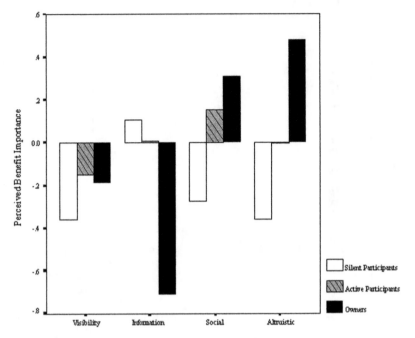

FIGURE 9–2.   Owners' and Members' Relative Benefit Importance Perceptions.

The degree to which participants' valued benefits from the groups also predicted their community-building work, over and above their type of membership and group attributes (group type, size, and content volume). People who valued social benefits reported performing more community building work of all types. Because social benefits include making friends and interacting socially, we also considered whether experiences outside of the list server were related to these motivations and to community work. In particular, we added respondents' estimates of the number of people on the list whom they knew in the real world to the analysis.[3] This analysis showed that the more people that members of the online community knew in the real world, the more time they invested in community building work, controlling for community benefits ($p < .05$). Knowing more list members in the real world was associated with higher levels of infrastructure maintenance, social encouragement, and content provision.

---

[3]Several respondents reported that they knew in excess of 200 list members outside the context of this list. To prevent undue influence of these outliers on the results, these responses were dropped from the analysis presented in Table 9.7.

TABLE 9.7.
The Relationship Between Benefit Perceptions and Community Building Work

	Total Time	Infrastructure Maintenance	Community Building Work Social Control	Social Encouragement	External Promotion	Content Provision	Audience Engagement
Intercept	7.744***	1.180***	.505	.270	.705*	.876**	-.301
Visibility	.341	.060	.008	.031	.101*	.078+	-.094
Information	.376	.069	-.107+	-.027	-.020	-.014	.102
Social	1.478***	.126+	.191**	.257***	.198**	.197**	.214*
Altruistic	.145	.011	-.035	.149*	-.046	.028	.105
No. of members known outside	.024*	.007***	.001	.004*	.002	.005**	-.001
Silent participants[1]	-1.294	-.963***	-.577**	-.033	-.483*	-.363+	.030
active participants[2]	-2.069+	-1.062***	-.565**	-.164	-.643***	-.326+	.028
Work-related group	-4.145*	-1.189**	.036	-.392	-.103	-.464	-.521
Log (size)	-1.140+	-.143	.003	-.058	-.089	-.310**	.133
Log (volume + 0.01)	1.188**	-.007	.099	.121+	-.004	.133*	.063
Group type × silent participants	4.958*	1.238**	.106	.201	-.038	.769+	.583
Group type × active participants	4.351*	1.150**	.035	.282	.191	.460	.481

$N = 296 + :p \leq 0.1; *:p \leq 0.05; **:p \leq 0.01; ***:p \leq 0.001$.

[1]Coefficients indicate the results of comparing silent participants to owners.

[2]Coefficients indicate the results of comparing active participants to owners.

Other benefits were more narrowly associated with particular types of community-building work. People who valued altruistic benefits were more like to encourage others. People who valued personal visibility were more likely to promote the group externally.

CONCLUSION

Online community building entails work. In the case of a list server, this work involves infrastructure maintenance, social control and encouragement, external promotion, and writing and reading messages. We have shown that members of list servers report spending substantial time each week doing this work. People with a formal leadership role—owners of the list servers—did more community-building work than others did. But other members also invested time to make their groups successful. Moreover owners and other members who valued different benefits contributed to the online group in different ways. Social benefits were especially powerful in driving community building work and led to a wide range of community-building activities, but other benefits were important as well.

The work presented here is subject to many limitations. We sampled only from unmoderated, unrestricted public list servers. We did not sample support groups. Thus we cannot estimate the extent to which our findings generalize to other types of online groups and communities. Moreover, our survey respondents may not be representative of the entire population of all list server members. Although the proportion of owners and other members responding to the survey were comparable to those in the population, the absolute number of owners, as well as the overall response rate, was low. All of the individual-level measures were based on self-report and may be subject to reporting biases.

Despite these limitations, our analyses suggest an interesting perspective on leadership in online groups. The formal leader role in online communities is the role of owner, administrator, or host. This role was originally defined with special access privileges so that the technical tools and network infrastructure of the online group could be maintained. However, unlike what seems to happen in many real world groups and organizations, technical responsibility in online groups goes hand in hand with social responsibility. Historically, owners often have had the original idea to start their online groups, or they have taken over the role after being active members. Owners therefore probably acquired their technical role with more community commitment than the typical online group member, and, as our data show, they have taken on broad social responsibilities and social community building work as well. Thus list owners not only do the work of maintaining the infrastructure but they also take on tasks such as promoting the group, sending messages to other members to encourage them or moderate their behavior, and posting messages. Thus, the role definition of owner seems to include social as well as technical tasks.

As we noted earlier, this evidence of in-role volunteer participation and community commitment by owners is consistent with the theory and research of Piliavin and her colleagues, who have studied real world volunteers. Owners are motivated more by altruistic motives than other members are. And owners are putting in substantial amounts of time on both technical and social tasks, and differentiating themselves from other members in their degree of active, as compared with passive, participation. In comparison with other members, they spend more time contributing content and composing messages than reading messages.

Despite this evidence that the formal leadership role is important, our data also show that other members also engage in time-consuming, community-building work. Our analyses showed that perceptions of community benefits predicted how much community building work members of the group did. One of the interesting personal benefits offered by an online community that may be less prominent in most real-world communities is personal visibility. Our data showed that those who valued this benefit were likely to do the work of external promotion of the community (and probably of themselves as well), such as cross-posting messages to other groups and websites.

For all members, and especially for owners of nonwork-related lists, social behaviors seemed to motivate a wide range of community-building effort. In addition, the more people that they knew in the real world, the more time they spent in community-building work, controlling for community benefits. Of course, this significant association does not tell us about causality. It is possible that online community members got to know other members in the real world as a result of their interactions in the online community, or that they already knew these people outside the online group. However, this finding is consistent with other work we have done that shows that participation in an online group can be stronger for those with real world group ties (Cummings et al., 2002b). Real-world community leadership also predicted some kinds of online community-building work: Those who had taken on real-world community leadership roles were more likely to engage in social encouragement and external promotion in the online community. Again, it is possible that real world ties were partly implicated in this activity.

In conclusion, our data suggest that if leaders want to increase community-building work done by other members, they can focus on increasing the social benefits and relationships that members derive from the group.

Online communities are interesting in large part because they are emergent. The more centralized and formalized community-building work becomes, the more "community" begins to resemble traditional formal organizations, or in the extreme, traditional mass media. For this reason it is important to understand why people, on their own initiative, invest their time, energy, and attention in the activities of community building.

REFERENCES

Baym, N. (1999). *Tune in, log on: Soaps, fandom, and on-line commmunity.* Thousand Oaks, CA: Sage Publications.

Bell, D. G., Bobrow, D. G., Raiman, O., & Shirley, M. H. (1998). Dynamic documents and situated processes: Building on local knowledge in field service. In T. Wakayama, S. Kannapan, C. M. Khoong, S. Navathe, & J. Yates (Eds.), *Information and process integration in enterprises: Rethinking documents* (pp. 261–276). Norwell, MA: Kluwer Academic Publishers.

Butler, B. S. (1999). *The dynamics of cyberspace: Examining and modelling online social structure.* Ph.D. Dissertation, Graduate School of Industrial Administration. Carnegie Mellon University. Pittsburgh, PA.

Callero, P. L., Howard, J. A., & Piliavin, J. A. (1987). Helping behavior as a role behavior: Disclosing social structure and history on the analysis of prosocial action. *Social Psychology Quarterly, 50,* 247–256.

Constant, D., Kiesler, S., & Sproull, L. (1996). The kindness of strangers: On the usefulness of weak ties for technical advice. *Organization Science, 7,* 119–135.

Cummings, J. N., Butler, B., & Kraut, R. (2002a). The quality of online social relationships, *Communications of the ACM, 45*(7), 103–108.

Cummings, J. N., Sproull, L., & Kiesler, S. (2002b). Beyond hearing: Where real world and online support meet. *Group Dynamics, 6*(1), 78–88.

Deaux, K., & Stark, B. E. (1996, May). Identity and motive: an integrated theory of volunteerism. Paper presented at the annual meeting of the Society for the Psychological Study of Social Issues, Ann Arbor, MI.

Finholt, T., & Sproull, L. (1990). Electronic groups at work. *Organization Science, 1,* 41–64.

Galegher, J., Sproull, L., & Kiesler, S. (1998). Legitimacy, authority, and community in electronic support groups. *Written Communication, 15,* 493–530.

Grube, J. A., & Piliavin, J. A. (1996, May). Role-identity, organizational commitment, and volunteer perofrmance. Paper presented at the annual meeting of the Society for the Psychological Study of Social Issues, Ann Arbor, MI.

Kollock, P., & Smith, M. (1996). Managing the virtual commons: Cooperation and conflict in computer communities. In S. C. Herring (Eds.) *Computer mediated communication: Linguistic, social, and cross-cultural perspectives* (pp. 226–242). Philadelphia: John Benjamins Publishing.

Kraut, R., Mukhopadhyay, T., Szczypula, J., Kiesler, S., & Scherlis, B. (2000). Information and communication: Alternative uses of the Internet in households. *Information Systems Research, 10,* 287–303.

Lerner, J., & Tirole, J. (2000, February 25). The simple economics of open source. Retrieved July 13, 2000 from http://www.people.hbs.edu/jlerner/simple.pdf.

Ogan, C. (1993) List server communication during the Gulf War: What kind of medium is the bulletin board? *Journal of Broadcasting and Electronic Media, 37,* 177–196.

Omoto, A., & Snyder, M. (1995). Sustained helping without obligation: Motivation, longevity of service, and perceived attitude change among AIDS volunteers. *Journal of Personality and Social Psychology, 68,* 671–687.

Organ, D. W. (1994). Personality and organizational citizenship behavior. *Journal of Management, 20,* 465–478.

Piliavin, J. A., & Callero, P. (1991). *Giving blood: The development of an altruistic identity.* Baltimore: Johns Hopkins Press.

Penner, L. A., & Finkelstein, M. A. (1998). Dispositional and structural determinants of volunteerism. *Journal of Personality and Social Psychology, 74*, 525–537.

Rheingold, H. (2000). *The Virtual Community*, revised edition. Cambridge: The MIT Press.

Sproull, L., & Faraj, S. (1995). Atheism, sex, and databases: The net as a social technology. In Brian Kahin and James Keller (eds.), *Public Access to the Internet* (pp. 62–81). Cambridge: The MIT Press.

Sproull, L., & Kiesler, S. (1991). *Connections: New ways of working in the networked organization.* Cambridge, MA: MIT Press.

Snyder, M., & Omoto, A. M. (1992). Who helps and why? The psychology of AIDS volunteerism. In S. Spacapan & S. Oskamp (Eds.), *Helping and being helped*: *Naturalistic studies* (pp. 213–239). Newbury Park, CA: Sage.

von Hippel, E. (2001). Open source shows the way: Innovation by and for users—no manufacturer required!, *Sloan Management Review*, forthcoming, Retrieved April 7, 2001 from http://opensource.mit.edu.

Wellman, B., Quan, A., Witte, J., & Hampton, K. (2001). Does the Internet increase, decrease or supplement social capital? Social networks, participation, and community commitment. *American Behavioral Scientist, 45*.

10

Cultural Challenges to Leadership in Cyberinfrastructure Development

Jeremy P. Birnholtz
University of Toronto

Thomas A. Finholt
University of Michigan

OVERVIEW

In this chapter, we show how Hofstede's cultural constructs help explain the leadership dysfunction we observed in the early history of NEESgrid, the cyberinfrastructure component of the George E. Brown Jr. Network for Earthquake Engineering Simulation (NEES). The goal of the NEESgrid effort was to design and deploy a collaboratory to link researchers and students with earthquake engineering data, experimental facilities, and computational simulations. The NEESgrid project involved participants from three distinct professional cultures: civil engineering, computer science, and program managers at the National Science Foundation (NSF). Using Hofstede's categories, we demonstrate how miscommunication arising from orthogonal orientations on Hofstede's dimensions complicated leadership within the NEESgrid team. In particular, NEESgrid succeeded only when the leadership shifted from cyberinfrastructure developers to civil engineers. In the discussion we consider why this leadership succession worked and suggest general leadership principles that will help future cyberinfrastructure projects avoid the problems we observed within the NEESgrid effort.

Geographically distributed project teams repeatedly experience difficulties when compared with their collocated counterparts (e.g., Cummings & Kiesler,

2003; Herbsleb, Mockus, Finholt, & Grinter, 2001; 2002; Jarvenpaa & Leidner, 1999; Olson & Olson, 2000). For example, the visibility and informal communication afforded by collocation can dramatically increase team effectiveness through constant monitoring of and participation in coworkers' activities (Teasley, Covi, Krishnan, & Olson, 2000; 2002). Another benefit of collocation is that workers have or develop shared cultural orientations, such as similar attitudes toward risk, equality, and collectivism (Hofstede, 1980). These shared orientations can play an important role in team members' ability to communicate and work effectively by creating a common ground for interpreting others' actions and statements (Clark, 1996). In the absence of common ground, communication breaks down with corresponding reductions in levels of trust and performance. Specifically, we believe that the dysfunction observed in the NEESgird project was in large part a result of diminished common ground among the project participants. The lack of common ground was exacerbated by conflicting cultural orientations among the target users of NEESgrid (civil engineers), the funders of NEESgrid (NSF program officers), and the initial NEESgrid leadership (cyberinfrastructure developers).

RESEARCH CONTEXT AND METHODS:
AN EXPERIENTIAL CASE STUDY

The creation of NEES was an $89 million cyberinfrastructure project funded by the NSF engineering directorate. Cyberinfrastructure is a concept used to describe the combination of computers, networks, services, and applications that scientists and engineers increasingly rely on to conduct their research (Atkins et al., 2003). In the NEES case, the cyberinfrastructure activity focused on a $10 million effort over the period 2001–4 to build NEESgrid. NEESgrid was envisioned to be a collaboratory for earthquake engineering, where a collaboratory uses cyberinfrastructure to join resources (e.g., instruments), people, and data via computer-supported systems (Finholt, 2003).

In addition to NEESgrid, during the development phase, NEES consisted of two other critical elements. First, $66 million went to construct 16 new earthquake engineering research laboratories at 15 universities. Figure 10–1 shows the location and capabilities of these new labs. Second, $3 million went to the Consortium for University Research in Earthquake Engineering to build and launch the NEES Consortium, Inc., or the nonprofit entity that NSF would fund over the period 2004–14 to maintain and operate the NEES systems. As of October 1, 2004, operational control of NEES passed to the NEES Consortium, and the grand opening ceremony for NEES was held on November 15, 2004.

Our role in the NEES program was to investigate and enumerate the user requirements for NEESgrid. Thus, we were an interface between the earthquake engineers (the target users of the system), the NSF program managers (the funders), and the cyberinfrastructure developers (the system integrators

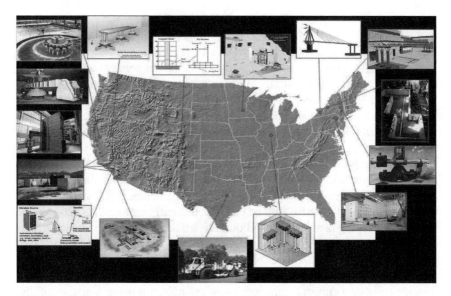

FIGURE 10–1.   Type and geographic distribution of the sixteen NEES sites.

and initial leaders of the NEESgrid team). In the process of gathering user requirements during the period 2000–3, we attended 10 national meetings and workshops of engineers, program managers, and cyberinfrastructure developers; attended six site reviews of the project by an independent panel; and participated in weekly videoconferences on the progress of the project with engineers, developers, and program managers. We also visited each of the 15 NEES equipment sites and conducted over 75 semistructured interviews with earthquake engineers, and conducted four national surveys of communication and collaboration practices within the earthquake engineering (EE) community. All of our data gathering activities were approved by the behavioral science institutional review board (i.e., human subjects) at the University of Michigan. All data collection, observation, and interviews were conducted with the informed consent of the NEES participants. Through these activities we had many opportunities to observe key participants in the NEES program and to catalog various breakdowns of communication and trust.

The conclusions drawn from the data are our own and do not reflect official positions of the leadership of the various NEES projects or of the National Science Foundation. The object of our analysis is to highlight general problems that can arise in interdisciplinary collaborations around the development of cyberinfrastructure and not to cast blame on specific individuals or groups. Finally, consistent with ethical social science research practice, we have removed any information that might identify specific individuals or groups.

CULTURAL ORIENTATION

In his famous analysis, Hofstede (1980, 1991), proposed four fundamental dimensions—uncertainty avoidance, power distance, gender, and individualism—that reliably differentiate national cultures. With some modest adjustment, these same dimensions can be used to describe differences in what might be called "professional cultures." Professional cultures are to people who work and were socialized in different fields as national cultures are to people who live and were socialized in different countries. In this case, we argue that the NEES project brought together participants from three areas of work, each area with its own unique professional culture (i.e., earthquake engineers, NSF program managers, and cyberinfrastructure developers). Despite broad endorsement of NEES by all participants, early interactions between the main groups were problematic and quickly led to mistrust.

Difficulties in NEES had the character of a "first contact gone awry." That is, in accounts of European exploration in the New World (e.g., Diamond, 2004; Ruby, 2001), a recurring theme is the inability of the Europeans to step outside their own cultural framework—with one result being a history of disastrous relations with native populations, such as the struggle (a depiction of first contact between the English explorer Frobisher and Inuit natives). Similarly, in the NEES project, representatives of the three key groups entered their initial collaborations assuming a common worldview. Subsequent discovery of divergent perspectives was initially a cause of communication failures and later the basis for open hostility. Hofstede's dimensions, when applied to the professional cultures represented in NEES, provide a helpful starting place for understanding why the start of the NEES project was so hard—and also why changes to the project over time eventually corrected some of the early problems and increased the likelihood of success.

While Hofstede provides four dimensions on which cultures can be distinguished, we found two of these to be particularly relevant in characterizing the NEES participants:

- Uncertainty avoidance: The extent to which individuals take steps to control risk and the unknown.
- Power distance: The extent to which individuals prefer formal and hierarchical relationships compared to more informal and egalitarian relationships.

The subsections that follow characterize each type of NEES participant according to these two dimensions with particular attention to how groups differed and how these differences led to negative consequences for project development.

Earthquake Engineers

Earthquake engineering is concerned with the seismic performance of the built environment (Sims, 1999). The research work of EEs typically consists of experiments conducted on large, physical models of buildings, bridges, and soil retaining structures (e.g., retaining walls, building foundations) that are outfitted with hundreds of sensors that record details of strain and motion in simulated earthquakes generated by means of large shaking platforms or hydraulic actuators. EE researchers are trained as civil engineers (and many are certified as professional engineers) and tend to apply computational simulations in support of physical simulations (rather than as substitutes, which is to say there isn't any analog yet in EE research for the computationally based subdisciplines that have emerged in other fields, such as computational chemistry or biology).

Uncertainty Avoidance. Earthquake engineers generally seek to avoid or control uncertainty. Experimental specimens in EE are typically built of steel or reinforced concrete, as are the real-world structures that these specimens represent. Such materials are difficult to modify once constructed, and there is therefore a tremendous amount of planning and analysis that goes into the design of an experimental specimen. Uncertainty, and the accompanying potential for changes, errors, and unpredictable structural behavior, are thus seen as significant potential liabilities in this community and are actively avoided. This risk aversion in experimental work is indicative of a generally conservative orientation among earthquake engineers that makes them suspicious of tools and methods that are new and untested.

Power Distance. Earthquake engineering is generally distinguished by high power distance. Among earthquake engineers there is a tendency to defer to authority figures both within local laboratories and in the field more generally. Power distance is reflected at the field level in the distribution of experimental apparatus. A small number of large-scale facilities define a clear set of elite institutions that are better ranked (e.g., by the National Research Council), publish more, obtain more funding, and attract better graduate students. At the local level power distance is reflected in the division of labor in the laboratories with some tasks clearly intended for masters-level students versus doctoral students versus technical staff and faculty. Additionally, graduate students work primarily on projects initiated and led by their advisors, rather than on projects they devise independently.

Cyberinfrastructure Developers

The NEES cyberinfrastructure development effort was based on a number of open source software codes, notably those needed to enable "grid-based" systems

(Foster & Kesselman, 1999). As a result, although not strictly an open source project, NEES developers did resemble open source programmers described elsewhere (DiBona, Ockman, & Stone, 1999). In other words, they exhibited an egalitarian orientation with a preference for informal organization.

Uncertainty Avoidance. The cyberinfrastructure developers were not risk averse and can therefore be characterized as low on the uncertainty avoidance dimension. Specifically, the developers worked using spiral software development models (Boehm, 1995) that advocated rapid iteration and prototyping. The spiral approach encourages risk taking and sometimes underspecified development activities because it is assumed that problems can be eliminated in the next iteration, which is never far away and does not have a high cost. Thus there was little perceived need to eliminate uncertainty early in the project because errors were expected and would be addressed in the subsequent development cycles. This is captured well in one of the NEES software developers' frequent use of the motto "don't worry, be crappy" to describe the incremental approach to risk inherent in the spiral model.

Power Distance. Power distance among cyberinfrastructure developers was low. Individual programmers often had broad latitude to determine how to proceed with development, provided they remained consistent with overarching design directions. Furthermore, in interactions among the developers, people participated largely independent of their status or seniority with the exception of sometimes deferring to others with deeper technical expertise.

NSF Program Managers

Program officers in the National Science Foundation are responsible for overseeing the distribution and management of resources in ways that promote the goals of the foundation. With much grant-based research, this tends to be accomplished via a reasonably "hands-off" approach. NEES, however, differed from typical grants in critical respects. First, NEES was a high profile project in terms of funding level and was awarded as a "cooperative agreement" which imposed a higher than typical oversight burden on NSF. Second, NEES was the first major research equipment and facility construction (MREFC) project in the engineering directorate. MREFC projects are line items in the NSF appropriation and are therefore subject to special congressional scrutiny. And finally, NEES was the first attempt by NSF to build a network of facilities linked by cyberinfrastructure and intended to be operated primarily as a collaboratory.

Uncertainty Avoidance. Uncertainty avoidance was high among the NSF managers. First, many came from the earthquake engineering and civil engineering cultures and shared the pervasive risk aversion of colleagues from these communities. Second, because of the cost and visibility of NEES, the stakes were quite high for individual managers, particularly in terms of career advancement.

Power Distance. Power distance among the NSF managers was high. That is, particularly because of the cooperative agreement governing NEES, NSF managers intervened more actively in the conduct of the project. Because this differed from the usual experience with grant-based research, NEES investigators chafed under the closer scrutiny of the NSF staff. For example, rather than the collegial relationship characteristic of grant-based activity, the cooperative agreement created a hierarchical relationship. In some cases, particularly around NSF requests for documentation and justification, NEES investigators felt they were treated as subordinates or mere contractors rather than as leading researchers in computer science or earthquake engineering

Consequences of Cultural Differences

One episode that illustrated the gulf between earthquake engineers and cyberinfrastructure developers emerged around the release of the initial user requirements report by the cyberinfrastructure development team. The report, grounded in the principles of user-centered design and based on substantial interview and survey data, outlined at a high level the comprehensive user requirements for the NEESgrid collaboratory. The earthquake engineers were almost universally disappointed with the user requirements report. Specifically, the earthquake engineers and the cyberinfrastructure developers had divergent notions of what constitute "requirements" that at least partially reflected differences in their professional cultures.

The engineering notion of requirements was specific with detailed characterization of functionality, implementation, and relationship to other requirements. This approach to user requirements was consistent with both the engineers' cultural bias against uncertainty and their preference for formal and hierarchical relationships. That is, a precise and exhaustive requirements document early in a project allows for elimination of potential problems and for clear division of labor. The cyberinfrastructure developers, on the other hand, had a less rigid view of requirements. The spiral development model they adopted suggested that it would be difficult or impossible to resolve all uncertainties early on, so the best approach was to specify requirements at a high level, implement to satisfy these initial requirements, and then iterate to improve both requirements specification and implementation. This approach struck the earthquake engineers as sloppy and unnecessarily risky. Differences about the meaning of requirements served to create a rift between the developers and earthquake engineers because neither side believed the other knew what "requirements" were or how to correctly document them. This fostered mistrust and vastly increased the need for communication and bridge-building between the communities. Similar conflict and dysfunction between engineers and physicists is discussed by Galison (1997) in his discussion of the increasingly complex design and construction of particle accelerators.

Another episode that underlined the difficulty of negotiating cultural differences among the NEES players was the emergency "all hands" meeting convened by NSF program managers just a few months after the project began. The primary issue at this meeting was a misunderstanding over the nature of project deliverables. The cyberinfrastructure developers argued that they had received funding to produce a set of grid-based telecontrol protocols and Application Program Interfaces (API's) for integrating equipment at different laboratories and for providing telepresence functionality (i.e., the ability to remotely observe and control laboratory equipment). The earthquake engineers, and to some extent the NSF program managers, thought they were getting a turn-key system and were shocked to learn that they would have to hire programmers and learn to use API's in order to make the NEES system functional. After one long discussion in which the cyberinfrastructure developers fended off a growing list of deliverables as "out of scope," a disgusted earthquake engineer observed of the cyberinfrastructure developers that "we wouldn't buy a used car from you guys," reflecting the sense that, with respect to NEESgrid, the engineers had been sold a "lemon."

Again, this conflict can be explained along cultural lines. The desire of the earthquake engineers to avoid costly uncertainty explains the extent to which they bristled at the surprising discovery of what they perceived as the deficient scope of the cyberinfrastructure development activity. Similarly, the response of the cyberinfrastructure developers reflected their cultural orientation toward maintaining flexibility to address interesting issues as they arose rather than being firmly committed to carry out tasks that might prove to be dead ends or time sinks. One measure of the cultural disconnect between the two sides was that at this meeting, and other subsequent sessions, the cyberinfrastructure developers brushed off the engineers' concerns (often using humor), not realizing the growing irritation on the part of the engineers. Specifically, at a moment when both sides needed to develop common ground, their cultural dispositions caused them to dig in and oppose each other. At this point, NSF program managers understood that significant steps were needed to bridge the deepening cultural gulfs and unite the team around a shared understanding and interpretive framework.

LEADERSHIP: BRINGING THE GROUP TOGETHER

After a problematic start to the NEES development and deployment, key players from each of the participating groups explored and adopted strategies to help overcome cultural differences. Many of these strategies involved participants stepping forward to exercise leadership. First, there was a general agreement that all parties needed more opportunities to communicate informally and in real time. One important step, therefore, was taken halfway through the first year of NEES development when a set of cyberinfrastructure developers, earthquake engineers, and NSF program managers took the initiative to convene a weekly multipoint videoconference (Hofer, Finholt, Hajjar, & Reinhorn, 2004). The format of these conferences allowed for presentation and discussion of a specific concern each week along with some time for general discussion. Responsibility for these meetings was traded off between the earthquake engineers and the cyberinfrastructure developers. These weekly conferences were widely viewed as tremendously helpful in getting the NEES project participants to understand each other better and to negotiate a shared understanding of the project.

A second strategy for overcoming cultural differences involved explicit efforts to increase the diversity of the overall project leadership. For the first two years, the project directors for the NEES collaboratory effort were part of the cyberinfrastructure development team and strongly aligned with the computer science culture. As the project progressed and relations between groups became more strained, the lack of a strong earthquake engineering voice in the NEESgrid development process became a focus for criticism from both earthquake engineers and the NSF program managers. This motivated a critical leadership change at the start of the third year of the project. The new leader of the collaboratory effort was a prominent earthquake engineer who was affiliated with the same university as much of the development team and had cultivated strong relationships with all three communities. This had a tremendously positive impact on relations between the participating groups in ways that are important for the present discussion of leadership. In particular, the new project director was able to do two things.

First, he was able to utilize his existing relationships with key players in all three communities and serve as a translator or broker between the groups. When one group made demands of another that were perceived as "unreasonable," for example, the new project leader was able to talk with members of both groups and negotiate an effective solution. In his review of similar approaches in the high-energy physics community, Birnholtz (2006) observes that this is called "managing by having coffee." This broker–translator function also proved useful when the development team presented ideas to the earthquake engineers and the NSF program managers. These ideas could be run past the new director, to gauge their likely reaction, or they could even presented by him to avoid potential conflict. A key component of this broker–translator role is the notion of what might be called "translated awareness." As was noted above, awareness information and communication exchanged between the three groups prior to the changed management approach were largely used in negative ways that hindered the project. One key role of the new project leader was to help all groups interpret and use this information in more productive ways. In part, of course, this was a function of increased opportunities (e.g., the weekly videoconferences) for informal interaction. At the same time, however, it was up to the new project director to help all three groups stay focused on shared goals.

Second, the new project director provided the earthquake engineers (and, to a lesser extent, the NSF program managers with whom he had a strong relationship) with an important sense of representation on the development team. As the "we wouldn't buy a used car from you guys" comment mentioned earlier strongly suggests, there was a great deal of mistrust between the earthquake engineers and the cyberinfrastructure developers. This stemmed, in part, from the fact that the engineers felt their interests were not well represented on the NEESgrid development team and that the cyberinfrastructure developers did not share the engineers' interests. In particular, this was fueled by the developers' desire to carry out "interesting" computer science tasks (such as the development of novel technologies and APIs) and define the more mundane tasks, such as figuring out how to make the software work with existing lab equipment, as "out of scope." Having an earthquake engineer leading the project gave the earthquake engineers a much stronger sense that their interests were being represented. Given the existing strong relationship between the new project leader and the development team, the developers generally did not feel that they were being "infiltrated" or lead by an outsider. Under different circumstances, though, this could clearly be cause for concern.

LESSONS LEARNED FROM THE NEES EXPERIENCE

We believe the experience with NEES during the period 2001–4 offers a set of general lessons that can be applied to other collaborative, multisite, multidisciplinary projects.

First, we have shown the role that significant differences in professional culture played in complicating the development of NEESgrid. These cultural gaps meant that even when information was communicated in seemingly objective ways common to project management (i.e., reports, requirements documents), this information was interpreted differently by the different groups involved in the project. In some cases this was detrimental to the progress of the project. This suggests that in carrying out projects that involve communities that may come from different professional cultures, it is important to identify cultural gaps. We found Hofstede's (1980) framework helpful in this analysis, but additional dimensions of culture may prove useful in other settings. This is an area ripe for future work, as multidisciplinary collaboration becomes increasingly common in research.

Second, we observed the importance of strong leadership in bridging these cultural gaps, once they had been identified. The new project leader in this case had two critical functions. First, he was able to leverage strong relationships with key players in all groups to act as a translator and broker between the groups, thereby ensuring that communicated information did not contribute to the "vicious cycle" identified here. That is, effective leadership helped the participating groups to constructively utilize shared information rather than to continue to view this information as evidence of deficiencies on the part of the other groups. Second, he increased the representative nature of the project leadership team by simultaneously being a part of the earthquake engineering and development teams. This gave the earthquake engineers the important sense that their needs and interests were being taken into consideration by the cyberinfrastructure developers and, for the same reason, afforded increased legitimacy to the development team in the eyes of the earthquake engineers.

Third, we observed the importance of not just formal project-related communication and encouragement but informal communication and negotiation as well. The cultural gaps between groups involved in the project meant that additional opportunities for interaction were necessary to ensure that the groups understood each other. This communication was encouraged by the new project leadership.

CONCLUSION

This chapter highlights professional culture conflict as an important and largely unexplored source of risk in multidisciplinary project initiatives, particularly with regard to cyberinfrastructure. Because this project involved the blending of effort between cyberinfrastructure developers and one or more communities of domain scientists or engineers, there was a greater than normal chance for misunderstanding and mistrust arising from cultural differences. Furthermore, because of the cost and visibility of this and other cyberinfrastructure projects, federal program managers may typically represent a third cultural perspective, often at odds with the other perspectives. As the preceding sections have shown, failure to understand and accommodate cultural differences can result in awkward first contacts and subsequent difficulty in building understanding and confidence among participants from separate professional cultures. We have described some of the steps taken to overcome cultural barriers in the NEES project and then use these experiences to describe a general set of lessons learned that can help other cyberinfrastructure efforts to avoid repeating the NEES mistakes.

ACKNOWLEDGMENTS

The work described in this chapter was supported in part or in full by the National Science Foundation under grants CMS 0117853. We are grateful for the assistance and advice from our colleagues on the NEESgrid project, particularly Randy Butler, Joseph Hardin, Dan Horn, Chuck Severance, and Bill Spencer. In addition, we appreciate the insights shared by the members of the earthquake engineering community.

REFERENCES

Atkins, D. E., Droegemeier, K., Feldman, S., Garcia-Molina, H., Klein, M. L., Messerschmitt, D. G., et al. (2003). *Revolutionizing science and engineering through cyberinfrastructure: Report of the National Science Foundation blue-ribbon advisory panel on cyberinfrastructure.* Arlington, VA: National Science Foundation.
Birnholtz, J. P. (2006). "What Does It Mean To Be An Author? The Intersection of Credit, Contribution and Collaboration in Science," *Journal of the American Society for Information Science and Technology, 57*(13), 1758–1770.
Boehm, B. W. (1995). A spiral model of software development and enhancement. In R. M. Baecker, J. Grudin, W. A. S. Buxton, & S. Greenberg (eds.) *Human computer interaction: Toward the year 2000.* San Francisco, CA: Morgan Kaufman.
Clark, H. H. (1996). *Using language.* New York: Cambridge University Press.
Connaughton, S. L., & Daly, J. A. (2005). Leadership in the new millennium: Communicating beyond temporal, spatial and geographic boundaries, *Communication Yearbook, 29*, 187–213.
Cummings, J., & Kiesler, S. (2003). *KDI initiative: Multidisciplinary scientific collaborations.* Arlington, VA: National Science Foundation.
Diamond, J. (2004). *Collapse: How societies choose to fail or succeed.* New York: Viking.
DiBona, C., Ockman, S., & Stone, M. (1999). *Open Sources: Voices from the Open Source Revolution.* Cambridge, MA: O'Reilly.
Finholt, T. A. (2003). Collaboratories as a new form of scientific organization. *Economics of Innovation and New Technologies, 12*(1), 5–25.
Foster, I., & Kesselman, C. (1999). *The grid: Blueprint for a new computing infrastructure.* San Francisco, CA: Morgan Kaufmann.
Galison, P. L. (1997). *Image and logic: A material culture of microphysics.* Chicago: University of Chicago Press.
Herbsleb, J. D., Mockus, A., Finholt, T. A., & Grinter, R. E. (2001). An empirical study of global software development: Distance and speed. In *Proceedings of ICSE 2001* (pp. 81–90). Washington, D.C.: IEEE Press.
Herbsleb, J. D., Mockus, A., Finholt, T. A., & Grinter, R. E. (2002). Distance, dependencies, and delay in a global collaboration. In *Proceedings of CSCW 2002* (pp. 319–328). New York: ACM Press.
Hofer, E. C., Finholt, T. A., Hajjar, J., & Reinhorn, A. (2004). The Internet2 Commons: Supporting Distributed Engineering Collaboration. *Syllabus Magazine* (January).
Hofstede, G. (1980). *Culture's consequences.* Newbury Park, CA: Sage Publications.
Hofstede, G. (1991). *Cultures and organizations: Software of the mind.* London: McGraw-Hill.
Jarvenpaa, S. L., & Leidner, D. E. (1999). Communication and trust in global virtual teams. *Organization Science, 10*, 791–815.
Olson, G. M., & Olson, J. S. (2000). "Distance matters." *Human-Computer Interaction, 15*(2/3), 139–178.

Ruby, R. (2001). Unknown shore: The lost history of England's arctic colony. New York: Henry Holt & Company.

Sims, B. (1999). Concrete Practices: Testing in an Earthquake Engineering Laboratory. *Social Studies of Science, 29*(4), 483–518.

Teasley, S. D., Covi, L., Krishnan, M. S., & Olson, J. S. (2000). How does radical collocation help a team succeed? In *Proceedings of CSCW 2000* (pp. 339–346). New York: ACM Press.

Teasley, S. D., Covi, L., Krishnan, M. S., & Olson, J. S. (2002). Rapid software development through team collocation. *Transactions on Software Engineering, 28*(7), 671–683.

11

Trial by Water: Creating Hurricane Katrina "Person Locator" Web Sites

Christopher Scaffidi and Mary Shaw
Institute for Software Research, International

Brad Myers
Carnegie Mellon University

OVERVIEW

We interviewed six people who led teams that created web sites enabling Hurricane Katrina survivors to report their status. We learned that interviewees did not discover and communicate with other teams when they started their projects, which resulted in redundant sites. The absence of a shared task impeded trust between teams, ultimately inhibiting data collection and aggregation. Moreover, communication within teams was problematic; developers who had adequate technical skills to work alone were more positive about their sites' success compared to developers who had to shore up skill weaknesses through collaboration. These problems did not simply result from team leaders' oversized egos because site creators were generally motivated by concern for other people instead of self-interest. Rather, these problems highlight the need for improved development methods and systems to help developers discover and communicate with other teams' leaders in order to collaborate on widely distributed, time-critical projects.

A shorter version of this work previously appeared as C. Scaffidi, B. Myers, and M. Shaw. Challenges, Motivations, and Success Factors in the Creation of Hurricane Katrina "Person Locator" Web Sites, *Psychology of Programming Interest Group (unpublished workshop)*, 2006.

On August 29, 2005, Hurricane Katrina made landfall near New Orleans, Louisiana. The storm breached levees, cut off phone and electricity service, flooded homes, and displaced hundreds of thousands of people throughout the Gulf Coast. In this tragedy's wake, people turned to the web to learn whether friends and family had survived and, if so, where they took shelter. To assist in this search, dozens of people led teams that created websites so users could store and retrieve data related to survivors' locations. The decision to lead these teams required significant investments of time, emotions, and skills. These leaders' efforts proved instrumental in reassuring and reconnecting many people.

We interviewed the creators of six Hurricane Katrina sites (HKS) to investigate two primary issues: What challenges did they encounter? What factors motivated their volunteerism and contributed to success? Because HKS creators operated under tighter time pressure than other volunteer software developers (for example, in the open source community), we anticipated that interviewees would provide unique answers to the questions here.

Next, we summarize our sample and method. Following that, we describe challenges to helping users locate people, and then we focus on related data quality issues. We then discuss interviewees' motivations, which differed somewhat from motivations of volunteer software developers in the open source community, followed by our analysis of success factors. Finally, we outline opportunities for future research aimed at facilitating highly distributed, time-critical software development.

SAMPLE AND METHOD

Our research group's objective is to help "nonprofessional programmers" with minimal training effectively create software such as web applications. Therefore, rather than interviewing every HKS creator, we wished to focus on sites that appeared to have been constructed by volunteers on a tight budget without the sponsorship of a large corporation.

Consequently, of 22 sites located using search engines, we narrowed our interest to those that did not display any corporate sponsors' logos, had only a few pages, and lacked fancy graphics. Combining these criteria yielded 10 sites. In addition, we targeted one "aggregator" site that consolidated other sites' records; we included this site because a companion Wiki site displayed numerous postings from volunteers who had worked on this site. As will be discussed below, each site contained records for hundreds to thousands of hurricane survivors. We regularly browsed the 11 sites from September through December 2005 and screen-captured many pages on November 29, 2005, in the event that teams took their sites down.

We used DNS registration and information on the sites to determine each site owner's email address and phone number. Six HKS creators agreed to participate in one 30-minute semi-structured telephone interview each between

November 4 and November 11. We tailored questions to address our primary focus: motivation and success factors.

We performed cross-case analysis by question to identify common concepts mentioned by respondents. Based on question-level commonalities, we coded responses into a matrix (respondents on rows and questions on columns) to identify patterns spanning questions. We reviewed preliminary findings and raw data with another researcher from outside our group to verify that the data adequately and consistently supported our findings.

Experiences of HKS Creators

HKS creators' first spur to action was a sense of chaos. One watched television, another read a blog, a third got a phone call, a fourth was unable to complete a phone call; they each realized that hundreds of thousands of people were fearing for one another and unsuccessfully searching for loved ones.

By August 31, one interviewee had created a PHP-based site with web forms that visitors could use to store location information in a publicly viewable database. Over the next four days, two more PHP-based sites and one blog-based site came up.

At this point, interviewees were unaware of one another's sites; they simply took the tools that they knew—PHP[1] or blog—and built as fast as they could. They sought simplicity in design. For example, the blog lacked a web form for posting information; users had to email the blog's owner so he could post the information. Some interviewees did not plan, build, or host their site entirely on their own but rather sought help.

These sites drew an overwhelming response. One site received over 9,000 unique visitors per day for the first week; another had traffic exceeding 60 MB/second during the same period, tapering off over a month. Testimonials poured in through email and sites' "Contact Us" forms. HKS creators happily posted some notes online, such as "Thank You!!!!!!!!!!!!!!!! Thanks for your site. . . . Out of 10 people, seven so far are fine, and found thanks to you!"

Sadly, not all notes to HKS creators were joyful. Many interviewees spent most of their waking hours answering hundreds of messages from site visitors asking about loved ones. HKS creators could tell them no more than the information already posted on the site, and the frustration and long hours gradually took an emotional toll. One person described the experience as "playing the role of counselor," while another "was in bad shape" and "wasn't well." He compared it to the creation of a similar site after September 11, which "also ate my life for a couple of weeks."

---

[1]http://php.net/

Three main challenges made it hard for HKS creators to help users find each other:

- Users had to search dozens of person locator sites.
- HKS creators had to fend off requests by distrusted aggregators for databases.
- Infrastructure damage impeded getting data out of hurricane-stricken areas.

Redundant Sites.   Users had to search dozens of person locator sites, each of which had a unique user interface and database. Unfortunately, HKS creators had no way to know that other people were in the process of creating sites. Even search engines, the best existing tools for locating websites, were of little use immediately after this disaster because they take time to "notice" new sites as they crawl the web. Interviewees who asked the media to advertise their sites were generally disappointed. In fact, one HKS creator mentioned that when he told radio and television stations about the site, they each opted to create an HKS of their own! (Fortunately, bloggers, newspapers, and government agencies advertised sites over the course of several weeks.)

Recognizing these inefficiencies, two interviewees collaborated with other people to build a site that aggregated data from many other sites; this site went live on September 5. In addition, one of these two interviewees also contributed to a second site that published an XML standard related to the aggregator site. The aggregator site was Java-based; the XML site was static HTML.

Whereas earlier person locator sites grew as visitors manually entered data, aggregators tried to populate their site automatically using screen-scraper scripts that read data off older sites. Some source sites, particularly those based on free-text tools like blogs,[2] were not amenable to this approach; in this case, aggregators browsed those sites and manually copied data items from old sites into the new site. (The new site also had a page where owners of older sites could upload XML containing data, although they did not use this page as heavily as anticipated.)

Distrusted Aggregators.   Three interviewees said the biggest challenge was fending off requests by aggregators for databases. They primarily resisted sharing with aggregators to protect their users' privacy. Not to be dissuaded, aggregators screen scraped to acquire data. (Ironically, one of the three interviewees who complained about aggregators was himself an aggregator, and his

---

[2]For an overview of blogging, see http://en.wikipedia.org/wiki/Blog

team was eventually threatened with a lawsuit because they had aggregated data from a site without permission.)

One illustrative case was a nonprofit organization that requested data from these three interviewees. In addition to a desire to protect their users' privacy, the HKS creators refused to share data because they perceived the organization's staff as unresponsive to questions, technically incompetent, and generally pushy. Moreover, interviewees felt that the organization's HKS was too late to be useful, not user-friendly, and lacking in search features. The HKS creators' resistance is understandable because their interactions with this organization lacked the five ingredients necessary for trust in distributed virtual teams: enthusiastic social communication, competent and timely responses, individual initiative and leadership, focus on a shared task, and a cool reaction to crisis (Jarvenpaa & Leidner, 1999). Without these ingredients, the relationships between HKS creators and the nonprofit organization soon grew antagonistic.

Broken Infrastructure. Although getting content for web sites is a common complaint among web application developers (Rosson, Ballin, Rode, & Toward, 2005), this challenge was exacerbated by a lack of infrastructure for getting data out of hurricane-stricken areas. Many shelters lacked computers, and some even lacked phone service for modems. In response, two teams sent volunteers to shelters to relay information and photos using cell phones. Compounding the problem, one HKS creator said that some shelters strangely kicked out these volunteers to protect the survivors' privacy, even though the survivors apparently welcomed the chance to report their whereabouts.

Discussion of Experiences. Interviewees were unable to discover and communicate with one another at the inception of their projects. This led to redundant sites. The ongoing absence of a shared task and good communication produced distrust between groups. This inhibited data aggregation as well as data collection from places where in-person data collection was necessary due to infrastructure damage. Later, we will return to this theme and expand upon it.

Aggregating a Mishmash of Data

Two interviewees responded to the plethora of redundant sites by leading a team that created scraper software to aggregate many sites into a single database. The team ran into data quality issues that prevented automatically scraping some sites; although scrapers processed over 500,000 records, volunteers had to type in another 100,000 manually. Hundreds of volunteers worked many hours each day for several weeks to achieve this. Not surprisingly, the labor took a physical toll, leading one person to write on the aggregator email list that he was "taking it light today due to CTS [carpal tunnel syndrome]. . . . My hand is hurting today in a big ugly way."

In short, these data quality issues made aggregating sites much more difficult. Whereas the three challenges addressed by the previous section represented general challenges to helping users find survivors, the following three data quality issues were specific to aggregating data.

Using Invalid Data.   HKS creators of the source sites generally did not implement much validation on their respective web forms. One writer on the aggregators' email distribution list recognized that this "loosey goosey data entry strategy" was suitable for getting sites up fast, and one HKS creator indicated that he intentionally omitted input validation in order to provide end users with maximal flexibility.

Unfortunately, the lack of validation on the source sites led to semantic errors that scrapers carried over into the aggregate database. For example, one end user put "12 Years old" into an "address" field on one site, which a scraper copied into the aggregate database. Repairing errors like these required manual labor.

Reformatting Fields.   Because each source site was built independently from the others, they used differing data formats. Moreover, data sometimes varied in format within each site. In effect, volunteers had to write a custom scraper program to read fields from each source site and transform them into a common format before inserting into fields of a uniform XML schema.

For example, one site used the format "09.04.2005" for dates, while another used "9/10/2005 11:41:17 A.M.," and still another used "2005-09-04 12:10:02." A few source sites had RSS data export features (and so did not require scraping raw HTML), but even these had varying formats (e.g., "22 Oct 2005 15:38:07"). The custom scrapers transformed each date/time field into the format "2005-09-03T09:21:12Z" before inserting it into corresponding date/time field of the common XML schema. However, in addition to specific date/time fields, the XML standard had freeform "notes" fields, and these fields still ended up containing embedded date/times in arbitrary formats such as "09/10/05 05:25 P.M."

Other types of data also varied in format, and scrapers generally did not reformat these into a common format. For example, most scrapers did not attempt to fix capitalization errors on names, and some even introduced errors related to character encoding (e.g., turning "O'Neal" into "O27Neal," by replacing the apostrophe with its Unicode equivalent, hex 27).

Finding Duplicate Records.   Because names could appear in a variety of formats, it was sometimes difficult to determine whether entries on different sites or within the same site referred to the same person: Is "Michael Smith" the same person as "Mike Smith?" This greatly inhibited automatically re-moving duplicate records. One interviewee from the aggregator project took the philosophy "Don't worry about dups," thus burdening end users with the job of mentally weeding out duplicates. On the other hand, another intervie-wee said that data entry volunteers often manually found and removed dupli-cates. Although they differed in their response, these two interviewees agreed that no good mechanism was available for automatically finding duplicates.

Discussion of Validition.   We believe that HKS and scraper creators omitted validation, in part, because it would have taken too much effort to implement high-quality validation. Consider, for example, how hard it would be to catch subtle errors like "12 Years old" in an address field.

Moreover, some HKS creators stated that validation would limit end users' flexibility. We believe this highlights the need for a new approach to web form validation that would deter end users from entering certain values yet would not forbid those values outright. For example, the validation code might detect a potentially erroneous input and display a popup asking, "This value does not have the expected format. Are you sure you meant to enter it?" Such an approach is attractive when errors are undesirable but erroneous data is preferable to no data at all. Suggestive validation of this sort is uncommon on the web, and HKS creators apparently did not consider it.

The diversity of data formats resulted from the lack of validation and the plethora of redundant websites. We believe that the ensuing mishmash under-scores the need for an easy way to transform data types automatically from one format to another. This would also help with the problem of finding du-plicates because scripts could automatically transform values into a common format to permit testing for equality.

Motivations of HKS Creators

What motivated interviewees to create and aggregate sites and to endure the difficulties described above? While analyzing the data, we recognized that HKS developers demonstrated a subset of the motivations demonstrated by open source software (OSS) developers, which is reasonable because volun-teer developers compose both groups. However, some differences did appear, chiefly the fact that OSS creators demonstrated more self-interested motiva-tions than HKS developers did.

Differences.   Certain OSS motivations were not very visible in inter-views with HKS creators. For example, whereas some OSS developers created software for their own use and then incidentally shared it as OSS (Lakhani & Wolf, 2005), only one interviewee hoped to make personal use of the site (be-cause his sister was lost).

In addition, some developers contributed to OSS projects because their companies paid them to do so (Lakhani & Wolf, 2005). Likewise, in general, most web developers have started projects because it was part of their job (Rosson et al., 2005). In contrast, only one HKS interviewee initiated his site because he worked for a company with a stated corporate goal of disaster relief.

Several OSS motivations were entirely absent in interviews. For instance, opportunity to learn has been a strong motivator for OSS creation (Lakhani & von Hippel, 2003) and web development in general (Rosson et al., 2005), but it did not appear to motivate HKS creators because none mentioned using new skills or tools during HKS projects.

In addition, developers were often motivated by enjoyment from coding OSS, mainly for intellectual stimulation lacking in day-to-day work (Lakhani & Wolf, 2005). In general, some web developers have created web applications for recreation (Rosson et al., 2005). In contrast, no interviewee mentioned such stimulation or enjoyment—indeed, four handed off some coding to other people, and answering fearful emails was anything but stimulating.

Finally, desires for reciprocal OSS and reputation among peers have motivated OSS developers (Lakhani & Wolf, 2005). HKS creators apparently had little concern for reputation: Most did not post their identities in an obvious place but instead provided anonymous-looking email addresses or "Contact Us" forms. Moreover, none mentioned reciprocity or reputation during interviews. Indeed, one said humility and "not taking credit" was a key to successful collaboration.

Similarities. HKS and OSS creators' motivations were not entirely different. For example, many OSS developers valued benefiting "the good of the group" and "helping the cause" (Lakhani & von Hippel, 2003). When asked what prompted them to create HKS, all interviewees cited other peoples' needs. Specifically, four HKS creators focused on the absence of "person locator" sites; three made comments like "there was no one system people could refer to." However, although these may be important HKS and OSS motivators, civic-mindedness is not a commonly cited motivation by web developers in general (Rosson et al., 2005).

Moreover, like HKS creators, OSS developers were motivated because success at coding contributed to feelings of achievement or efficacy—"a sense that they have some effect on the environment" (Lakhani & von Hippel, 2003). To varying degrees, most interviewees took pride in their achievements. For example, two praised their site's support for heavy query load, and most expressed pride in how quickly their site was completed.

Discussion of Motivations. In general, OSS developers demonstrated a greater number of self-interested motivations compared to HKS creators. We suspect that the differences largely resulted from the fact that OSS development has typically involved a long-term commitment of many months or years whereas HKS development required an intense short-term commitment of only a few weeks aimed at addressing an urgent social need.

Of course, this is not to say that HKS creators were entirely disinterested in their own well-being. However, our interviews do suggest that some programmers may be willing to lead highly draining, sacrificial projects like HKS creation, as long as they know that the engagement will be short-lived and targeted to a significant social need.

Skills, Collaboration, and Success

Because of the wide availability of easy-to-use software such as Microsoft Access and FrontPage, we anticipated that most sites in our sample would be implemented by people with limited technical skill. Yet we knew that some tasks, such as database design, might benefit from the assistance of technically skilled workers, so we suspected that collaboration be a strong success factor.

Interviewees had varying levels of technical skill. Five worked in software development firms or computer science departments; the sixth sold retail goods. Five had created entire websites on their own in the past; the sixth could edit HTML but had always obtained graphical design help. Three had created databases on their own in the past and continued to do so at least monthly as part of their jobs. Four were managers, one was a student, and one was a graphic designer. All six had 10 to 30 years' experience using computers. One had a BS in computer science, one had an HTML tutor several years ago, and all were greatly self-taught. (All interviewees were male.)

Only two interviewees actually *implemented* the site on their own. (One had database skills; the other did not, so he used a tool that automatically generated a blog and its back-end database.) Two others coded part of the site and then had a professional programmer coworker finish it, and the remaining two just handed off requirements to programmers who implemented the HKS.

Three interviewees relied on teammates for assistance in *evaluating* what features should be present and whether the site was a viable project at all. In general, interviewees had known their fellow planners through prior shared projects. All six HKS creators relied on existing relationships when choosing where to host their sites; four hosted in-house within their respective firms, and two hosted at firms with whom they had an existing relationship.

These observations indicate that interviewees shored up their skill weaknesses through collaboration but did not develop new trust relationships during HKS projects. Yet this pattern had two exceptions. First, half of the interviewees contacted the media and bloggers by email, phone, or press release to advertise the site; most contacts with the media relied on prior relationships, some did not. Second, two sites benefited from volunteers who found the site and sought to help. Volunteers answered emails from site users, visited shelters to relay data, typed data into the site manually, or wrote scripts to populate the database automatically. (Most volunteers apparently lacked the technical skills for this last task.) The aggregator had hundreds of volunteers, so some volunteers set up an email list and Wiki to coordinate work.

A desire for a sense of accomplishment motivated many HKS creators in the first place, so perceived success may affect whether they respond to future disasters. Therefore, after we asked interviewees to state the site's primary goal, we asked whether they felt the site was a success overall; if they said it was a success, we asked why they believed it was a success. To assess if they would "do it all over again," we asked what advice they would give to two hypothetical friends who wanted to create an HKS; one "friend" had no programming experience, and the other had the same programming experience as the interviewee.

In general, the most technically skilled people expressed the most positive views on their site's success. For example, the two most skilled interviewees (who had created sites and databases in the past and coded much of their HKS) both cited high query volume and user testimonials as evidence of success. Moreover, they both would encourage their hypothetical friends to build similar sites.

In contrast, the two least skilled interviewees (neither of whom had created databases in the past nor helped implement their HKS) did not mention visitor testimonials, nor were they enthusiastic about their site's overall success. Moreover, they suggested that their hypothetical friends should collaborate with another HKS creator instead of creating their own. One moderately skilled person was happy with his site's technical capability but said it "just contributed to decentralization" overall.

Discussion of Technical Skills and Success. Several interpretations might explain the pattern described above. First, prior studies suggested that "developing an application . . . predisposes an end user developer to be more satisfied with the application than they would be if it were developed by another end user" (Lakhani & Wolf, 2005). Thus, it is possible that technically skilled HKS creators, who tended to be more involved in actually implementing their sites, were predisposed to view their work favorably.

Another reasonable interpretation is that because less technically skilled interviewees relied more on teams, they were more prone to feeling emotionally worn down through friction with other people and through a feeling that the HKS was out of control. This may have colored their view of their site's success. Among interviewees with low self-perceived success, the most commonly reported interpersonal stresses usually related to whether or how to share data with other sites. Stresses also built up within teams; for example, one organization that hosted an HKS did not trust teammates from other organizations to touch the code on the "live" site, so the hosting organization ultimately became a bottleneck when feature additions were necessary.

A final potential explanation is that existing development tools for building this type of site required significant up-front learning. After this disaster, there was little time to learn complex new tools. Therefore, HKS creators used whatever tools were already understood or easily understandable (such as blogs) to cobble together a site. Interviewees with more skills could draw on more tools, perhaps yielding a better site. While the data are consistent with this interpretation, it would be desirable to check whether a more objective measure of success, such as number of lives saved or people found, correlated with the HKS creator's skills. However, no such measure is available, to our knowledge.

CONCLUSION

Our study highlights several challenges related to developing time-critical websites in an environment lacking any central coordination mechanism. It appears that these challenges did not result from mean-spiritedness or from leaders' egos: To the contrary, it appears that HKS creators were driven by few of the self-interested motivations that apply to OSS creators. Because concern for "helping the cause" strongly motivated HKS creators, we suspect that most of them would have collaborated with other site creators rather than creating their own site, if they had been aware of each other earlier. Thus, these challenges ultimately owed to the difficulty of discovering other developers' work at an early enough stage to facilitate coordination.

Raising the visibility of projects might also have made it easier for people to match their own skills to specific project tasks so people with technical skills could have focused on technical tasks and left counseling to someone more qualified. We suspect that better matching of skills to tasks could lead to more successful projects, further reinforcing workers' motivation to participate.

The key ingredients for HKS creators' problems seem to have been (1) an event that simultaneously inspired several teams to begin projects, (2) the fact that these teams did not know each other when the event occurred and (3) the rapid accumulation of resources (data) that were valuable enough to protect and that were somewhat incompatible between projects. Little about these three ingredients is unique to Hurricane Katrina, so we suspect that similar challenges arise in other circumstances. For example, we hypothesize that these problems might arise if a large software corporation is caught off guard by a significant event, such as the surprise release of a competitor's product. If the corporation is large and disconnected enough that most of its workers do not know each other, then multiple departments may begin planning responses to the event. These independent projects may yield valuable artifacts such as software code that are difficult to merge later, which might lead to interteam distrust and infighting rather than collaboration.

In short, we believe that there is a need for improved systems to help workers discover and collaborate with one another early in widely distributed, time-critical projects. Realistically, even with these systems, it is likely that the workers will create some redundant artifacts before discovering one another. However, the systems should help workers discover one another as quickly as possible, in order to keep the number of redundant artifacts to a minimum. Moreover, the systems should help the workers evaluate the quality of whatever redundant artifacts do exist, and it should help the workers merge those artifacts into a unified, high quality whole.

In addition, these systems should facilitate the rapid establishment of trust among workers. Prior research reveals that this requires enabling workers to perceive competent and timely progress by other workers on their shared task (Jarvenpaa & Leidner, 1999). Consequently, the systems should help workers discover and evaluate the work of others. Moreover, to help workers focus on tasks that they will be competent at doing, these systems should help workers to match their skills to tasks remaining to be done.

Existing systems for supporting widely distributed projects do not meet all of these criteria, mainly because they do not facilitate rapid discovery of other workers. For example, there are dozens of websites dedicated to the coordination of OSS projects; therefore, discovering whether anybody is working on a certain type of project requires searching all of these sites with a search engine. However, in a time-critical situation, web-wide search engines do not spider these projects quickly enough to be of use. Moreover, teams probably do not bring sites online until after investing a substantial amount of work or even finishing their respective sites. By the time a traditional search engine becomes applicable, the teams have already created redundant artifacts.

In closing, our interviews provide a point of comparison for future studies concerning software development after crises. Developers have continued producing new "person locator" sites and similar applications after natural disasters, including hurricanes, typhoons, and earthquakes. It would be interesting to investigate whether leaders of these projects were familiar with the problems that surrounded HKS creation, and if so, whether more recent "person locator" projects have been more successful. If people have led multiple projects of this type, perhaps they have developed promising approaches for dealing with the difficulties outlined in this paper. Studying their experiences may provide additional perspectives on highly distributed, time-critical software development and generate more data to support deeper analyses yielding new solutions to these challenges.

ACKNOWLEDGMENTS

We thank the interviewees for participating in this study and Sara Kiesler at Carnegie Mellon University for assistance with analysis. This work was funded in part by the EUSES Consortium via the National Science Foundation (ITR-0325273), by an NDSEG fellowship, by the National Science Foundation under Grant CCF-0438929, by the Sloan Software Industry Center at Carnegie Mellon, and by the High Dependability Computing Program from NASA Ames cooperative agreement NCC-2-1298. Opinions, findings, and conclusions or recommendations expressed in this material are the authors' and do not necessarily reflect sponsors' views.

REFERENCES

Jarvenpaa, S., & Leidner, D. (1999). Communication and trust in global virtual teams. *Organization Science, 10*(6), 791–815.

Lakhani, K., & von Hippel, E. (2003). How open source software works: Free user to user assistance. *Research Policy, 32*(6), 923–943.

Lakhani, K., & Wolf, B. (2005). Why hackers do what they do: Understanding motivation and effort in free/open source software projects. In J. Feller, B. Fitzgerald, S. Hissam, and K. R. Lakhani (Eds.) *Perspectives on Free and Open Source Software*, (pp. 3–22), MIT Press, Cambridge, MA.

Rosson, M. B., Ballin, J., Rode, J., & Toward, B. (2005). 'Designing for the Web' revisited: A survey of informal and experienced web developers. In D. Lowe & M. Gaedke (Eds.), *International Conference on Web Engineering 2005—Lecture Notes in Computer Science, 3579* (pp. 522–532). Berlin: Springer-Verlag.

12

Approaches to Authority in Online Disaster Relief Communities After Hurricane Katrina

Cristen Torrey, Moira Burke, Matthew Lee, Anind Dey, Susan Fussell, and Sara Kiesler
Carnegie Mellon University

OVERVIEW

The Internet is widely valued for distributing control over information to a lateral network of individuals, but it is not clear how these networks can most effectively organize themselves. This chapter presents a descriptive study of distributed networks of volunteers that emerged online following Hurricane Katrina. Online communities responded to the disaster by facilitating the distribution of donated goods from individuals directly to hurricane survivors. These "connected giving" groups faced several challenges: establishing authority within the group, providing relevant information, developing trust in one another, and sustaining the group over time. Two forms of computer-mediated connected giving were observed: small blog communities and large forums. Small blog communities had a centralized authority figure in the form of a moderator. These groups were more immediately successful in managing information and developing trust, but over time blog communities were difficult to sustain. Large forums with more decentralized authority structures had greater difficulties focusing the community's communication and developing trust but sustained themselves over a longer period of time.

Hurricane Katrina flooded 80% of New Orleans and left four million residents of the southern United States in need of assistance (American Red Cross, 2006). The magnitude of the disaster overwhelmed institutions normally responsible for providing relief, such as the Red Cross and the Federal Emergency Management Agency (FEMA). Displaced residents of the city of New Orleans waited days for shelter, clothing, and financial aid. Meanwhile, people around the United States felt compelled to help. Some used Internet bulletin boards to offer jobs, services, and financial assistance to hurricane evacuees.

When the Red Cross specifically discouraged "in-kind" donations of goods due to sorting and delivery overhead, website owners created online spaces to promote "connected giving." Connected giving allowed people with goods to donate (such as clothing, tools, or diapers) to connect with people in the disaster area (Harris, 2005). Donors saw their distributed efforts as an appropriate complement to the distributed needs of those affected by the disaster. They saw gaps left by large, institutionalized organizations that could be filled by a peer-to-peer approach. Individuals with no training in disaster relief found one another through online communities and organized the distribution of an ad hoc collection of resources. People appropriated the Internet technologies that were readily available to them—forums, bulletin boards, blogs, and personal websites—to coordinate a massive grassroots response to the disaster.

Two forms of computer-mediated connected giving were common: small blog communities and large forum communities. Small communities benefit from the strong relationships between members; these strong ties make cohesive, trusting groups. Large communities have the advantage of more resources, larger networks of participants, and diverse information (Granovetter, 1973). Weak ties within large communities link people to new sources of information whereas the information from strong ties—which are often based on interpersonal similarity—may be redundant.

Some connected giving communities used a moderator to establish authority and group norms. In Usenet groups, owners assume administrative authority, maintain the technical infrastructure, and help sustain the viability of the community by monitoring and encouraging on-topic posts (Butler, Sproull, Kiesler, and Kraut, chapter 9, this book). Other communities distribute authority equally to members and establish group norms by consensus. The Internet is widely valued as a technology that connects people directly to one another without formal leadership. For example, Wikipedia allows the public to author a continually evolving encyclopedia and relies on its members to monitor one another's contributions (Bryant, Forte, & Bruckman, 2005). Open source software communities grant commit privileges to a subset of participants in order to maintain quality (Mockus, Fielding, & Herbsleb, 2002). Slashdot uses thousands of moderators to rate the information the group receives (Lampe & Resnick, 2004). The absence of a single centralized authority does not imply that these groups lack organizational structure. Communities that distribute authority must establish group norms as well, but they do so collectively. Committed members often emerge in these groups as informal leaders to sustain norms, initiate activity, and inspire members.

In order to investigate the successes and challenges encountered by small blog communities and large forums, we sampled four representative sites. Connected giving groups faced several challenges: establishing authority within the group, providing relevant information, developing trust in one another, and sustaining the group over time. We observed small blog communities utilizing a centralized authority structure that appeared more immediately successful in managing information and developing trust, but over time blog communities were difficult to sustain. Without a centralized authority, large forums appeared to have greater difficulties focusing the group's communication and developing trust but managed to sustain themselves over a long period of time.

CHALLENGES OF CONNECTED GIVING

A connected giving community includes both donors and hurricane survivors, a mix of people offering and seeking help. Donors post offers online along with their contact information. Hurricane survivors tell their stories and request specific items for their families. Other members offer logistical information, such as which zip codes are not flooded and are open for postal deliveries.

Working remotely, groups coordinating disaster relief face challenges beyond those of face-to-face groups. For example, remote teams often take longer to complete tasks (Herbsleb, Mockus, Finholt, & Grinter, 2000) and have more disagreements than teams working locally (Straus, 1997). Like many groups, connected giving communities after Hurricane Katrina had to coordinate information and establish trust, but they did so with a unique sense of urgency. The pressing need for disaster relief attracted large numbers of potential participants in a very short time and increased the likelihood of organization and communication failure.

Connected giving communities faced several challenges—establishing authority, accessing information, establishing trust, and sustaining group activity.

Establishing Authority

A centralized authority exists when decisions are made by one or a few individuals, such as a moderator or blog owner. Centralization helps achieve two goals: quality control and accountability. A moderator establishes interaction norms and standard operating procedures for the site. Contributions from visitors are subject to review by the moderator to determine appropriateness. In some cases a moderator may establish interaction norms simply through leading by example, but moderators may actively edit or delete posts of community members as well.

Decentralized authority structures are those in which decisions are made locally, distributed among members of the community. Decentralization has an advantage in making use of local expertise and on-the-scene contextual knowledge. However, no single person is accountable for problems.

In decentralized online communities, the burden of developing interaction norms and standard operating procedures occurs through open discussion. Some decentralized communities use voting systems to influence the behavior of other members, such as allowing members to flag inappropriate posts. Heavily flagged posts are removed.

In theory, there is no right answer as to which authority structure is better for an online community. Centralized authority supports smooth coordination, accountability, and consistency. Decentralized authority supports speedy action and local expertise.

Accessing Information

In order for joint work to be successful, people must have access to the right information and people at the right times. Individuals often join online communities to exchange information (Ridings & Gefen, 2004). In context of urgent disaster relief, the need for access to information becomes even more important. Potential donors want their offers to be accepted; requestors want to be heard.

Developing Trust

People coordinating disaster relief work under time pressure with complete strangers, and so trust is critical. In this context, trust is the willingness to be vulnerable beyond rational risk, based on the expectation of positive action from another person (Mayer, Davis, & Schoorman, 1995). In online communities without time pressure, members establish relationships over time; trust develops through their interaction history (Boon & Holmes, 1991). When a trusted relationship is established, that individual becomes a conduit to other trusted contacts. Trust can be assisted by the involvement of a trusted third party; if the third party is trusted, then trust can be extended through that individual (Uzzi, 1997).

Under these emergency conditions, however, a kind of swift trust may be at work. Research on swift trust suggests that strangers attempting to develop temporary groups may rely upon simple, category-based judgments—such as similar socioeconomic status or religion—to build trust (Meyerson, Weick, & Kramer, 1996). Individuals also identify another person as a member of a trusted group and transfer trust to that person (Postmes, Spears, & Lea, 2000; Turner, 1978). Group members also bond and identify with one another. Bonding to other group members can occur through frequent interaction, mutual disclosure, and interpersonal similarity (McKenna, Green, & Gleason, 2002).

In the present research, one method for measuring trust was to observe its absence. Conflicts related to the lack of interpersonal trust within the group can be highly noticeable, amplified by third-party gossip (Burt & Knez, 1995). Suspicious or distrustful behavior within the group may have destructive effects beyond those of trust-building events (Slovic, 1993).

Sustaining Group Activity

Retaining existing members and recruiting new ones is critical; to achieve these goals, groups must display a record of activity and encourage member contribution (Beenen et al., 2004). Visible content helps newcomers develop expectations about group benefits, and interaction leads to increased commitment of existing members (Moreland & Levine, 2001). When people receive replies to their messages, they are more likely to post again; the effect is particularly strong for newcomers (Lampe & Johnston, 2005). The benefits of recruitment and retention do have their limits, however. Groups must maintain a size appropriate to their goals. Though large groups have access to more resources (McPherson, 1983) and diverse information (Granovetter, 1985), they also face coordination problems (Steiner, 1972), potential for conflict (Cummings & Kiesler, 2005), and decreased contribution (Karau & Williams, 1993).

METHODS AND SAMPLE

Thirteen connected giving communities were observed for a period of six months. Four representative communities were selected for study in more detail, and a portion of their website communication was coded for further qualitative analysis. In order to understand the experience of the volunteers from their perspective, we interviewed five participants about their successes and failures.

Katrina relief sites were gathered with a snowball sampling method, beginning with Google searches for Hurricane Katrina relief sites and then following links from posts on Craigslist, searching Friendster and Orkut for "Hurricane Katrina" and "New Orleans," and following website references from newspaper stories and blogs. Our initial sample of websites included several different formats for communication (see Table 12.1). Blogs and forums are examples of preexisting websites that were repurposed by their owners to be used for coordinating relief efforts.

In this chapter we focus on the use of forums and blogs by connected giving communities because these types of community technologies were the most prevalent. The appropriation of blogs and forums is particularly interesting because their creation and use has become accessible to those without any technical training. In contrast, databases and wikis generally require host-

TABLE 12.1.
Formats of Relief Sites

Website URL (http://)	Format
forums.ebay.com/forum.jspa?forumID=1000000000	Forum
forums.craigslist.org/?forumID=52	Forum
www.nola.com/forums/reachingout	Forum
groups.google.com/group/Katrina-Hub	Forum
www.citizenactionteam.org	Forum
www.reliefspark.org	Database
www.katrinasangels.org	Database
gracedavis.typepad.com/katrinablog	Blog
wheretosenddonationsforkatrina.blogspot.com	Blog
beenthere.typepad.com	Blog
katrinahelp.blogspot.com	Blog
katrinahelp.info	Wiki
www.projectbackpack.org	Wiki

ing one's own server. Another compelling aspect of blogs and forums is that they facilitate visible communication between participants, an essential element for online community development. The interaction on forums and blogs is structured by the format of the communication and the size of the group.

Communication Format of Forums and Blogs

Forums are designed for discussion. Participants open conversations by starting new discussion threads and continue conversations by replying to others' threads. The threaded structure allows replies to messages to be easily tracked (see Figure 12–1). Forums are commonly hosted by high-traffic websites, and

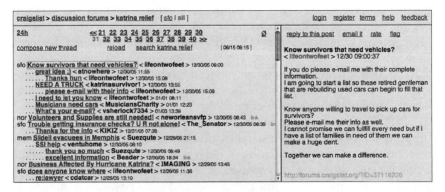

FIGURE 12–1.   Threaded structure of forums.

participants go through a minimal registration process to post and reply to messages.

On blogs, messages are posted by date in reverse chronological order (see Figure 12–2). Blogs generally have a dedicated group of readers and participants. Unlike forums, blogs do not allow visitors to post directly on the blog, but they often allow readers to comment in response to a blog author's post after a simple registration process, usually requiring a username and email address. Blog readers do not have the ability to address another reader's comment directly; additional comments are instead appended to the list.

Group Size of Forums and Blogs

Online communities exist in many different sizes. Some communities support the communication of a small circle of close friends, and others support thousands of people in a single group. Assessing a group's true size is difficult because there is an unknown number of potential "lurkers," people observing the group without actively participating (Nonnecke & Preece, 2000). It is possible, however, to compare group size on the basis of active participation and define group members as those who post to the website.

Websites Sampled

Communication format and group size did not vary independently in these communities. Blogs were small and forums were large. We selected four rep-

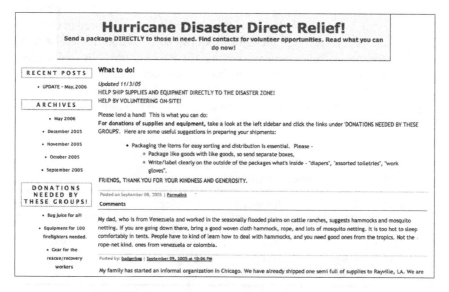

FIGURE 12–2. Post-and-comment structure of blogs.

resentative websites, two of each type, with observable activity focusing on in-kind donations of relief goods (see Table 12.2). From these four websites, we collected communication activity between August 28, 2005, and February 25, 2006. For the blogs, content consisted of posts made by the blog owner and comments left by readers. For the forums, content consisted of threads and the associated responses.

When it was first created, the Been There blog focused on parenting. In response to Hurricane Katrina, the blog authors posted an entry asking readers to offer clothes, toys, or other supplies to victims in the comments section of the post. Visitors to the site who were in need posted comments about their backgrounds and specific requests. The blog authors occasionally marked the offers and requests that had been fulfilled by editing the comment. An overwhelming response from readers offering and requesting goods motivated the blog authors to launch a new version of their site solely dedicated to matching people in need with donors. This new site had different sections for posting offers of goods, posting requests for goods or information, telling stories, and connecting donor families with needy families. Most of the communication appeared in the long list of comments.

The Direct Relief blog was also created by a long-time author of a personal blog. After contacting a person coordinating donations to shelters and churches in the disaster area, the blog author launched Direct Relief to publicize what donations were most needed and where they could be shipped. The blog author subsequently added a section dedicated to connecting people with families affected by the hurricane and coordinating the donation of goods to meet their longer-term needs. The owner-authored content consisted of contact information and lists of items needed by shelters or families. Most of the requests for goods were contributed by the blog owner and appeared in the main posts. Visitors read through the list of requested goods and mailed items to the given address. The comments section of each blog post allowed readers to ask questions or post information about others that needed help, the overall donation process, and goods they had to offer. Most of the messages offering and coordinating goods were contributed by the blog readers and appeared in the comments.

TABLE 12.2.
Connected Giving Community Sample

Community	Format	Group Size	Participating Members
Been There	Blog	Small	549
Direct Relief	Blog	Small	92
Craigslist Katrina Relief	Forum	Large	3,549
Nola.com Reach Out	Forum	Large	2,119

The Craigslist Katrina Relief forum was set up shortly after the disaster to allow people to discuss anything related to the hurricane relief effort. The Katrina Relief forum is one of many discussion forums found in a popular online classifieds site.

Nola.com's Reach Out Forum was hosted on a New Orleans newspaper site. Reach Out focused on helping people connect with New Orleanians to offer assistance in donations, housing, and jobs.

Website Activity

For each of the four sites, we gathered statistics about the communication and membership activity over time. We counted the number of new threads and messages per week, and calculated how many times each participant posted.

Communication activity for the four sites was broken into two categories, posts made by the site owner and those from the public. The proportion of messages contributed by the blog author gives a rough indication of how much authority the moderator exerted in the group. To investigate the emergence of community leaders—core contributors without administrative control over the site—the frequency of repeat posters within the community was counted.

Content Coding

A subset of 250 messages from each site was coded in order to analyze the communities' task and social content (see Table 12.3). A single post was coded with any combination of the two codes, such as "other relief info" and "distrustful." The task content codes addressed the community's ability to access information, and the social content codes addressed the development of trust in the community.

Access to Information.   The primary activity of these communities is coordinating information. One person may know where goods are needed; another may have the needed goods. Both kinds of information must be accessible. The distraction of off-topic chatter was a concern for creators of these

TABLE 12.3.
Content Coding Scheme

Task Content: Access to Information	*Social Content: Development of Trust*
Donation info	Supportive
Other relief info	Distrustful
Off-task	Neither

communities. One website (not included in our detailed analysis) specifically informed participants to keep their communication focused on disaster relief:

> "We do understand you're wanting to post and talk to each other and to be a community-based board. Under normal circumstances we would be doing cartwheels to see this occur. The problem we face on this board is if the front page is full of chat threads when a disaster situation is in effect important information that people need would be lost among the OT [off-topic] threads."

For each site we measured access to on-task information, that is, how easy it was for people to find the necessary information to fulfill their goals. We coded the sample posts and identified those that contained "on-task" information such as requests, offers, and confirmations of shipping or receiving:

> "I have used clothes in very good condition for boys 2–6 years, boots, shoes and toys. Also, nice stroller and crib w/mattress for the Katrina victims. Email me for more info. God Bless all, my heart and thoughts are with you."

On-task posts also included information about the general relief effort such as updates from the disaster area, contact information for shelters or families that required assistance, suggested links to other online or offline resources, and instructions for shipping:

> "can anybody help explain to me why my mother is not receiving any financial help at all from the red cross? I have spoken to quite a few people who are in much better financial situations than she is and have received 2 installments from the red cross. any insight would be helpful. thanks."

> "Seems that Amazon will ship, they just say it will take about 10 days."

Off-topic posts were not directly related to the task of donating goods, e.g., chat about personal lives, rants about politics or beliefs, or advertisements:

> "So so true. If you are poor you usually get the shaft no matter where you are in this world. A powerful industrialized nation or the third world."

> "goodnight all I am turning in"

Development of Trust. For each site, we measured how participants identified themselves with the group by coding posts for the presence of supportive content. It included praise for the accomplishments of the group, thanking other participants for their (potential) contributions, or displays of positive affect toward the group:

> "Hey guys, Glad to help. Would love to hear the story if possible. Thanks for keeping an eye out for the ones that truly need help. You are both amazing to me! Hugs!"

> "Thank you for all that you are doing to get the word out and get help!"

For each site, we coded posts for the presence of distrust, including questions regarding the accuracy of information or the authenticity of an individual:

> "and just for the record, I WAS scammed by one that posted on this board. However, all it did was make me more cautious."

> "[name], at this particular time, I really think that the last thing we need is someone yanking people's chains just for the hell of it. Back off."

Posts about government officials or scam websites were not coded as distrust here. A post fell into the distrust coding category only if it questioned the legitimacy of a participant or the content of the online community.

Coding Reliability.   Our sample included 250 messages from each website for a total of 1,000 messages. To assess interrater reliability, two judges coded a subset of 50 messages from each site, for a total of 200 messages. Cohen's kappa (Cohen, 1960) for task content was 0.77 and for social content was 0.76.

RESULTS

We observed small blog communities and large forums in order to provide a descriptive comparison of their respective abilities to establish authority, provide access to information, develop group trust, and sustain activity over time.

Establishing Authority

Although generally it is possible for blog authors to distribute authority equally to all members, we did not find evidence of equality in our sample. As previously discussed, the format of the communication on a blog lends itself to one or more central moderators supported by a group of readers. Readers interact by posting comments, but the blog author has ultimate responsibility for the site content and procedure.

The moderators' activity on the two blogs differed. For Been There and Direct Relief, the moderators contributed 8% and 71% of all communication to the discussions, respectively. The majority of the content of Been There came from the community whereas the majority of the content on Direct Relief came from the blog author.

The small blog communities established authority by focusing on the personality and reputation of the moderator or moderators. Neither of the moderators we observed needed to explicitly dictate group norms; their communication behavior as well as their encouragement of others' behavior was enough to establish a standard for group communication. The Direct Relief moderators posted packing instructions and roughly prioritized shelter lists, and they distributed tasks to the community, such as requesting that members generate a list of zip codes to match the shelter addresses.

> (Direct Relief Moderator, at the top of the page): "Packaging the items for easy sorting and distribution is essential. Please:
> • Package like goods with like goods, so send separate boxes
> • Write/label clearly on the outside of the packages what's inside—"diapers," "assorted toiletries," "work gloves".
> For your convenience, we listed links to shippers on the left sidebar."

> (Direct Relief Poster, in the comments section): "Are there any shippers that are still providing free shipping to the affected areas?"
> (Direct Relief Moderator, in response): Hey there, we don't know of any organizations offering free shipping. We sure would post it here. Maybe you could research that for us and you—? Thanks!

Both the Direct Relief and Been There moderators used the affordances of the blog to lead the relief effort. They posted news and instructions on the front page and sidebars of the site—prominent screen real estate where the public could not write—and posted thank-yous and clarification messages within the comments section, where the rest of the community was talking.

The large forums did not use moderators to establish authority. Though the administrators of the sites—Craig Newmark and the New Orleans Times-Picayune newspaper—are the ostensible leaders, their presence was negligible or completely absent. A few discussions of authority, including decisions for prioritizing and coordinating donations, were present in the forums, but we observed no clear consensus on these issues. Given the sheer volume of new threads appearing every day on the forum, it would be difficult for any single committed member to provide direction to the group. In the first two weeks, the Katrina Relief forum received over seven thousand messages. A volunteer that sought to directly moderate a forum of that size would have little time for coordinating disaster relief.

Accessing Information

The number of posted messages varied greatly between the large communities in forums and the small communities on blogs. On all four sites we observed, a large percentage of messages were posted in the two weeks following the hurricane. Table 12.4 shows the number of messages at each site in the first two weeks as a percentage of the total messages posted in the entire six-month period. This means that connected giving communities had the most resources—people and information—in the very beginning of their development, in some cases before the communities had established procedural norms.

TABLE 12.4.
Number of Messages in First Two Weeks as Percentage of Total Activity

Community	Format	First Two Weeks	% of Total	Total Messages
Direct Relief	Blog	34	21%	159
Been There	Blog	369	43%	868
Katrina Relief	Forum	7,257	44%	16,505
Reach Out	Forum	3,104	72%	4,299

None of the websites we observed had official policies for propriety. Nonetheless, there were de facto norms in the actual content. We looked at the distribution of on-task messages, those focused on the donation of goods, in order to compare the effort expended by members of different communities to access the information they needed.

As shown in Figure 12–3, the moderated blogs (Direct Relief and Been There) had a higher concentration of task-specific information. The blogs were created with the goal of coordinating the donation of goods, and the messages largely reflect the task-focused nature of the communication. In contrast, the forums were created for general Katrina relief discussion. These forums had far fewer donation-relevant posts, but they also contained a lower percentage of on-task information than the blogs. We did not formally analyze the remaining message content on the forums because the present analysis focused on donation coordination, but we observed a large amount of political and social debate. Participants on one of the forums immediately identified this type of communication as a distraction and wanted off-task posters to take their discussion to another board in order to make the relief information more accessible. One person wrote, "I did post several times in the first few days after Katrina, when an idiotic troll posted every few minutes." Trolls are posters that seek to create trouble; their messages are also called "flamebait" (Donath, 1998). Because the forums had no moderator, no individual had the authority to enforce a single content norm. Over time, the group had to agree on appropriate uses of the board. On the Katrina Relief Forum, members flagged posts, identifying inappropriate ones. If enough members flagged a post, it was removed, but it took time.

Developing Trust

The social challenge for these distributed groups is the problem of developing trust with strangers. In all of the communities we sampled, participants had to create an online identity to post a message. Most identified themselves with unique screen names, although some used their real names and addresses. We observed people expending effort verifying their identities to one another.

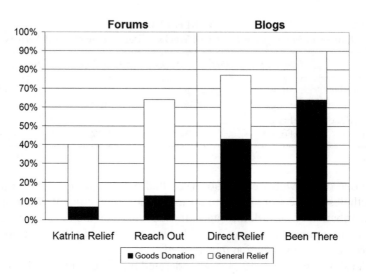

FIGURE 12–3.   Percentage of on-task messages.

They sometimes emailed scans of their driver's licenses to members who questioned their identities; some offered their FEMA identification numbers or
even their social security numbers in forum posts as evidence of their identity. Different communities required different strategies to develop trusting,
working relationships with one another.

Trust Developed Through Interaction History.   Visible histories of interaction led to trust in the blogs. Blog moderators posted inspiring stories
about the donated goods reaching their destinations and thank-you messages
from recipients demonstrating task-based leadership. The impact of the
group's work and the legitimacy of the blog author were clear. The visibility of
the collective effort motivated participants, and it also helped establish the
blog owner's reputation, providing information to newcomers about the
group's trustworthiness.

> "[We] checked in with Sunny (she's been feeding the town from her deli) to see
> if her trucks has arrived. She is totally exhausted but so very happy at this huge
> level of generosity. They are working with a couple of the churches in great need
> to distribute the items. She said to tell you: THANK YOU THANK YOU
> THANK YOU! You have no idea the good you have done and so many people
> you have helped. . . . You can see all those donations piling up at Sunny's place
> in this photo from a volunteer who made deliveries to Sunny's store."

The reputation of the blog moderator was then used to transfer trust to
the moderator's contacts; the moderator functioned as a trusted third party.

When a potential recipient was introduced by the moderator, community members trusted whomever the moderator vouched for. One blog poster wrote, "This is from [the moderator], therefore it is real and has been verified." In another instance, one moderator requested goods for her son's coworker's family. Even though the information was removed several times from its source, the reputation of the moderator was so strong that community members trusted the recipients and organized donations for them.

Communities that utilized a distributed authority structure could not rely on the visibility and resultant trust in a single moderator. Participants in forums still needed to establish interaction-based trust, but they had a more difficult time establishing credibility. One participant invited another to investigate her reputation: "You can ask multiple people on this board and many others that can back my reputation." As a result of the sheer number of participants, members of forums had to work harder to remain visible to one another. Participants vouched for each other explicitly: "[A] is someone you can trust . . . she has lots of links and places if you need info she is like a library!! . . . and a very good woman!!!" However, the large volume of communication made specific testimonials less salient.

Forum participants made themselves visible by actively responding to others' questions and threads. Many threads contained direct dialogue between posters, and some members posted dozens of times (see Figure 12–4). On the Katrina Relief Forum, there was a core group of around 20 individuals that posted to the forum over 100 times each; one individual posted over 900 times.

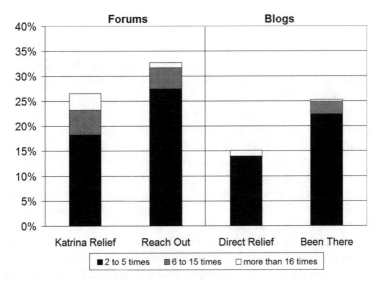

FIGURE 12–4.   Percentage of participants posting more than once.

Trust Developed Through Group Membership.   Trust can be transferred to individuals simply by identifying them as members of a trusted social category. Connected giving participants often casually identified themselves in the process of making an offer: "I just recently became a stay-at-home mom, so I have suits or casual clothes." Participants also identified their collaborators by group membership, referring to the "supermom-on-the-ground" or "she's a Steel Magnolia." On the blogs we studied, community members seemed to be fairly similar to the blog moderators and to each other. Members often identified themselves as mothers.

> "As a mother of 3, my heart goes out to the many displaced people of the Gulf Coast. . . . I and a lot of my friends and neighbors want to help. I am a member of or know others who are active in several mothers' groups in my area. We all feel a very real NEED TO HELP!"

Members also wanted to help those who were like them. One donor considered her own experience trying to find the right formula for her child and felt compelled to help others in the same predicament.

> "I have a child who has struggled with severe reflux/dairy/soy allergy, and I have some of his very costly ($50/can) formula left over that is still good. Children who need this formula and don't get it can suffer SERIOUS physical pain! These children cannot tolerate your typical milk- or soy-based formula, or even the special broken down formulas. I know what my baby went through (horrendous screaming for MONTHS), and I am picturing these few special babies who are being fed normal formula because that is all their poor mothers can get their hands on."

In comparison, the diversity of participants on large forums may have inhibited some of the benefits of this kind of self-disclosure. When participants on forums disclosed personal information, especially politics or religion, the disclosure was as likely to create conflict as it was to create trust.

In addition to establishing trust on the basis of off-line categorical identities, membership in the online community itself translated into trust because a group identity formed around the participants themselves. For all four of our sample communities, we coded the number of times participants said supportive things to one another: "You guys rock," and "This is a great idea." There was a large difference between the moderated blog communities and the forums. Roughly 25% of blog messages in our sample contained group encouragement; this may have translated into a more salient group identity. The samples of messages from the forums contained approximately 7% support posts. Forums could not rely on trust in a single authority, and the lower frequency of supportive posts as compared to the blogs may indicate that the strength of their identification to the group was lower as well.

Evidence of Distrust.   We found few instances of suspicion or interpersonal conflict on either of the moderated blogs we observed. Likely due to the moderator presence and the subsequent development of group identity, blogs showed little distrust. Members recognized that there were some people taking advantage of the generosity of donors; one member asked those requesting donations to send "a full sentence about who you are so I can determine if I'm getting spam or a real request." Of course, participants in blogs may have chosen to verify the trustworthiness of recipients over email, rather than communicate publicly on the blog.

In contrast, approximately 5% of the forum messages sampled contained accusations and distrust. Examples of distrust were primarily suspicions of falsified stories.

> "you do not know me personally but i had read your postings and was organizing a group of people at my business to help you, but was warned by people on this forum that my help would be better directed elsewhere. People seem not to trust you."

Indeed, some members went to significant lengths to research and monitor members of whom they were suspicious. One member warned, "The one thing that we ask when we offer our help is that you be HONEST with us. If you are NOT honest we WILL find out." There were also more general messages discouraging the donation of goods to unknown people. The posts included links to news stories about Internet scams and online auction listings of previously donated items.

The forums are self-policing, so there was no official moderator to make a decision about potential wrongdoing. When someone on the board was challenged, often there was a public discussion on the board about the disagreement, but there was rarely a definitive outcome. Participants had to simply agree to coexist in the community.

> "Regardless, we obviously have nothing to offer each other, as we disagree on certain aspects of the ethics of helping. I wish you the best and trust that all will be revealed in its proper time. Until then, everyone has the right to trust, not trust, believe, question, admire, like or dislike whomever they please."

The atmosphere of suspicion was discouraging to those doing volunteer work. Several members posted farewell messages, informing others they were unwilling to participate any longer.

> "first off i will say this is my last post on here . . . it is just too much going on here it is so hurting to see what is going on . . . sorry we have to come here and see all the distrust by ones who are to help. my heart goes out to the real ones on here."

It is difficult to quantify the precise effect that the distrust messages had on the development of trust and subsequent social coordination of the forums. Nonetheless, the level of suspicion on the forums was not an obstacle that the blog communities faced.

Sustaining Group Activity

For each site, we counted the number of new posts over time to identify which sites sustained group activity. As illustrated in Figures 12–5 and 12–6, all websites experienced an initial spike of activity in the first one or two weeks after the disaster. Activity waned in the weeks that followed.

Of the four sites we studied, only the Craigslist Katrina Relief Forum, a large community with decentralized authority, remained active six months after the disaster. After the same period, the two blogs exhibited little activity. Comparing the two blogs, we found that activity at Direct Relief, where the owner provided most of the content, extinguished more quickly than Been There, where the community provided the majority of the content.

DISCUSSION

At the outset of this study, we assumed that a decentralized authority structure would better support speed for channeling relief where it was urgently needed. We expected that a large, distributed network of people would have

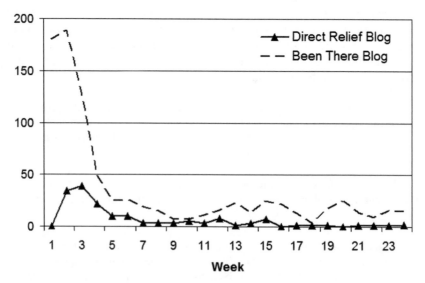

FIGURE 12–5.   Number of posts (blogs).

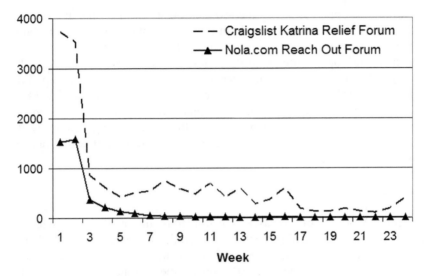

FIGURE 12–6. Number of posts (forums).

the information and resources to best cope with the quickly changing situation. The results demonstrate an important tradeoff between small, moderated groups and large, decentralized groups that has consequences for how trust is established and the extent to which the community is sustained.

The presence of a moderator in the small blog communities seemed to address the challenges of providing information and developing trust quickly. The strength of the moderator's presence dictated how the group would function and what constituted appropriate content. Blogs afforded high moderator visibility and both task- and relationship-focused leadership. The history of the group's activity demonstrated the outcome of the group's effort and established legitimacy for the moderator. Participants similar to the moderator rallied around their leader creating the potential for trust based on group membership. Unfortunately, moderated groups could not sustain themselves absent the participation of the moderator. Over time, moderated groups were not long lasting; the continued participation of the community was contingent on communication from the moderator. Moderators scaled back their contributions to the disaster relief blogs and shifted their focus back to their own personal blogs. As a result, six months after the disaster, the disaster relief blog communities had very little or no communication.

In contrast, the large forums we investigated did not use a centralized authority structure, or moderator, to establish group norms and appropriate behavior. Their collective model of authority relied on group consensus and group bonds, which take time to develop. Activity in the Reach Out forum community dropped to negligible levels a few weeks after the disaster. We speculate that these members did not invest the time to create bonds, build consensus, and take collective ownership of the community. In contrast, the Katrina Relief forum initially appeared less cohesive than the blogs but ultimately lasted longer than all the other communities because ownership of the group was distributed to multiple members. There is some evidence that Katrina Relief members formed subgroups that communicated frequently over email and on other blogs as well. Although there was no single authority, the forum may have served as fertile recruiting grounds for several leaders of other smaller communities.

Limitations

The generalizability of this research is limited by the small sample size. The sample comprises a small percentage of overall communication and only that which was public. Group members exchanged email directly with one another that we were not able to observe. Additionally, the size and authority structures of the sites were intertwined. Because we observed neither large blog communities nor small forums in the disaster relief context, we cannot be certain how communication format and group size operate independently of one another.

Future Work

We found that groups using a decentralized authority structure often struggled to create consensus around group norms and group identity. Once consensus was created, the group appeared stable and members committed, but often the process was lengthy and difficult. Could the process of creating consensus be made more efficient, thereby increasing the overall productivity of the group? It seems possible that conflict may be necessary to instigate an evaluation of the group's norms. One forum weathered the conflict that arose and ultimately bonded together; this forum remained active six months after the disaster. The other forum had fewer visible conflicts, and the group never seemed to cohere. Six months later, participation had slowed considerably. An interesting question for future research is how conflict functions in creating group solidarity and identity. It may not be possible to sustain a community with a decentralized authority structure without responding to a certain amount of conflict. It is possible that when the group is challenged, members either leave or become motivated to stake out an agenda and a group identity. Further analysis of the group's communication may expose a more detailed picture of the mechanisms that establish group norms and create solidarity among members. Another potentially fruitful investigation would be on the question of transformational leadership (Bass, 1985). Some disaster relief communities seem to embody the idea of transformational leadership, in which highly charismatic leaders inspire members to make sacrifices for a meaningful cause, beyond any expectations of reward (Bass, 1985). Finally, online disaster relief communities provide a particularly interesting context to study relationship- and task-focused leadership (Fiedler, 1978). These groups might benefit from a relationship-focused leader to help strangers form ties or from a task-focused leader, and to get the work done rapidly. In that few leaders have both qualities, which would be more effective?

CONCLUSION

Our work on connected giving communities expands the literature by observing the immediate online collaboration of a large number of people on a time-critical task. We found that small blog communities efficiently managed challenges with the help of a moderator's presence, but these communities were not sustained without the moderator's continued participation. The large forums we observed had difficulties managing their content and developing trust. To the extent these challenges were met, large forums were maintained.

ACKNOWLEDGMENTS

The authors wish to thank Robert Kraut and Irina Shklovski for their suggestions and feedback on this project. This material is based upon work supported by the National Science Foundation under Grant Nos. IIS-0325047, IIS-0121426, IIS-0325049, and DGE-0333420. Any opinions, findings, and conclusions or recommendations expressed in this material are those of the authors and do not necessarily reflect the views of the National Science Foundation. This work is also supported by an AT&T Labs Fellowship.

REFERENCES

American Red Cross. (2006). *Red Cross: Hurricane Season 2005 Six-Month Report* (No. HIS 20170): American Red Cross.

Bass, B. M. (1985). *Leadership and performance beyond expectations.* New York: Free Press.

Beenen, G., Ling, K., Wang, X., Chang, K., Frankowski, D., Resnick, P., et al. (2004). *Using social psychology to motivate contributions to online communities.* Paper presented at the Computer Supported Cooperative Work (CSCW 2004). November 6–10, 2004, Chicago, IL.

Boon, S. D., & Holmes, J. G. (1991). The dynamics of interpersonal trust: Resolving uncertainty in the face of risk. In R. A. Hinde & J. Groebel (Eds.), *Cooperation and Prosocial Behavior.* New York: Cambridge University Press.

Bryant, S. L., Forte, A., & Bruckman, A. (2005). *Becoming Wikipedian: transformation of participation in a collaborative online encyclopedia.* Paper presented at the Conference on Supporting Group Work (SIGGROUP 2005). November 6–9, 2005, Sanibel Island, FL.

Burt, R., & Knez, M. (1995). Third-party gossip and trust. In R. M. Kramer & T. R. Tyler (Eds.), *Trust in Organizations*. Thousand Oaks: Sage Publications.

Cohen, J. (1960). A coefficient of agreement for nominal scales. *Educational and Psychological Measurement, 20*, 37–46.

Cummings, J., & Kiesler, S. (2005). Collaborative research across disciplinary and organizational boundaries. *Social Studies of Science, 35*(5), 703–722.

Donath, J. S. (1998). Identity and deception in the virtual community. In M. Smith & P. Kollock (Eds.), *Communities in Cyberspace*. London: Routledge.

Fiedler, F. E. (1978). The contingency model and the dynamics of the leadership process. In L. Berkowitz (Ed.), *Advances in experimental social psychology*. New York: Academic Press.

Granovetter, M. (1973). The strength of weak ties. *American Journal of Sociology, 78*(6), 1360–1380.

Granovetter, M. (1985). Economic action and social structure: The problem of embeddedness. *American Journal of Sociology, 91*, 481–510.

Harris, L. (2005). Connected giving. Salon.com. http://dir.salon.com/story/mwt/feature/2005/09/10/charity/index.html

Herbsleb, J. D., Mockus, A., Finholt, T. A., & Grinter, R. E. (2000). *Distance, dependencies, and delay in a global collaboration*. Paper presented at the Computer Supported Cooperative Work (CSCW 2000), December 2–6, 2000, Philadelphia, PA.

Karau, S., & Williams, K. (1993). Social loafing: A meta-analytic review and theoretical integration. *Journal of Personality and Social Psychology, 65*(4), 681–706.

Lampe, C., & Johnston, E. (2005). *Follow the slash(dot): Effect of feedback on new members in an online community*. Paper presented at the Conference on Supporting Group Work (SIGGROUP 2005). November 6–9, 2005. Sanibel Island, FL.

Lampe, C., & Resnick, P. (2004). *Slash(dot) and Burn: Distributed Moderation in a Large Online Conversational Space*. Paper presented at the SIGCHI Conference on Human Factors in Computing Systems (CHI 2004), Vienna, Austria, April 24–29.

Mayer, R. C., Davis, J. H., & Schoorman, F. D. (1995). An integrative model of organizational trust. *Academy of Management Review, 20*, 709–734.

McKenna, K., Green, A., & Gleason, M. (2002). Relationship formation on the Internet: What's the big attraction? *Journal of Social Issues, 58*(1), 9–31.

McPherson, M. (1983). The size of voluntary organizations. *Social Forces, 61*(4), 1045–1064.

Meyerson, D., Weick, K. E., & Kramer, R. M. (1996). Swift Trust and Temporary Groups. In R. M. Kramer & T. R. Tyler (Eds.), *Trust in Organizations* (pp. 166–195). Thousand Oaks: Sage Publications.

Mockus, A., Fielding, R. T., & Herbsleb, J. D. (2002). Two Case Studies of Open Source Software Development: Apache and Mozilla. *ACM Transactions on Software Engineering and Methodology, 11*(3), 309–346.

Moreland, R., & Levine, J. (2001). Socialization in organizations and work groups. In M. Turner (Ed.), *Groups at work: Theory and research* (pp. 69–112). Mahwah, NJ: Lawrence Erlbaum Associates.

Nonnecke, B., & Preece, J. (2000). *Lurker demographics: counting the silent*. Paper presented at the Conference on Human factors in computing (CHI 2000). April 1–6, 2000, The Hague, The Netherlands.

Postmes, T., Spears, R., & Lea, M. (2000). The Formation of Group Norms in Computer-Mediated Communication. *Human Communication Research, 26*(3), 341–371.

Ridings, C., & Gefen, D. (2004). Virtual community attraction: Why people hang out online. *Journal of Computer-Mediated Communication, 10*(1).

Slovic, P. (1993). Perceived risk, trust and democracy. *Risk Analysis, 13*, 675–682.

Steiner, I. (1972). *Group process and productivity*. New York: Academic Press.

Straus, S. G. (1997). Technology, Group Process, and Group Outcomes: Testing the Connections in Computer Mediated and Face-to-Face Groups. *Human-Computer Interaction, 12*, 227–266.

Turner, J. C. (1978). Social comparison, similarity and ingroup favouritism. In H. Tajfel (Ed.), *Differentiation between social groups* (pp. 233–250). UK: Academic Press.

Uzzi, B. (1997). Social structure and competition in interfirm networks: The paradox of embeddedness. *Administrative Science Quarterly, 38*, 628–652.

V

Conclusion and Future Directions

13

Lessons About Leadership at a Distance and Future Research Directions

Suzanne Weisband
University of Arizona

OVERVIEW

With the diverse range of distant leadership settings considered in this book, the lessons about distance and leadership that run across many of the chapters are highlighted. Research questions are then posed to suggest future directions for conducting research on leadership at a distance.

This book challenges researchers interested in leadership to confront a world in which people work across boundaries of time or organization, culture, and geography. In this world, leadership itself is a complex construct, difficult to pin down with a few words like "vision" and "goal setting." In this conclusion, I draw some lessons from the chapters in this book. My aim is not to summarize each chapter, or to recommend what leaders should do when working at a distance. Instead, I want to offer some lessons from the book as a lens toward future research.

LESSON 1: EXERCISING LEADERSHIP AT A DISTANCE REQUIRES NEW SKILLS AND COMPETENCIES

This book began with a focus on the challenges facing leaders today. Bikson et al. (Chapter 2) found that the U.S. track record regarding international leadership was disappointing, especially for the public and non-profits sectors. Their data suggest that recruiting leaders is difficult due to salary differences, poor grounding in the industry's core business, and a long hiring process. Most importantly, there is a shortage of desired skills and competencies in the future leadership cadre. Bikson et al. recommend a multidimensional and well-integrated set of competencies for international leaders. These include *substantive depth* (professional or technical knowledge) related to the organization's primary business processes, *managerial ability*, with an emphasis on teamwork and interpersonal skills, *strategic international understanding*, and *cross-cultural experience*. Though in great demand, this skill repertoire is in short supply. As today's senior managers and professionals near retirement, it is not at all clear that succeeding cohorts will have the required competencies for leadership in this changed world.

But there is hope. Respondents in the Bikson et al. study remarked that "each new cohort of employees was more IT-savvy and more motivated to keep up with state-of-the-art IT uses" (Chapter 2, p. 25). Technological advances, in turn, may widen the eligible pool of employees when flexible hiring strategies are considered. For example, telecommuting can allow employers to hire people who are homebound or who live far away, including in other countries.

We also learned that young people who have proficient technical skills can turn the tools they know—PHP or blog—and build a website quickly to deal with crisis situations (see Chapters 11 and 12).

If seasoned leaders do not have the skills organizations need for its growing global missions, what kind of technical training is needed to prepare for leadership roles in a highly interconnected world, where technical skills are a premium? Future research should look into the skill sets required to lead at a distance. For example, Butler et al. (Chapter 9) and Scaffidi et al. (Chapter 11) suggest that formal leaders of an online community need to have more than technical skills to maintain the online site, but they also require social responsibilities to build relationships and motivate members to contribute.

Understanding what motivates leaders to serve civic and humanitarian goals may help explain why distant leaders are willing to work so hard to contribute to the public good without compensation. As Scaffidi et al. (Chapter 11) point out, there are some similarities between Hurricane Katrina sites (HKS) and open source software (OSS) developers in that both valued benefiting "the good of the group" and "helping the cause." But there are also many differences. Clearly, there are many reasons that may account for why people are motivated to lead others at a distance. Future research may want to probe further on why people decide to build, develop, and lead large-scale distributed collaborations.

LESSON 2: NEW TECHNOLOGY HAS INCREASED THE LIKELIHOOD THAT PEOPLE WILL BE MEMBERS OF GROUPS THAT LACK A FORMAL LEADER

The four studies on large-scale collaboration described groups that had no leader designated formally, that were selected by organizational authorities, who had the proper rank and seniority, and that had monetary rewards. With a motivation to change the way things are currently done, a person today can assume leadership and encourage new groups to help build online communities of mutual interest (Chapter 9), develop new techniques and services (Chapter 10) and software tools to find people in a crisis (Chapter 11), as well as monitor progress (Chapter 3). It's this emergent leader who brings these loosely connected people together and, in doing so, can affect change (Chapters 11 and 12) and influence outcomes (Chapters 9 and 10).

Leaders sometimes emerge to build relationships, as when groups experience crises and conflict (Chapters 10, 11, and 12), and to solve task-related problems, as when groups experience a work delays and uncertainty about how to proceed (Chapter 10). Many of them are self-taught, relying heavily on existing relationships to help them navigate an environment lacking any central coordination mechanism (e.g., Chapter 11).

If this phenomenon of emergent leaders in large-scale, geographically distributed communities and organizations is increasing, how do we study them? Balthazard et al. (Chapter 7) suggest that group interaction styles may help explain why people emerge as leaders. For example, a constructive interaction style was characterized by a balanced concern for personal and group outcomes, cooperation, creativity, and respect for others' perspectives. Defensive styles included limited information sharing, impartiality, and aggressive behavior. Thus group interaction style was theorized to impede or enhance team members' abilities to bring their unique knowledge and skills to bear on the task and may determine who emerges as a leader.

Recently Ajay Mehra and his colleagues (e.g., Mehra, Smith, Dixon, & Robertson, 2006a; Mehra, Dixon, Brass & Robertson, 2006b) used social network analysis to examine distributed leadership in work teams. They argue that leadership research has been preoccupied with understanding how the style, personality, and other characteristics of the leader influence team dynamics and performance, with little regard for the informal, emergent leader. In this more recent line of work, distributed leadership focuses on two issues: (1) leadership is not just a top-down process between the formal leader and team members, and (2) there can be multiple leaders within a group. Mehra et al. (2006a) found that distributed leadership networks were not associated with higher team performance, but that a distributed–coordinated structure was related to higher team performance when compared to traditional leader-centered leadership networks. Team performance was not simply a matter of having more leaders but also whether the leaders perceive each other as leaders.

Bradner and Mark (Chapter 4), Birnholtz and Finholt (Chapter 10), and Torrey et al. (Chapter 12) also found evidence of multiple leaders within a large, distributed group. For example, Bradner and Mark studied engineers that reported to several engineering "leads" who reported to two "project leads." The project leaders were senior engineers who had been promoted to management after 20+ years of service and were assigned to manage the work at the Phoenix, Arizona, and Houston, Texas, sites, respectively. In the Birnholtz and Finholt chapter, multiple professional groups with noticeable cultural differences and leadership styles had to work together to design and deploy a collaboratory to link researchers and students with earthquake engineering data, experimental facilities, and computational simulations. Torrey et al. observed that blogs tend to have one or more central moderators supported by a group of readers, whereas large web forums did not use moderators to establish authority.

What other large-scale, geographically distributed communities can be studied where leaders emerge and are not formally chosen, where leaders have stronger technical skills than leadership skills, and where trust is hard to establish because of cultural differences? Research that probes the context of this work in more detail holds promise for future work on distant leadership.

LESSON 3: LEADERSHIP AT A DISTANCE INVOLVES MULTIPLE COMMUNICATION STRATEGIES

Many of the chapters in this book discussed the important role communication played for distant leaders. Cummings (Chapter 3) found that group leaders were able to mitigate the consequences of geographic dispersion by ensuring frequent communication with members. He suggests that leaders can act as models to the rest of the group by displaying behavior early on that allows members to feel comfortable visiting, calling, or emailing other members. Similarly, Bradner and Mark (Chapter 4) told of the benefits of having all the engineers meet in one location before the start of the project to help them later when they were distributed, in terms of understanding the work norms and domain expertise.

Communication also varied among team members. In Xiao et al. (Chapter 5), the leaders of a trauma team were attending physicians in a teaching hospital. Part of their duties included helping fellows (senior residents) learn how to conduct surgery without the attending physician present. The study investigated how physicians communicated when they were with the surgery team in the same room and when they were remotely observing the surgery with videoconferencing technologies. The investigators found that communication patterns and team composition had to adapt on the fly in crisis situations. When the leader was distant, the team hierarchy was predominant in the respect that there was more communication from leader to senior fellow and from the senior fellow to the junior resident than when the leader was collocated with the team. Distant leaders also tended to ask more questions and give fewer instructions compared to local leaders.

Stasser and Augustinova (Chapter 8) found that teams needed to know how information access was distributed among team members to develop efficient communication strategies. They argued that "simply connecting knowledgeable people and letting them communicate is not sufficient . . . to pool diverse knowledge effectively" (Chapter 8, p. 164). As discussed earlier, distant leaders need to foster a climate that encourages problem-solving, critical thinking, and consideration of diverse points of view. They should also consider composing teams with complementary and relevant expertise and ensure that the members have the time and take the time to explore and integrate information (see also Bradner and Mark, Chapter 4, for a similar recommendation).

Cummings (Chapter 3) recommended that members of geographically dispersed teams should have at least two members in the same location because they will be more likely to communicate with others if they aren't alone. Recent studies on geographic dispersion (e.g., Mortensen & O'Leary, 2006; O'Leary & Cummings, 2002) have found that different configurations among dispersed teams had implications for how teams communicate and perform. What would also be interesting is to understand how different leadership configurations in geographically dispersed teams affect outcomes. This book certainly has much to say on the topic (see for example Chapters 3 and 8), but a focus on distant leadership configurations, both experimentally and in the field, may help tease apart the factors responsible for communication strategies across leaders and teams in distributed collaborations.

Birnholtz and Finholt (Chapter 10) demonstrated that the emergent leader in the NEESgrid project was able to negotiate an effective solution between culturally diverse groups. A prominent earthquake engineer, this leader had cultivated strong relationships with all three professional communities. Thus, he was able to serve as a "translator" or "broker" between the groups because he could help all groups interpret and use information in productive ways. Another communication strategy this leader used was to provide earthquake engineers with an important sense of representation in the development team, something they didn't feel they had previously. Future research may want to look into the details of why people who take on leadership roles or who have relevant professional expertise are able to able to bridge cultural gaps and effectively help teams succeed (see also Boh, Ren, Kiesler, & Bussjaeger, in press).

LESSON 4: LEADERS AT A DISTANCE ARE SUPPORTED BY A VARIETY OF COMMUNICATION TECHNOLOGIES AND USE THEM WITH VARYING DEGREES OF SUCCESS

Much of the experimental work on leadership at a distance investigates leadership using specific technologies as a way of understanding behavior when leaders must rely on electronic communication (see for example Chapters 6, 7, and 8). Studying leadership in experimental settings has advantages, especially when the research questions are related to important dimensions of leading at a distance, for example, in understanding different types of leaders (e.g., transformational or charismatic leaders as in Chapter 6), and when leaders emerge and why (Chapter 7). Stasser and Augustinova who communicate electronically (Chapter 8) point out that seemingly small changes in the communication software (e.g., SAS task) can have striking effects on the amount and kinds of information that are communicated. They caution that communication software offers a powerful tool that must be carefully considered and more adequately studied.

The Xiao et al. study (Chapter 5) used a pseudoexperimental design to capture what real trauma resuscitation teams do when the attending physician is observing the team remotely from a "distant command center." Because they had to work with critical events in the lives of real patients, the researchers went to extra lengths to make sure the technology physicians used was reliable and relatively trouble-free. This was very sophisticated technology. The "distant command center" was set up so the attending surgeon could have visual access to the rest of the team through three camera views and two-way audio communication. The communication system operated with an infrared wireless bone-conducting headphone system to minimize interferences with other electromagnetic devices and to keep the wearer's ear channels unobstructed for the use of stethoscopes and for regular auditory perception (e.g. communicating with collocated team members and the patient, and listening to signals from patient monitors). The audio system, once activated, allowed hands-free operation. With such a setup, it was technically feasible to manipulate the distance from which the leader of a trauma team collaborated with the rest of the team. Extensive consultation was carried out with the management clinicians of the trauma center to define field experiment procedures to ensure the standard care and the welfare of the patient.

Much can be learned from what real people do when experimental conditions can be manipulated to answer important research questions related to communication and technology use. Many of the authors in this book describe leaders with a great deal of technical savvy (Chapters 3, 4, 9, 11, and 12) and willingness to use—and even struggle with—multiple communication technologies to improve their work (e.g., Chapter 5). These leaders have special access privileges so technical tools and network infrastructures and communities are maintained to encourage use (Chapter 9) and to help others in need (Chapter 11). These technologies include sophisticated cyberinfrastructures (Chapter 10), blogs and web forums (Chapters 11 and 12), online communities (Chapter 9), group support systems (Chapter 6), videoconferencing and audioconferencing (Chapters 4 and 5), and email and cell phones (e.g., Chapters 3, 4, and 7).

Bradner and Mark (Chapter 4) demonstrated a variety of drawing, rendering, meeting, and communication technologies to support engineers working on the sophisticated design of an airplane tail. The project involved

NetMeeting (mostly used by two project leads as an informal meeting to exchange documents and ideas), CAITA, a computer-aided design program used in the teleconference, and 3-D View, a rendering tool that integrates geometric data for CATIA models, to produce three-dimensional images of drawings. All of these technologies were used in place of face-to-face meetings, some with greater success than others.

These sophisticated uses of technology to coordinate distributed groups of people has been studied extensively, but the careful ethnographic and empirical analyses conducted by many of the authors here (Chapters 4, 10, 11, and 12) suggests that leadership performance outcomes are hard to measure directly, that distant leaders adapt and learn on the fly. The global world we live in suggests that future research may want to consider how we lead in environments that lack any central coordination mechanism, or how multiple leaders work together to innovate, create, and help others. We think this book is a start in that direction, and we look forward to research that continues to challenge our sensibilities and theories on what it means to lead people at a distance.

REFERENCES

Boh, W. F., Ren, Y., Kiesler, S., & Bussjaeger, R. (in press). Expertise and collaboration in the geographically dispersed organization. *Organization Science.*

Mehra, A., Dixon, A., Brass, D. J., & Robertson, B. (2006b). The social network ties of group leaders: Implications for group performance and leader reputation. *Organization Science, 17*(1), 64–79.

Mehra, A., Smith, B., Dixon, A., & Robertson, B. (2006a). Distributed leadership in teams: The network of leadership perceptions and team performance. *Leadership Quarterly, 17*, 232–245.

Mortensen, M., & O'Leary, M. B. (2006). *Isolation and ambiguity: Subgroup members' perceptions of local and distant teammates in geographically distributed teams.* Paper presented at the Interdisciplinary Network for Group Research (INGRoup) Conference, Pittsburgh, PA, July 27–29, 2006.

O'Leary, M. B., & Cummings, J. N. (2002). *The spatial, temporal, and configurational characteristics of geographic dispersion in teams.* Paper presented at the Annual Meeting of the Academy of Management, Denver, CO, August 11–14, 2002.

Author Index

Subject Index